Personal Evangelism for Today

Personal Evangelism for Today

G. William Schweer

BROADMAN PRESS
Nashville, Tennessee

4262-41

ISBN: 0-8054-6241-4

Dewey Decimal Classification: 248.5

Subject Headings: WITNESSING

Library of Congress Catalog Card Number: 83-70003

Printed in the United States of America

Library of Congress Cataloging in Publication Data

Schweer, G. William, 1926-
  Personal evangelism for today.

  Bibliography: p.
  1. Evangelistic work. I. Title.
BV3790.S34 1984   269'.2   83-70003
ISBN 0-8054-6241-4

Dedicated to Wanda,
wife wonderful,
who has walked, worked, wept,
and witnessed with me over many years.

Contents

Preface

This book is intended as a textbook for classes in personal evangelism, but hopefully it will serve as a refresher for many pastors, staff members, and church leaders as well. It is a nontechnical theme and should be readily digestible by laypersons.

Much has taken place in recent times to influence thinking about personal evangelism. A continuing secularization and pluralization of society, the growing concern about large numbers of inactives and dropout members, the evangelism claims of some segments of the electronic church, the looming importance of spiritual gifts and lay ministry, new insights from persons skilled in communications and persuasion, new appraisals of traditional methods, and the timely emphasis on follow-up and discipleship have all contributed to the desire to put together a new text. I have tried to draw together in one book some of the best materials which arise out of the above stimuli, as well as some basic matters necessary to any course in personal evangelism. I am by no means the only one who has done so.

My indebtedness to others is monumental. I have tried to give credit for many borrowed ideas. Many things, however, I have heard or read, assimilated, preached, or taught; and the source has long since been forgotten. As I studied and wrote, I was often reminded of Pietist Philip Jacob Spener's words as he began to make different emphases than Luther. When he compared himself with the great Reformer, he said:

> A giant remains great and a dwarf small, and there is no comparison to be made between them; but if the dwarf stands upon the shoulders of the giant, he sees yet further than the giant, since this great stature lifts him above himself. Therefore, it is no wonder that often a dwarf, who is far enough from being a great teacher like Luther, finds something in the Scripture which Luther had not found, after having the advantage of all Luther's learning, without which he could not have found it (Brown 1978,95).

I have felt myself very much the dwarf, and I have been aware of standing on the godly shoulders of many giants who have gone before me. By profiting from their insights, I sincerely hope I have drawn the material together in a helpful way.

The book constitutes an appeal for responsible evangelism. If it seems somewhat critical of certain emphases or methods of the past, it is not without great appreciation for what has been accomplished and for the many who have been won. It is written with the conviction that we should profit from inadequacies of the past and make such improvements that appear wise. In many ways the book expresses the evolution of my own thinking and practice in evangelism. A few years ago at a California State Evangelistic Conference, I heard W. A. Criswell say that "the seminaries ought to be hotbeds of evangelism." I said a hearty "Amen," and I earnestly hope these chapters may contribute to that end.

Textbooks can teach evangelism only up to a certain point. Any person who would be a witness must finally launch forth and speak. Silent lips must move. Practice must complement the theory—much practice. I entertain the hope that readers will experience a holy inclination to overflow about the Savior in the marketplace, the home, the school—in short, everywhere, and that their joy in the doing of it will cause them never again to rest in silence and inaction.

I owe special thanks to a number of people. Dr. Roger Skelton, retired professor of religious education at Golden Gate Baptist Theological Seminary, has read the manuscript and offered many helpful suggestions. Dr. John Havlik, retired director of evangelism development of the Home Mission Board of the Southern Baptist Convention, read the first chapter and has responded to many questions in a most gracious way. My fall 1983 class in personal evangelism has used this material and helpfully raised questions and offered suggestions from the standpoint of those for whom it is primarily designed. Of course, I alone am responsible for the deficiencies that remain.

Mrs. Clif Ingram, student and office secretary, has seen the chapters through several typings beginning with my illegible scrawl. Golden Gate student Kay Woodley has used her considerable proofreading skills to my great advantage, and Mrs. Donald Patterson of Secretarial Services has put it on the word processor. Not least, my dear wife has served as encourager and proofreader and often as resident thesaurus and dictionary in a most patient and loving manner. I owe all of these more gratitude than I can express.

The book goes forth baptized in prayer that it might be useful, and perhaps even inspirational, in many hearts.

1
Personal Evangelism and Its Urgency

We had returned from furlough and moved with keen anticipation into a new mission house in a quiet but churchless area of our equatorial city. It offered the advantages of sparse traffic, a large yard, and the opportunity of beginning a new church on weekends.

Moving day was long and hard, and we retired quite late. Our intention was to sleep late the next morning and catch up before the regular routine began. But such was not to be. At precisely 6:00 AM, the militant sounds of the national anthem from a blaring radio somewhere across the street startled us out of bed. We learned later it was from an old Dutch mansion then occupied by a number of national army families. The result was that we became involuntary early risers, although our decided preference and practice was to work late and sleep late. As for radios, it was just prior to the day of transistors. Import fees and customs charges made the old-time models extremely expensive.

One day my wife was visiting the seminary campus and chatting with one of the national teachers. During the conversation, the instructor asked about our new accommodations. In reply, my wife explained the radio problem. When my wife had finished, she said, "I believe I know what has happened.

One family in that house has had the rare good fortune to acquire a radio, and they feel that it is only right to turn it up loud enough so that everyone can hear it."

My wife must have unconsciously registered a "you-don't-mean-it" look, for after a few moments our friend exclaimed, "But Mrs. Schweer, if one has something so precious, is it not right that all should be able to hear it?"

My wife quickly realized that the question she had asked was so appropriate to the reason for our being there that she found herself nodding and saying, "Yes, indeed, it is right that all should be able to hear it."

Our national friend had unwittingly stated a great principle of evangelism. It, too, has to do with sharing something of great value. Though totally undeserved, by the grace of God some possess the secret of salvation and have become members of God's new community. It is a story so precious that all should be able to hear it. The sharing of that good news is the most basic meaning of evangelism.

Defining of Personal Evangelism

Preliminary Considerations

At the outset it is clear that personal evangelism is more limited than evangelism in general. It is one kind of evangelism. It is directed towards a certain individual or individuals as opposed to varieties such as media, street, or mass campaigns directed toward many. It is personal as opposed to impersonal and specific as opposed to general. It is face-to-face encounter with an individual in contrast to preaching to many from afar. It is without intervening barriers such as podiums, television screens, platforms, or distance. Here the witness is most vulnerable and, consequently, most effective.

Important Words

One way to discover the meaning is to examine the main words that have to do with evangelism. The verb $\epsilon \vec{v} \alpha \gamma \gamma \epsilon \lambda \acute{\iota} \zeta \epsilon \sigma \theta \alpha \iota$ is one of those. It means "to bring" or "to announce good news." It is found fifty-two times in the New Testament in the middle form and three times in the active, but the meaning is the same. It is, with few exceptions, translated by the appropriate form of "preach" or "bring good news." There is at least one clear example of the use of this word where the preaching was directed to an individual. "Philip . . . told him the good news of Jesus" (Acts 8:35). There are other instances where it is implied (Acts 8:4; 11:20; 14:7), and it is a safe assumption that phrases such as "preached the gospel in many villages" (Acts 8:25, KJV), tells us that the evangelizing was directed to both individuals and groups. In Acts 8:4 where the Jerusalem Christians "went about preaching the word," personal encounter with individuals was almost certainly a major aspect of the activity described.

There is a close connection between this verb and the nouns $\epsilon \vec{v} \alpha \gamma \gamma \acute{\epsilon} \lambda \iota o \nu$

(gospel) and εὐαγγελίστης (evangelist). The word *gospel* will be discussed later in this chapter, but the use of the word εὐαγγελίστης is noted now. It is used three times in the New Testament and refers to persons who have special ability in evangelizing. It is used of Philip (Acts 21:8), who won the eunuch on the road to Gaza, of specially gifted persons who were to help equip the church for ministry (Eph. 4:11), and of young Timothy who was to do the work of an evangelist in his pastoral situation at Ephesus (2 Tim. 4:5). Face-to-face encounter was surely a large part of the evangelist's work.

A second important verb is κηρύσσειν. It can mean "to announce" or "to make known," but in the New Testament it is the declaration of an event. Its true sense is "to proclaim" (Friederich 1965, 702). It is used sixty-one times and is most often translated with the appropriate form of the word *preach*. It is frequently used with a direct object such as "the kingdom" or "Christ," indicating what is preached or with a dative or locative following, showing to whom the preaching is directed or where it is done. Sometimes it is used absolutely as in Mark 3:14: "He appointed twelve, to be with him, and to be sent out to preach." It is usually used in precisely the same way as εὐαγγελίζεσθαι.

Once again it is a safe assumption that the proclamation was both to groups and individuals, but there are at least two passages where the implication of personal evangelism is more specific. When Paul was at Miletus bidding farewell to the Ephesian elders, he addressed them as those "among whom I have gone preaching the kingdom" (Acts 20:25). Just prior to that, however, there is an explanation of how he had gone about it. "I did not shrink from declaring to you anything that was profitable, and teaching you in public and from house to house" (Acts 20:20). In a second passage, Paul recounted that he was incarcerated in a rented house chained to a guard (Acts 26:29; 28:16). He was able to welcome "all who came to him, preaching the kingdom of God and teaching about the Lord Jesus Christ quite openly and unhindered" (Acts 28:30-31).

We have already seen that these two major verbs are synonymous in meaning, but sometimes εὐαγγελίζεσθαι is used in a very broad sense for the whole of Jesus' activity. In Luke 8:1, the evangelist used the two verbs in the same verse. Jesus was "preaching (κηρύσσων) and bringing the good news of the kingdom of God (εὐαγγελιζόμενος τὴν βασιλείαν)." This phrase, Friederich says, "gives us a comprehensive picture of the whole activity of Jesus. His whole life was proclamation of the Gospel" (Friederich 1964, 718). Then, concerning of his birth as good news (εὐαγγέλιον) in Luke 2:10 and his preaching peace (εὐαγγελίσατο εἰρήνην) in Ephesians 2:17, Friederich says, "His manifestation, not merely His preaching but His whole work, is described in terms of εὐαγγελίζεσθαι" (ibid.)

In the strictest sense, these verbs have to do with preaching, proclaiming, bringing the good news. The major thrust of this book is to discuss evangelism

in that light. Yet, here εὐαγγελίζεσθαι clearly has a larger meaning as
Friederich has stated. One has only to look at the contents of Luke 8 to see
the affirmation of that assertion.

We can see the same thing in regard to Paul. "He can use εὐαγγελίζεσθαι to describe his whole activity as an apostle" (1 Cor. 1:17) (ibid., 718). This
is a very important consideration in framing a definition of personal evangelism. While the strict sense of evangelism is clear, there is this important larger
sense in which evangelism includes the total ministry of Jesus and Paul.

A third word and its cognates which speak of New Testament evangelism
is μαρτύρειν, meaning "to bear witness" or "to be a witness." Various forms
are found where the idea of witness is used in a legal sense or in the sense of
good report, but it is in the Book of Acts and in John's writings that we find
the special Christian sense of the terms.

Luke tends to restrict the use of the word *witness* to refer to those who were
eyewitnesses of Jesus' life, death, and especially the resurrection. These were
able to bear witness both to the historical facts about Jesus as well as to the
significance of the events which they had come to understand by faith. Luke
does move away from this in the final chapters of Acts where he uses the term
witness for both Paul (22:15; 26:16) and Stephen (22:20), who were not eyewitnesses in the same sense as the original apostles. Thus the term took on the
sense of a confessing witness as opposed to those who were both eyewitnesses,
in the full sense of the word, and confessing witnesses. This enabled the term
to survive as the eyewitnesses died (Strathman 1967, 493-94).

It is John who makes large use of the terms μαρτύρειν and μαρτυρία
(that is the verb and noun forms of witness), while avoiding κηρύσσειν and
εὐαγγελίζεσθαι (verbs for preach and bring good news) altogether, except
in Revelation. Michael Green reminds us that the reason these terms are so
important to John is that they are in keeping with the nature of his Gospel
which was intended as a μαρτυρία to lead readers and hearers alike to Jesus.
He further points out that the only way the eyewitnesses could pass on their
faith was by, first, testifying to their own belief and experience that the claims
of Christ were true and, second, by sharing the evidence that led them to
believe. This was what John did. His Gospel became a model of witness (Green
1970, 75).

Jesus is always the focus of witness. The Baptist bore witness to him (1:14-
18,29-34), and Jesus gave witness to himself (3:11,32-33; 8:12-13; 18:37). The
Father bore divine witness to him (5:32,36-37; 8:18, etc.) as do the inspired
Scriptures (2:22; 5:39; 19:24,28,36; 20:9). The same is true of the Holy Spirit
(15:26) and, in addition, he bears that special witness within the believer as to
the reality of their salvation (14:26; 1 John 5:10) (ibid., 75).

Green concludes that John has given us "the most profound understanding
of the place of testimony in faith to be found anywhere in the New Testament"
(ibid., 76). John's emphasis on the unity of word and deed as witness is
especially noteworthy. Words and deeds are seen as inseparable and dependent

upon one another. It was John who gave us the clearest examples of the personal evangelism of Jesus, as well as some of the models that are so valuable for teaching and instruction.

The fact that the word *witness* is both a verb and a noun should not escape our notice. It is something we must be as well as something we must do.

While these are the most important words that have to do with sharing the message, there are others. For example, the message was taught (forms of $\delta\iota\delta\acute{a}\sigma\kappa\epsilon\iota\nu$, Matt. 4:23; Acts 5:42; 15:35, etc.), spoken (forms of $\lambda\acute{a}\lambda\epsilon\iota\nu$) to large groups (Mark 2:2; Luke 9:11) and to individuals (John 3:11); argued or reasoned (forms of $\delta\iota\alpha\lambda\acute{\epsilon}\gamma\epsilon\sigma\theta\alpha\iota$ Acts 17:2,17; 18:4,19; 20:7,9, etc.), proclaimed solemnly ($\kappa\alpha\tau\alpha\gamma\acute{\epsilon}\lambda\lambda\epsilon\iota\nu$, used only once in Luke 9:60), and made known (forms of $\gamma\nu\omega\rho\acute{\iota}\zeta\epsilon\iota\nu$, 1 Cor. 15:1; Eph. 6:19), and these do not exhaust the expressions of the gospel. In each case, it seems clear that the gospel was conveyed to both large or small groups and to individuals as the opportunity came.

A Descriptive Definition

The following definition is an effort to state as concisely as possible just what personal evangelism is as seen in its New Testament context. I define it as the Spirit-led, person-to-person communication of the gospel of the Kingdom by one or more Christians in such a way or ways that the individual recipient has a valid opportunity to accept Jesus Christ as Lord and Savior and become a responsible member of his church.

Explanation

Spirit-led.—Few things are more important in sharing our faith than the recognition that we are dependent upon the work and power of the Holy Spirit. Evangelism is the human aspect of God's effort to bring the lost to himself. It is not so much something we do as something God does through us. Witnesses are simply instruments of the Holy Spirit in this activity. The praying 120 who remained in Jerusalem were to become witnesses only after the Holy Spirit came upon them (Acts 1:8). John represented the Holy Spirit to be the converter or convincer of sin, righteousness, and judgment (John 16:7-11). In Acts 8:29 the Spirit directed Philip to join himself to the chariot where the Ethiopian official was pondering a scroll of Isaiah.

Men had been given entirely too much credit for the converts in the Corinthian church where there was a tendency toward personality cults. Paul pointed out that these men, himself included, were only servants through whom they had believed. People could plant and water seed, he said, but God is the one who brings forth life (1 Cor. 3:3-7). It is altogether essential for every witness to recognize and practice this relationship of dependence and instrumentality.

Person to person . . . individual recipient.—These terms distinguish personal evangelism from other kinds as emphasized earlier. It sets it apart from the various less personal forms of proclamation to a group or groups.

Communication.—I have attempted to choose each word of the definition with care but this word especially so. Those who have read *Planning Strategies for World Evangelism* by Dayton and Fraser (1980, 80) will recognize that their definition has influenced mine, but it was also Charles Kraft's *Communicating the Gospel God's Way* that convinced me to use this word (Kraft n.d., 3). Kraft feels the word *communication* would be a good translation for the word usually rendered "preach" (a form of κηρύσσειν) in Mark's version of the commission. "Go into all the world *to communicate* the good news to all people" (Kraft's translation, Mark 16:15). This, of course, is not our strongest commission from the standpoint of textual criticism, but when we consider that the Great Commission of Matthew 28:19-20 is actually to "make disciples," it is clear that communication was God's intention.

The point is that there can be a vast difference between simply announcing the good news and communicating the message. The word *communicate* implies getting the message across. There could be any number of reasons why a mere announcement might not communicate. For example, there are always spiritual barriers such as blindness (2 Cor. 4:3-4) or satanic hindrance (Mark 4:15). Other obstacles may well be of a more mundane nature which care and study on the part of the witnesses might eliminate. For example, if there is a language barrier or if the form or mode of communication is not culturally acceptable or if the known conduct of the witness has served to damage his or her credibility, then communication is greatly hindered. E. Stanley Jones once heard a startling remark from a college principal who chaired one of his meetings in Asia.

> Jesus has stood four times in history before the door of India and has knocked. The first time he appeared in the early days he stood in company with a trader. He knocked. We looked out and saw him and liked him but we didn't like his company, so we shut the door. Later, he appeared, with a diplomat on one side and a soldier on the other, and knocked. We looked out and said: "We like you, but we don't like your company." Again we shut the door. The third time was when he appeared as the uplifter of the outcasts. We liked him better in this role, but we weren't sure of what was behind it. Was this the religion of imperialism? Are they conquering through religion? Again we shut the door. And now he appears before our doors, as tonight, as the disentangled Christ. To this disentangled Christ we say: "Come in. Our doors are open to you" (Jones 1968, 110).

The message had been announced, but there had been obvious commercial, political, and cultural barriers. The bearers of the good news were suspect because of their entanglements and associations, and they did not communicate.

It should not be lost upon us that Jesus engaged in a lengthy discussion with the Samaritan woman and seemed to extend his stay in that village because of the interest and response. He intended to communicate. Paul, too, was unwilling to proclaim the gospel on a "take-it-or-leave-it" basis evidenced by his use of words like *beseech* and *persuade.* The task we are sent to do "normally calls for the kind of loving that takes time" (Taylor 1966, 33).

Gospel of the kingdom of God.—The gospel is the content of the message about Jesus. The fact that one had arrived who fulfilled all the ancient prophecies about a coming Messiah was joyous news, and so it came to be designated by a term that meant good news, "the gospel."

In one sense everything about Jesus was good news, but there was a need to know the basic content or the indispensable aspects of the good news. What were the fundamental tenets that a non-Christian would have to understand in order to become a Christian? What was the essential content of the message proclaimed by the apostles and the early church as they evangelized?

One very influential attempt in that direction was made by C. H. Dodd in 1936. Based on his examination of Paul's epistles he came up with a seven-point outline of the basic content of the gospel (Dodd 1936, 17). Following an examination of the apostolic preaching in Acts he produced a six-point core that can be briefly summarized as follows:

> First, the age of fulfillment has dawned. "This is that which was spoken by the prophet" (Acts 2:16). . . . Secondly, this has taken place through the ministry, death, and resurrection of Jesus. . . . Thirdly, by virtue of the resurrection, Jesus has been exalted at the right hand of God, as Messianic head of the new Israel. . . . Fourthly, the Holy Spirit in the Church is the sign of Christ's present power and glory. . . . Fifthly, the Messianic Age will shortly reach its consumation in the return of Christ. . . . Finally, the *kerygma* always closes with an appeal for repentance, the offer of forgiveness and of the Holy Spirit, and the promise of "salvation," that is, "the life of this Age to Come" to those who enter the elect community . . . (Dodd 1936, 21-24).

Dodd then adds, "We may take it that this is what the author of Acts meant by 'preaching the Kingdom of God' " (ibid., 24).

This basic core of the gospel has come to be called the *kerygma,* a Greek word meaning "preaching." It refers not to the act of preaching, but to the content of the message. "It pleased God through the folly of what we preach ($\tau o\hat{v}\ \kappa\eta\rho\acute{v}\gamma\mu\alpha\tau o\varsigma$) to save those who believe" (1 Cor. 1:21).

While Dodd's theory has had wide influence and acceptance, it has also been the subject of continuing debate. His work has been revised and rethought by many. Various scholars have produced their own basic *kerygma* with five, four, or three main points, although they do not always agree on what these points should be (Green 1970, 61). Michael Green's work in his fine book *Evangelism in the Early Church* is an example. He presents a three-point *kerygma:*

> First, they preached a person. Their message was frankly Christocentric. . . . Second, they proclaimed a gift. The gift of forgiveness, the gift of the Spirit, the gift of adoption, of reconciliation. The gift that made "no people" part of the "people of God," the gift that brought those who were far off near. . . . Third, they looked for a response. The Apostles were not shy about asking men to decide

for or against God who had decided for them. They expected results" (Green 1970, 150-53).

Besides disagreement on the number of basic points and what they should be, some feel that there is too much emphasis on a fixed *kerygma* and that it was not nearly as stylized as Dodd and others supposed. Not only do they see the variation of conviction among scholars about what the points were, but they see a wide variety of ways in which the gospel was presented. Others see the background and understanding of the listeners to be a factor in determining how the message was to be presented (ibid., 61).

Despite these disagreements, however, Dodd's work is seen by most to have great value, for it shows that "the gospel had a recognizable shape and content" and that there was a basic "common approach to evangelism" although there could be considerable variation in detail (ibid., 70). A study of these suggested basic points is vital as we plan our message, for this is an irreducible basic content which the witness must convey in order "to expect God's full blessing upon our preaching" (Drummond 1972, 102).

There is one point of unanimous agreement. It is that whatever the gospel is, it centers in the person and activities of Jesus Christ. Indeed, he is the gospel. Ladd's statement is a good summary. "The heart of the apostolic kerygma is the proclamation of the Lordship of Jesus (2 Cor. 4:5). Christians are those who have received Christ Jesus as Lord" (Ladd 1974, 339).

The kingdom of God has been the subject of vigorous debate, but a convincing stream of opinion sees it to be God's new order for the believer, embodied in Jesus Christ. It is God's kingly rule or reign which is a reality to persons of faith. It is what the rabbinic literature called the age to come and dates back to the Old Testament idea of contrast between the present order of things and the redeemed order to be introduced by the Day of the Lord (ibid., 45-46). It is that new age breaking into the present evil age, a new order to which a genuinely repentant person turns. It is unshakable and permanent (Heb. 12:28) in contrast to all man-made orders which are shakable and temporary. It is characterized by love, righteousness, justice, peace, and life, whereas the old order meant lust, greed, pride, injustice, and death. It is a new community made up of a new race for whom Christ is King.

It is an order both present and coming. It has broken in with the life and ministry of Jesus, but its complete fulfillment awaits his visible return.

Jesus spoke of it constantly. It was the central theme of his ministry (Matt. 4:23; Mark 1:14-15). It was what he sent the twelve to preach (Luke 9:2), and after his crucifixion, it was the theme of his instruction during the forty-day postresurrection ministry (Acts 1:3).

There are several key passages that help us understand the kingdom and its revolutionary meaning. When Jesus went to the synagogue in Nazareth and was given the opportunity to speak, he read the messianic passage Isaiah 61:1-2 about the coming of an anointed one who would proclaim the acceptable year of the Lord (Luke 4:18-19). Then he said, "Today this scripture has been fulfilled in your hearing" (Luke 4:21).

When John the Baptist was imprisoned, he sent two disciples to inquire if Jesus was the one whom they had expected as a fulfillment of Old Testament messianic prophecy. Jesus told the inquirers simply to go back and report what they saw.

In both instances, Jesus' own announcement and the encounter John's inquirers would report revealed the comprehensive personal and social dimensions of the Kingdom. The total needs of persons were receiving attention. The poor were hearing the good news, and injustice, oppression, and neglect were being rectified.

When the disciples asked Jesus to teach them to pray, a part of the Model Prayer Jesus gave reads,

> Thy kingdom come,
> Thy will be done,
> On earth as it is in heaven (Matt. 6:10).

If this is a case of parallelism wherein "Thy will be done, on earth as it is in heaven" explains "Thy kingdom come," as many scholars seem to think, then it is a reasonable conclusion that God's kingdom is manifested wherever his will is being done.

When Jesus cast a demon out of a poor dumb man (Luke 11:14 ff.), some said that he did it by the power of Be-elzebul. Jesus quickly showed the impossibility of such an idea. Then he said, "If it is by the finger of God that I cast out demons, then the kingdom of God has come upon you" (Luke 11:20). Such a miracle represented an attack upon Satan and a defeat of cosmic proportions. This is both a foreshadowing of his final demise as well as a present manifestation of the Kingdom.

What we must see is that God's kingdom has both personal and social dimensions. Social righteousness is as vital to God's will as personal righteousness. Personal and social goals are blended and intertwined. As E. Stanley Jones said when he came to understand the implications of Jesus' teaching about God's kingdom, "It wiped out the distinction between the individual and the social—they were two sides of one whole" (Jones 1968, 151).

Personal evangelism is concerned with the gospel of the kingdom. It will not offer cheap grace. Salvation must not be made to sound easy. The hard sayings of Jesus will not be hidden. The revolutionary implication of being a part of God's new community which demands an entirely new way of life now must be a part of the proclamation.

By one or more Christians.—This phrase is largely self-explanatory. True life-style witnessing usually involves one Christian seizing upon the opportunities discovered in the course of daily life, at work, the neighborhood, at school, in various social groups, or within the extended family. More formal witness, such as visiting in homes in the name of a church, usually involves two people.

Sometimes there are three where training is taking place, but more than that is usually unwise.

In such a way or ways.—There are a surprising number of ways to communicate the gospel. For example, it is verbalized by preaching, teaching, dialoguing, singing, and choral reading to mention a few. From the area of media, aside from television and radio, it can be conveyed through magazines, books, tracts, films, news and feature articles, pictures, diagrams, and drama. It can even be communicated nonverbally, to a degree, in that new converts often evidence their transformation to others without speaking a word.

From the standpoint of personal evangelism there are three categories of communication that are of the utmost importance. They must work together, for they need each other. At all costs they must not contradict one another.

First, there is the matter of being; second, the matter of doing; and third, the matter of telling. It takes all of these working in harmony if evangelism is to be complete and powerful.

Not a few feel there has been all too much emphasis on verbalization without appropriate support from being and doing. As Delos Miles puts it, "We have majored on telling, minored on doing, and made an elective out of being" (Miles 1975, 8). That is well said. Being and doing can constitute powerful witness. Peter acknowledged this clearly when he spoke of husbands being "won without a word by the behavior of their wives" (1 Pet. 3:1).

Yet the emphasis on being and doing does not mean a denigration of telling. It will always be important. The persons who say, "We will just witness by our lives" have really not thought deeply about the matter. Such an approach would be altogether inadequate for the simple reasons that even the best Christian lives still have many unattractive flaws, and to rely on that method alone would be extremely slow. It is deeply significant that the one person who could have witnessed simply by his matchless life modeled a powerful verbalization of the gospel as well. No communication of the gospel is really complete without proclamation somewhere in the process. D. T. Niles said it quite clearly years ago: "Making love is not enough. One must say, 'I love you.' Kind deeds are not enough. One must say 'I forgive you. . . .' One must perform the duties and obligation of being an ambassador (Eph. 6:20). One's credentials from his king must be presented, the word on behalf of one's king must be spoken" (Niles 1962, 126).

At the same time, a Christlike life does communicate powerfully, and proclamation is inadequate without it. I have never forgotten one of my earliest attempts to witness as a pastor. I stood on the back of a farmer's tractor and invited the man to accept Jesus. He said, "You know, if I thought I could become a person like Hubert Laffoon (one of the deacons in my church), I would become a Christian." The consistent Christian life of that godly man had influenced many in that community and had made a profound impression upon my prospect who had no trouble associating it with the verbalization I had conveyed.

God's supreme method of communication was incarnation. Jesus not only had a message; he was the message. He is the best possible illustration of the phrase "the medium is the message." This has a poignant application to the life of every witness. We must be good news before we can share good news (Aldrich 1981, 20). The world has seen far too much of spiritual hypocrisy. What it must see now is Christians who have incarnated their message and who are living as kingdom people and who can speak out of that context.

What a Christian does is also indispensable. Sharing must be manifested in service. Jesus' own works were salient testimony as to who he was. Nicodemus acknowledged their power when he said, "Rabbi, we know that you are a teacher come from God; for no one can do these signs [works] that you do, unless God is with him" (John 3:2). While he did not fully understand, and while flattery may have been involved, Jesus' works had carried a powerful message and had drawn Nicodemus to further inquiry.

This discussion will raise the question with some as to whether social ministry can be considered evangelism. This matter has generated no little debate, and it is not a question that will soon be settled. Not a few take the view that evangelism is one thing and ministry another, and these are kept in separate compartments with no overlap or mixture, even though the necessity of both may be readily admitted. I believe that social ministry in the Spirit of Christ is powerful evangelism. It is simply one of its forms (Rutenber 1960, 128). We must now see the task holistically, that is, that Jesus was equally concerned with social and spiritual needs and with temporal as well as eternal realities. These concerns were so wonderfully blended together in his activity that attempts to categorize them are usually artificial.

It is well known that prophets often symbolized their message by what they did. Jeremiah purchased a field at a very dark time to show his faith that the nation had a future (Jer. 32:6-15). Hosea married a harlot to symbolize God's love for his unfaithful people (Hos. 1:1-3). Jesus entered Jerusalem on the foal of an ass to symbolize the kind of kingdom he came to establish (Mark 11:1-10). These acts preached more clearly than if mere words had been spoken, and such is often the case in regard to evangelism.

Luke 8, mentioned earlier, sheds a floodlight on the question of the relationship between proclamation and demonstration. Luke says that Jesus "went on through the cities and villages, preaching ($\kappa\eta\rho\acute{v}\sigma\sigma\omega\nu$) and bringing the good news ($\epsilon\grave{v}\alpha\gamma\gamma\epsilon\lambda\iota\zeta\acute{o}\mu\epsilon\nu o\varsigma$) of the kingdom of God" (8:1). The latter word summarizes all that he did as we have seen. He spoke the parable of the sower and identified his true family as "those who hear the word of God and do it" (8:21). He demonstrated his power over the forces of nature by stilling a storm and saving his fearful disciples. He exorcised the demons from a poor man of the Gerasenes. He healed a woman who had suffered with a hemorrhage for twelve years, and raised Jairus's daughter from the dead (compare Watson 1976, 27-28). That was how he brought the good news. It was clearly by word and deed. Of these activities David Watson has remarked: "This surely was a tremendous powerful part of Jesus' evangelism. It was neither a prelude to, nor the consequence of, evangelism. It was simply evangelism, the bringing of good news" (ibid., 27-28).

In Luke's introduction to Acts it is not without significance that he refered to his first book as an account of "all that Jesus began to do and teach" (Acts 1:1). Jesus' ministry was not just preaching, but preaching so set into a context of compassionate deeds that the totality was bringing good news.

Paul described his own work in the non-Christian world in similar terms in writing the Romans (15:18-20). Christ had worked through him "to win obedience from the Gentiles, by word and deed, by the power of signs and wonders, by the power of the Holy Spirit." In that way Paul said he had "fully preached ($\pi\epsilon\pi\lambda\eta\rho\omega\kappa\acute{\epsilon}\nu\alpha\iota$, to set forth fully) the gospel of Christ" (ibid., 28). For Paul, an adequate setting forth of the gospel clearly consisted of preaching and demonstration. He goes on immediately to say that his ambition is "to preach the gospel" ($\epsilon\mathring{v}\alpha\gamma\gamma\epsilon\lambda\acute{\iota}\zeta\epsilon\sigma\theta\alpha\iota$, that is, the word used to describe his total ministry in 1 Cor. 1:17) where he does not "build on another man's foundation." It seems clear that for Paul there were no divisions of service and preaching. The total activity was frequently seen as evangelizing or bringing the good news.

A valid opportunity.—It is immediately obvious that this is a matter hard to measure. Yet, it is an extension of some principles expressed in regard to the matter of communication.

While admitting the difficulties involved, Dayton and Fraser have established several criteria of a valid opportunity. They are writing about a general evangelism strategy for world missions, but most of their principles apply, at least in degree, to personal evangelism. Important ones are that "the message must be phrased in the language and idioms, the thought forms and world view of the listeners. . . . The means of communication must be suitable to the social structure and communication patterns common to the people, . . ." and "the witness must be sustained long enough to be comprehensible to the average person of the group being evangelized" (Dayton and Fraser 1980, 83).

Obviously these suggestions do not solve all the problems of determining the perimeters of a valid opportunity. Spirit-led judgment and godly wisdom must play a large role. These do serve, however, to remind us again that "quickie" exposures are almost always inadequate and that many persons may require multiple exposures over what may be a lengthy period.

To accept Jesus Christ as Savior and Lord.—Our discussion of the gospel makes it unnecessary to add to what has been said about the person of Christ as Savior and Lord. To "accept" Jesus, however, may need some amplification. This is to internalize personally the gospel affirmations concerning him that he is Savior and Lord so that those truths can be sincerely confessed, "Because, if you confess with your lips that Jesus is Lord and believe in your heart that God raised him from the dead, you will be saved" (Rom. 10:9). It is sincere belief in the inmost being that constitutes acceptance. It is receiving Jesus into one's life (John 1:12) in such a way that there is not only a consciousness of his forgiveness, but he becomes the Master of one's life.

A responsible member of his church.—The New Testament pattern is very clear in Acts. It was belief (2:37-40), baptism (2:41), and incorporation into the church (2:41). This was not without reason, for in the new community they heard and absorbed the apostle's teaching (2:42; 5:42). They worshiped (2:42b,46,47) and experienced fellowship (2:42). They shared so as to meet needs (2:44) and stood in awe of the mighty power of God (2:43). Worship and instruction were altogether important to the survival of the newborn. The fellowship met the basic need of belonging. In that God created us as social beings, all stand in need of a community where each one draws and gives strength. The New Testament church was a deeply caring fellowship where members knew others and were known by them. Their experiences within the body, coupled with persecution, resulted in fervent witness and great enlargement of the church (Acts 8:1-4).

These Christians recognized that their commitment and love to Christ was to be expressed in ministry. They saw that their response must be a participatory one. They loved, sacrificed, shared, grew, fellowshiped, worshiped, witnessed, and served in Christ's name. They became active, functioning, responsible members of the church. Nothing short of this will suffice today.

The Urgent Necessity of Personal Evangelism

Authors concerned about evangelism have been writing about urgency for many years. That is not without reason. Evangelism is indeed a most urgent concern. It is more urgent than our minds can grasp, for we are always limited in vision perception by the dulling effects of evil which are a part of us all. Yet, we must try to internalize this concept as determinedly as we can, for urgency is a part of the very nature of evangelism. To fail to understand and to genuinely manifest urgency is to rob ourselves of an essential part of its meaning and to minimize the effectiveness of the evangelism we do. Like a plant that can only grow and produce in a tropical climate, evangelism's best health and productivity is experienced only in an atmosphere of responsible urgency. This does not mean, of course, that we do not recognzie that people need time to understand and that the Holy Spirit often takes time to do his work. Evangelism remains urgent, although it proceeds with a sensitive respect for persons and the utmost caution against running ahead of God or manipulating people.

It seems to me that there are theological, ethical, and practical reasons why evangelism is so urgent. Some are more crucial than others, but all are important and contribute to the exigent nature of the enterprise.

Theological Reasons

First, the Scriptures represent Christ to be the only God-given means of salvation. Here we can see the great influence of theology on the matter of urgency. If one believes, for example, that God will not allow anyone to be lost or that everyone is already saved and only needs to hear that fact announced, then preaching is not so imperative. If Christ is found in all religions, and if salvation in the classical sense is no longer relevant, then we would not expect much urgency to manifest itself in the proclamation of the gospel. One could seriously question whether the gospel, as historically understood, could be preached at all by a person who held one or more such views. On the other hand, if one believes that Christ is the only real hope of the world, that he alone is the source of redemption and new life, that one's present and eternal destiny depends upon the discovery of his significance, and that true fulfillment and purpose are only realized in him, one would wonder how evangelism could be anything but urgent. If the Bible is truly authoritative—and that is a presupposition of this book—then the latter pattern of conviction is basic to a proper perspective on the whole matter.

Jesus represented an individual's relationship to him to be a matter of life or death (John 3:18), and he was concerned not just that people might die without him but also that they might live without him. At the same time he spoke much about judgment and condemnation and, frequently, about the wrath of God (John 3:36; 5:24). Unquestionably, such was an important aspect of his message and a vital factor in urgency.

Second, evangelism is urgent because it is the human activity God uses to bring about the transforming experience from which all else that is Christian flows. One goal is conversion, without which the Christian life could not exist (Luke 13:3). All discipleship and productive ministry begins here.

It was at the Aldersgate Society meeting where John Wesley's heart was strangely warmed, and he trusted Christ alone, that his superb life began to be productive. He was already thirty-five years old and an ordained clergyman in the Church of England. If he had died before that experience, there would be little reason for us to remember him and even less to discuss his work. His conversion changed everything, and a Moravian named Peter Bohler played a personal evangelism role in the human side of that event. The same could be said for Augustine in the fourth century, William Carey in the nineteenth, or for Malcolm Muggeridge in the twentieth. Evangelism leads to the bottom-line experience where all else Christian begins.

Third, transformed discipled persons represent the best hope of a just society. Spirit-blessed evangelism produces a new humanity (Eph. 2:15), the new community that can learn love of neighbor and that will not "pass by on the other side." It is profoundly clear from history that serious Christians can change societies. The Wilberforces, Shaftesburys, Barnardos, and Nightingales of the world bear resounding testimony to that principle.

Urgency is seen in the fact that both individuals and societies suffer untold losses and deprivations when evangelism fails. Vast talents and energies are wasted in years of empty endeavor, and the transforming benefits society could enjoy from discipled lives remain unconceived and unborn.

Fourth, evangelism is urgent because the opportunities both to do and respond to evangelism are limited. First, there is the uncertain nature of life. James said we really do not know there will be a tomorrow and metaphorically referred to life as a "mist that appears for a little time and then vanishes" (Jas. 4:14). Life is "the valley of the shadow of death" (Ps. 23:4). Death is a daily possibility and a final certainty. While younger people may be far more concerned about meaning in life now, the final issue presses harder with each passing day if one does not learn how to cope with it. There are trials, hardships, burdens, and sufferings also which no one escapes. Christ came to help people live victoriously despite those things, and it is urgent—both to the lost person and the Christian witness—that Jesus' way be discovered before the day of opportunity is past. We do not have forever either to decide or serve.

The doctrine of the second coming is a second limiting factor. People must be prepared to receive him when he comes, for both the non-Christian's opportunity to believe and the Christian's opportunity to share, end at that moment (Heb. 9:27).

There is another theological source, however, from which the healthiest sense of urgency grows. That is out of our relationship with Christ. It is as we are more and more "in Christ" and he "in us" that we take on his concerns and intents. All too often we are like some of Paul's associates described in Philippians who were looking after "their own interests, not those of Jesus Christ" (Phil. 2:21). It is as we appropriate the mind of Christ (Phil. 2:5) that we begin to share his urgency.

Jesus often spoke urgently. "If your right eye causes you to sin, pluck it out and throw it away; . . . And if your right hand causes you to sin, cut it off and throw it away; it is better that you lose one of your members than that your whole body go into hell" (Matt. 5:29-30). In other words don't let anything, even something as important as an eye or a right hand, keep you from doing what God would have you do. Those are urgent words.

"We must work the works of him who sent me, while it is day; night comes, when no one can work" (John 9:4). The awareness that the night of his death was coming and that his days were numbered heightened his sense of urgency. What was true for Jesus is true for each of us. He did not have very long to do his work, nor do we.

"Follow me, and leave the dead to bury their own dead" (Matt. 8:22). Despite the fact that the proper burial of a Jewish man's father was a most sacred responsibility, the matter of following Jesus was far too urgent to wait upon such an earthly concern. The father in the incident was, of course, not yet dead. For Jesus, in the light of his inbreaking kingdom, those who still held customs sacrosanct were the spiritually dead. They could bury the dead. To follow him was an urgent call permitting no delays. These examples by no means exhaust his words of urgency.

One can also see the urgency of Jesus even more clearly in his spirit and demeanor. Recall his weeping over the blind, unrepentant city of Jerusalem

(Luke 19:41). See him moved with compassion at the sight of shepherdless sheep and spiritual desolation (Matt. 9:35-38). Remember how he was touched to the very depths when the leper asked his help (Mark 1:41). See his urgency supremely as Jesus left heaven to live among people, taking upon himself the form of a servant and going to the cross in order to open the way for sinful persons to stand before a holy God. Humanity's plight was that urgent. That was what it required.

It is as we begin to think his thoughts, follow his steps, do his works, and take upon ourselves his cares and concerns that we incarnate his urgency. And this urgency has much to do with the effectiveness of our evangelism.

Ethical Reasons

There are also pressing ethical considerations that make evangelism urgent. The first is that, for the person of faith, it is simply the right thing to do. If the gospel is all the Bible claims it is, then those who believe it know that this is true. Something of such value, that we received as a free gift, must not be selfishly grasped but shared as widely as possible.

There is a powerful Old Testament incident that gives substance to this idea. Syrian King Ben-hadad's seige of Samaria had caused a tragic famine to befall the city. It was so severe that four lepers at the city gate had all but given up hope. They decided that their last possibility was to go to the enemy camp on the chance that someone there might show mercy and give them food.

The Lord had already acted on behalf of Samaria. He had caused the Syrians to flee in panic, thinking that Israel had hired the kings of the Hittites and the kings of Egypt against them. When the lepers arrived, they found the abandoned abundance of the Syrians. After satisfying themselves and hiding some of the spoil, they suddenly came to an important realization. They said, "We are not doing right. This is a day of good news; if we are silent and wait until the morning light, punishment will overtake us; now therefore come, let us go and tell the king's household" (2 Kings 7:9). This incident is a parable of the Christian's situation. To fail to share the good news of our discovery is to fail in doing what is right. If we are serious about ethics, then sharing is a moral obligation.

But such sharing is not done simply because it is right; it is the ethical response of the transforming love of Christ in the light of overwhelming needs. It is not merely that God weeps over the growing millions who have never confessed Christ. He cares deeply also that multitudes are hungry, sick, oppressed, abused, and without hope of anything better in their lifetime. The Christian can no longer claim lack of knowledge as an excuse for inaction. World communication is now too efficient. These needs are too obvious to be ignored. There are wounds to bind up, empty stomachs to fill, suffering to alleviate, and the oppressed to set free. Kingdom evangelism is such that it will not and cannot ignore these needs.

Practical Reasons

The urgency of personal evangelism is particularly clear from the practical standpoint, although evangelism as a whole also addresses these concerns. First, personal evangelism is the only method by which many can be reached. Some years ago a career evangelist was participating in a Billy Graham campaign and rejoicing at the results. One night on the way to the stadium, however, he suddenly realized that he must have passed one-half million people heading the other direction. While he was convinced of the benefits of a powerful campaign, he realized anew that many people would never attend an evangelistic crusade irrespective of the fame of the evangelist (Edwards 1962, 31-32).

The only way a large segment of unsaved people can ever be reached is through responsible, thoroughgoing personal evangelism. While a campaign has the potential of reaching some, personal evangelism has the potential of reaching all.

Second, personal evangelism is essential to the success of most other types of evangelism. Few Christians realize the crucial role that personal evangelism plays in evangelistic efforts called by other names. It is not without reason that well-planned, city-wide campaigns are preceeded by large efforts in lay-witness training, personal prayer lists, and organized opportunities for visitation.

Recent studies have confirmed what thinking observers have long believed: most people do not make important decisions of this sort without face-to-face contact with another person whose experience and understanding has made them influential. One survey in Canada revealed that 90 percent of those responding in public crusades had been contacted first through the personal witness of another individual (*World Evangelization* September 1982, 6).

The powerful role of personal evangelism at Pentecost is often overlooked in our enthusiasm over the three thousand that were converted. Prior to that response, Luke is careful to point out the activity of the one hundred twenty Spirit-filled disciples (Acts 2:4); "each one heard them speaking in his own language" (2:6). Obviously there had been much individual and small-group discussion before Peter's proclamation to the multitude. The same is true today in regard to other types of evangelism. Personal contact will play the decisive role for the majority of converts. This important principle will be emphasized in the chapter on media and elsewhere, but it should be kept in mind from the beginning.

Third, churches simply expire without evangelism, and we have just seen how dependent evangelism is on the personal contact. Any given local church that ceases to evangelize will die in fifty to sixty years or, considering other interacting factors, perhaps a good bit sooner. Hundreds of churches die every year from various causes, but many die because they have failed to evangelize. This, of course, is never the motive for evangelism. The church that only evangelizes to keep from dying will die anyway, for without a deep sense of mission and a healthy measure of Christlike concern a church will succomb to a plethora of diseases.

Extinction, however, is not the only kind of death that a church can experience. Frequently, people refer to a particular church as "dead." They usually mean that although people still gather in a given building called the "church," there is a lack of spiritual vitality and growth and no detectable excitement or victory note about their activity. In short, nothing is happening. Churches can stagnate and evidence death long before they actually cease to exist.

The life of a church is dependent upon a certain inflow/outflow principle similar to that which is observable in nature. If a body of water is to remain fresh and life-giving, there must be both inflow and outflow. If there ceases to be either of those, the lake or pond "dies." The Great Salt Lake in Utah was once a huge body of fresh water named Lake Bonneville, but a combination of earth shifts and climatic changes stopped its outflow and minimized its inflow. The salt content increased until almost no life could be sustained. A church must have an outflow and outreach into the world, and this, in turn, brings the inflow that sustains its life. Without it a church stagnates and eventually dies.

The church that emphasizes and practices personal evangelism is an exciting church. The constant influx of new persons, the experience of seeing God's Spirit at work, the freshness of the testimonies of newborn Christians, and the sense of anticipation that looks toward Sunday are all signs of vigorous life.

Finally, it is an arresting thought that the task of evangelism was given exclusively to the church. The task of communicating the good news in such a way or ways as to give people the opportunity to know Christ as Lord is the responsibility of no other group or organization. Many things churches do are duplicated by other organizations. From a human point of view, some of those things can even be done better by secular groups who have greater financial resources and political clout. No other organization, however, will evangelize with the purpose of bringing humanity to God. If the churches do not do it, it simply will go undone.

Getting Started

Some reading this book should begin witnessing immediately, so a brief overview of some basic principles is appropriate here. Most of these will be treated in greater detail in later chapters, but it will be helpful to have them in mind from the beginning.

Commitment to the Task

Many readers will be students, pastors, or dedicated Christians who already know something about faith sharing. Some will have had training courses, perhaps even taught them, and done considerable witnessing. Many will have witnessed only in sporatic bursts and, consequently, carry a sense of failure. Nevertheless, a valuable underlying strata of experience is there. When this is the case, a serious new commitment is in order. One should not hesitate because earlier commitments have failed. That is all the more reason to make a new commitment and get at the task as quickly as possible. Enough time has been lost, and too many opportunities have already passed. Daily commitment to this task is one aspect of the prayer life of successful witnesses.

A basic presupposition of this book is that he "gave us the ministry of reconciliation" (2 Cor. 5:18). Witnessing is the task of every Christian. To fail is to stumble, not only in obedience but also in loving concern. It is a breach of both the Great Commission and the Great Commandment. The light must be retrieved from under the bushel and put on the lampstand, and the salt must be tasted in the world again (Matt. 5:13,15).

It has long been recognized that the best learning is experiential; that is, it takes place as one engages in the matter being studied. Thus, it is not simply obedience and a response to love but a means to the most efficient growth and progress in the task.

Others, of course, will have done little or no witnessing. Here, too, a commitment to the task is essential, even though it may be best to read a bit further in the book before going much beyond the personal testimony. We must determine at all costs to become what God has called us to be.

Catching the Vision

Beginners in personal evangelism sometimes ask, "To whom can we witness?" The answer is that opportunities are all about us. Jesus encountered or was encountered by people everywhere. At the seaside, in a boat, in the synagogue, in homes, at the tax office, on a mountainside, at a well, beneath a tree; in short, wherever there were people Jesus found ways to speak or demonstrate his message.

It was the same with the earliest disciples and with Paul. Any place persons would listen was a place of witness, and, though the message was essentially heard by the poor, all classes were included.

The late missionary statesman E. Stanley Jones often explained how he simply surrendered himself to God each morning, praying that he would be usable and sensitive to opportunities that came. He found no lack of persons to whom to witness once he made himself available and earnestly sought the Spirit's leading.

Jesus made it clear to his disciples that there was no lack of opportunity. The harvest was plenteous. The problem was lack of laborers (Matt. 9:35-38).

This book discusses methods elsewhere, but suffice it to say for now that God seems to use a wide variety. There is no one way to win people. A cultivative approach is certainly necessary for many people today, but God can use chance encounters as well.

I often ask students in my classes to tell how they became believers. Most credit the local church where they grew up or a friend who was a Christian, but some have been greatly touched through a chance encounter with a bold

Christian stranger. There was the young man who, when fourteen, sat by a witnessing Christian on a bus. By the end of that journey he had decided to become a Christian.

A young lady presented herself for membership in a church I pastored, so I asked her to tell me about her salvation. It had happened one day in her college dorm. She and her roommate had been discussing Christianity, wondering if there was anything to it. A new Christian engaged in a witnessing course was in the room next door. She could not help hearing through the cheaply constructed wall. She went next door and apologized for the intrusion but explained that she had recently had an experience with Christ that she must share. Her witness led to that young lady's conversion who became a fine member of my church. And how could I forget a twelve-year-old Indonesian boy we met in front of our missionary residence. He was looking for crickets (thought to bring luck) in our masonry wall. We took him with us to Vacation Bible School where he accepted Christ; later, over a period of years, he led the rest of his family and several neighbors to the Lord.

Personally, I emphasize friendship, ministry, cultivative evangelism related to a local church. Those are the most productive, and lasting kinds, but God is pleased to use many methods. None that are honorable and well motivated should be ruled out.

Often, many people play a part in another's decision. Our witness may simply move a person closer to a decision. We sow where we do not reap and reap where we do not sow. Such is the nature of evangelism. It is marvelous work, and we must be open to any method God's Spirit may choose and to whomever he knows is receptive.

Conquering Fear

The obstacle that defeats most would-be witnesses is fear. It is primarily a fear of rejection. The witness becomes very vulnerable. In one sense, he or she is offering what has not been requested, answering what has not been asked, and entering in where no invitation has been extended. If this is done without deep sensitivity to the prospect and the clear leadership of the Holy Spirit, people can react quite negatively. On the other hand, if concern is truly deep and sincere respect for the person is evident, there is often real appreciation for the interest.

Fear is something everyone feels. Even the most experienced admit that there is always a degree of apprehensiveness in approaching a lost person for the first time. In one sense it is an advantage. A degree of fear sharpens our senses and helps us be at our best for Christ.

I find that it is helpful to ask, "Within reason, what is the worst thing that could happen?" Except for the rarest circumstance, harsh words, a slammed door, or a hostile attitude would be the answer. Any Christian ought to be able to handle that for Christ's sake. "Consider him who endured from sinners such hostility against himself, so that you may not grow weary or fainthearted"

(Heb. 12:3). Besides, if we are misused in the process of serving Christ, we are promised a special reward for our trouble (Matt. 5:11-12).

Fear is something to be largely overcome, "for God did not give us a spirit of timidity [fear] but a spirit of power and love and self-control. Do not be ashamed then of testifying to our Lord" (2 Tim. 1:7-8). It is not without reason that Luke spoke approvingly of the boldness of the early church (Acts 4:31).

When we do the thing we fear, we soon discover new confidence. It is best to go with some experienced person at first, and then go on our own as the fear lessens. Fear is something to commit prayerfully to the Lord. Then launch out, and you will soon say with the psalmist, "I sought the Lord, and he heard me and delivered me from all my fears" (Ps. 34:4).

What a shame if D. L. Moody's Sunday School teacher had let fear defeat him. Edward Kimball confessed his apprehension as he set out to speak to the boy. He began to think of reasons not to go. He passed the store once without noticing. Then he said, "I determined to make a dash for it and have it over at once" (Pollock 1963, 13). He found Moody with a ready heart. What a privilege he would have missed if he had succumbed to fear.

Contact and Cultivation

Some believers today actually avoid non-Christians, but if we are to witness to the unsaved we must make contact with them. This important factor will receive emphasis throughout the book. Christians must be trained to befriend the lost. Such activity must be intentional and premeditated as well as prayerful and expectant.

Cultivation is a continuation of contact and it is important for two reasons. First, witnesses need time to establish credibility with the person for whom they are concerned. Most people need some time to grow in their understanding of the message if they are to respond appropriately.

Confronting the Issue

At some point, if one senses the prospect is ready, there should be an opportunity to say yes or no to the claims of Christ. This represents Christ's own invitation to the lost person conveyed by the witness. It may be accompanied by prudent persuasion, but it must not run past the Holy Spirit or go so far as to rule out another encounter.

Continuing the Concern

Whether the person makes a commitment or not, there must be continuing concern. Many people need time. If we have given a faithful witness, the Holy Spirit can use it at his pleasure. Our task is to continue caring, praying, and ministering to needs while waiting for another natural opportunity to share the Word. We do not give up. God is at work. Everyone's circumstances are changing. "Hostile yesterday, hungry today" is frequently the case when the Holy Spirit is at work.

If the person has made a commitment, our concern is for follow-up. Though much will be said later, it is desperately necessary to help that person become established in the faith and incorporated into a local church. A new-member class is indispensable and small-group Bible study a must.

2
Effective Witness and Spiritual Discipline

"I just don't have the spiritual energy to do all that work, and neither do my people." That was the resigned reply of a pastor who had asked why I thought his church wasn't growing. I had mentioned some of the things growing churches were doing, particularly emphasizing continuing lay-witness training and vigorous visitation. He was not excited to hear it. I sensed it made him tired, and his reply was honest. It was in the same vein as the answer of a layperson who was being urged to take a course in witnessing: "I don't need another course, Pastor. I need to be motivated to do what I already know."

That accounts in part for this chapter coming so early in the book. Spiritual lethargy is a widespread disease. Much of primary motivation occurs in the prayer closet, those quiet moments when our souls feast on the Word, and sincere prayers voiced to God recharge our spirits and rekindle our resolve. The personal devotional time is a major source of spiritual energy. Without it, dreamed dreams and spiritual visions (Acts 2:17) become merely unfulfilled fancies and the memory of what might have been.

One mistake we make is in assuming. We assume most pastors practice vigorous spiritual discipline, that lay leaders study their Bibles and pray, that seminary students hold their quiettimes inviolate. Some do, of course. The truth is, however, that this is the point of struggle for many and, consequently, the major determinant of spiritual energy and vitality, or the lack of it. John Stott's honesty is refreshing. When speaking of the priority of developing the inner life, he says: "The thing I know will give me the deepest joy—namely, to be alone and unhurried in the presence of God, aware of His presence, my heart open to worship Him—is often the thing I least want to do" (Little 1966, 130).[1]

People who share their faith effectively and consistently are a particular breed. Invariably, they have a vital personal relationship with God. Sharing the faith is spiritual work. It must be done in spiritual power. It is a work which faces all kinds of opposition from the adversary, and it is never the path of least resistance. Thus, it is only those who understand and practice spiritual discipline who survive. Others witness only in spurts and experience a large measure of defeat and discouragement.

The fact is that, not only lay Christians but many preachers witness very little despite all our evangelistic noise. Meager baptismal records are one clue. Many churches manage to baptize few besides the children of deacons and faithful members. Approximately 16 percent of Southern Baptist churches baptize no one in a year's time, and among the denominations they are known for their evangelism. Surveys among Southern Baptists indicate that "less than twenty-five percent of the pastors make one evangelistic visit a week" (Ramsey 1981, 3). If pastors do little, laypersons are almost certain to do less.

I am convinced that failure at the point of spiritual discipline is a major cause of our problem. Any new resolve with regard to becoming a productive witness must begin here.

The Emerging Picture

The Example of Jesus

Jesus' frequent recourse to prayer was a fact and a problem for his disciples. When crowds were seeking him, they found it hard to understand how he could be off praying (Mark 1:35-37). They preferred action to praying, as do many modern disciples, but in the matter of winning persons and ministering to them prayer was primary. There was a certain prayer rhythm to Jesus' life. It manifested itself in his going in to God and out to people, never remaining very long among people without a return to the place of prayer.

Luke tells us that "he withdrew to the wilderness and prayed" (5:16), but his grammatical usage indicates that it was his habitual practice (Fisher 1964, 27-28). Jesus spent the whole night in prayer prior to choosing the apostles upon whom so much of the work of evangelism would depend (Does any church follow such a practice prior to selecting key leaders today?), and the importance of prayer to Jesus is seen in the forty-two references to it in his life and teaching. Twenty-one of them have to do with instances where he prayed himself, and the other twenty-one to his specific teachings about prayer (ibid., 27).

When the disciples saw that they needed to pray, it was natural that they requested Jesus to teach them (Luke 11:1). He was clearly the the master of prayer. His great prayer example challenged them and continues to inspire us today.

Besides incidents mentioned above, Jesus prayed either prior to many of the great events of the Gospels or was praying when they occurred. This was true of the feeding of the 5000 (Mark 6:41), the feeding of the 4000 (Mark 8:6), asking the disciples the crucial question as to his identity (Luke 9:18), the transfiguration (Luke 9:28-29), the Lord's Supper (Mark 14:22-23), sharing bread with the two disciples met on the Emmaus road (Luke 24:30), Peter, prior to his denial (Luke 22:31-32); the raising of Lazarus (John 11:41-42), and his passion (the prayer in Gethsemane, two versions: John 17:1-26 and Mark 14:32-42; Matt. 26:36-46; Luke 22:39-46) (compare ibid., 28).

He prayed after other events such as his baptism (Luke 3:21) and the return of the seventy (Luke 10:21-22). Prayer was even on his lips during the crucifixion (Mark 15:34; Matt. 27:46; Luke 23:34,46).

The point is that prayer was a priority with Jesus. He could walk away from huge crowds in order to pray. He missed sleep in order to pray. He is found praying before, during, and after many of the great events of his ministry. His was an example to be followed.

The Postresurrection Thrust of the Church

To begin with an emphasis on prayer and spiritual discipline is to begin where the centrifugal thrust of the church began. Following Jesus' ascension, the church gathered in the upper room to pray. They continued praying for ten days. Then came the mighty outpouring of the Spirit and the explosive evangelism of the days and years that followed. It all began in concerted prayer. That is the logical place to begin our witness today. It is a case of "first things first." In many lives, however, the case has been "first things last" or not at all.

The Pattern of the Early Church

An Atmosphere of Prayer

Not only was Pentecost preceeded by ten days of praying, prayer became a vital part of the atmosphere in which the burgeoning church grew. Luke tells us that the converts "devoted themselves to the apostles' teaching and fellowship, to the breaking of bread and the prayers" (Acts 2:42). That this remained the practice is seen in the incidents which follow.

Adversity and Prayer

When persecution arose and they were threatened by the authorities, their recourse was prayer. They asked for boldness to speak the word and for further demonstrations of God's power (Acts 4:24-30). God answered and "they were all filled with the Holy Spirit," and they continued speaking both with boldness and great power (4:31-33). Thus did mighty evangelism find its strength in prayer.

The problem over assisting widows again revealed the primary place of prayer in the early church. Seven spiritual men were chosen to deal with the problem, so that the twelve might devote themselves "to prayer and to the ministry of the word" (Acts 6:4). These social needs were not neglected! In fact, caring for the poor was a primary concern which had already produced great generosity (2:43-45; 4:36-37). This wise disposal of the jealousy problem and the primary emphasis on prayer and sharing the Word resulted in extraordinary evangelism and expansion of the church.

When the first martyr died, he did so with an evangelist's prayer on his lips. He asked God that he not "hold this sin against them." Though they stoned him, Stephen hoped in his last moment that his executioners might be the recipients of God's forgiveness and salvation (Acts 7:60).

So it was when Peter was imprisoned. The response of the church was to make "earnest prayer for him . . . to God" (Acts 12:5). Such was the atmosphere in which tremendous evangelistic growth took place. Prayer was the fuel that fed the flames of evangelistic fire.

Paul and Silas found themselves imprisoned in Philippi because of their merciful ministry to a demon-possessed girl. They had been beaten and their feet placed in stocks, but they clearly demonstrated the nature of their life-style in that they prayed and sang praises to God (Acts 16:25). They had taken Jesus seriously when he taught that men "ought always to pray, and not to faint" (Luke 18:1, KJV).

Expansion and Prayer

Though the passage will be noted later, it is important to see that prayer was vitally involved in sensing and knowing God's leadership in various aspects of missionary enterprise. It was "while they were worshiping the Lord and fasting, the Holy Spirit said, 'Set apart for me Barnabas and Saul for the work to which I have called them' " (Acts 13:2). Prayer was surely a part of worship and was always the companion of fasting. With further fasting and prayer they "laid their hands on them and sent them off" (13:3).

Fasting and prayer was a central activity that accompanied the appointment of elders in the newly established churches (Acts 14:23). The selection of those leaders, who would be vitally involved in the strengthening and further evangelistic ministry of the churches, was a solemn, spiritual occasion. Much was at stake in churches and in individual lives by their appointment. It called for the most fervent prayer to the exclusion of concerns like eating.

A Matter of Obedience

Thus far most of what has been said has related directly to prayer. While prayer may be the most critical matter in spiritual growth in that it seems the most difficult matter to master, the concern of the New Testament is wider than that. Growth in every area of life is in view. Knowing the Scriptures, using gifts, serving others, and Kingdom living are all vital matters of spiritual discipline.

Growth Instructions to Individuals and Churches

Paul's command to his young friend in 1 Timothy 4:7 is one of the clear expressions of this theme. "Train yourself in godliness." Paul goes on to point out that "we toil and strive" to this very purpose (v. 10). It is something he and those with him were doing; and lest some think this was an admonition addressed only to a young preacher, Paul went on to say, "Command and teach these things" (4:11). The whole church should engage in this training in spiritual fitness.

Since Paul was using an athletic metaphor and comparing benefits of physical exercise with that of spiritual, it is well to point out one additional matter. Modern students of physical fitness have concluded that if exercise is to be beneficial, it must be vigorous and regular. In view of the prominence of the discipline theme in the New Testament, it is not too much to say that spiritual exercise must have the same characteristics.

One of my seminary professors, Dr. W. W. Adams, emphasized that the Holy Spirit is the "Spirit of truth." We can easily limit what God might be able to do with us by the meager amount of truth that we possess. Did not Jesus say, "Sanctify them in thy truth; thy word is truth" (John 17:17)? Those times in the prayer closet with open Bible should be times of learning and of listening to what God may say through his Word.

Some great saints of the past have read the Bible on their knees. George Whitfield was a prime example; and as an additional spiritual exercise, he read Matthew Henry's commentary on his knees. This devotion to spiritual discipline was basic to the unusually fruitful ministry which was his.

At 47 City Road in London is the restored home of John Wesley where he lived the last twelve years of his life. On the third floor is Wesley's bedchamber adjoined by a tiny room with a window and miniature fireplace which he used as a prayer closet. His table, kneeling bench, and candlestand are there along with his chair. On the prayer table someone had lettered on a card one of his remarks about that prayer room. It read: "I sit down alone; only God is here. In his presence I open; I read his book, and what I learn, I teach." Those hours of learning in the prayer closet obviously meant much to him and, consequently, countless others. The lessons absorbed in the quiet hours with God were impregnated with power. That process has not changed. It is a necessary, but often missing, element of Christian growth and witness today.

Praying for Others Who Witness

Paul saw a definite connection between sharing the message and the prayer of others. When he wrote to the Colossians, he first admonished them, "Continue steadfastly in prayer" (4:2). Then he said, "Pray for us also, that God may open to us a door for the word, to declare the mystery of Christ, . . . that I may make it clear, as I ought to speak" (Col. 4:3-4). Doubtless Paul prayed about these things himself, but it was of such importance that he commanded them to pray as well. He wrote a very similar instruction to the Thessalonians (2 Thess. 3:1), to the Ephesians (6:19), and, doubtless, repeated his request many times in his oral messages to the church. Sharing the Word is a matter worthy of the widest possible prayer support.

The All-Inclusiveness of Prayer

To be exhaustive concerning prayer in the New Testament would require a large book, and no effort of that sort is intended or possible here. Yet, in addition to the direct or indirect prayers surrounding and enveloping evangelism, there are certain commands or admonitions that emphasize the central place Paul intended prayer to have. For example, he wrote (author's italics): "Pray *at all times* in the Spirit, . . . with all perseverance, making supplication for *all the saints*" (Eph. 6:18); "Have no anxiety about anything, but *in everything* by prayer and supplication with thanksgiving let your requests be made known to God. And the peace of God, which passes all understanding, will keep your hearts and your minds in Christ Jesus" (Phil. 4:6-7); "Pray *constantly,* give thanks *in all circumstances,* for this is the will of God in Christ Jesus for you" (1 Thess. 5:17-18); "I urge that supplications, prayers, intercessions, and thanksgivings be made for *all men*"(1 Tim. 2:1); and "I desire then that *in every place* the men should pray, lifting holy hands without anger or quarreling" (1 Tim. 2:8). Christians were to pray and give thanks at all times, for all the saints, in all circumstances, in everything, and in every place. This was the spiritual backdrop against which evangelism played its role in the New Testament world. It is little wonder that the early witnesses were amazed at the effectiveness and power of the message.

A Prerequisite to Power

Jesus' Unforgettable Words

One particularly salient passage of Scripture that shows spiritual power to be dependent on prayer is in Mark 9:14-29. While Peter, James, and John had gone to the mount of transfiguration, a distraught father with a deaf, dumb, epileptic son came seeking the help of Jesus. Since Jesus was gone, he asked the remaining disciples for help. They tried to minister to the boy and failed completely, much to the disappointment of the father.

When Jesus returned, the crowd, including some scribes, was still there enjoying the embarrassment of the disciples whose failure had been so public. The father explained about the boy and his symptoms and said, "I asked your disciples to cast it out, and they were not able" (v. 18). Interestingly enough, "they were not able" could just as well be translated, "they had no strength" or "they had no power." Facing such tragic need these disciples were powerless and ill prepared, a sad story, all too often the case of the church in history and in contemporary Christian experience.

Jesus' disappointment in them is clear, "O faithless generation, how long am I to be with you? How long am I to bear with you?" (v. 19). He obviously expected more of them than they had shown.

It is noteworthy that when this man asked Jesus for help he did so with words of doubt and uncertainty. "But if you can do anything, have pity on us and help us" (v. 22). Gutzke points out that this is the only case in the New Testament where one seeking help came with such a spirit of skepticism (1975, 120).

The contrast is shocking indeed when we compare it with other cases like the leper, "If you will, you can make me clean" (Mark 1:40); or the woman with the issue of blood, "If I touch even his garments, I shall be made well" (Mark 5:28); or the centurion with the sick servant, "Lord I am not worthy to have you come under my roof; but only say the word, and my servant will be healed" (Matt. 8:8); or the four men who were so convinced that Jesus was the answer to their friend's need that they dug through the roof to get the paralytic to him (Mark 2:2-5).

We do not have to look far to find the reason for the father's doubt. He had just asked help from Jesus' disciples who claimed to know him and to be very close to him. They had shown themselves, however, to be utterly powerless. It was natural after such a disappointing experience with his disciples to suppose that Jesus would not be able to help either. Is that not a reason so many are skeptical about Jesus today? They have seen too many of his disciples who claim to be close to him who manifest an unmistakable powerlessness in daily life. It is natural for them to suppose that Jesus would be powerless to help them as well.

There is another lesson of extreme importance. To try to do spiritual work without spiritual power may not only be unfruitful; it *may do great harm.* The father was obviously worse off faithwise after his encounter with the disciples than before he met them. By the time he addressed Jesus, any sense of expectation was almost gone.

After Jesus had drawn out such faith as the father had and healed the boy, the disciples asked why they had failed. Jesus told them plainly, "This kind cannot be driven out by anything but prayer" (Mark 9:29). In other words, they had failed in the matter of prayer. That sort of problem yielded only to prayer, and they, apparently, had not done any.

In a very real way the boy's sad condition symbolizes the world to which we are to minister. It is deaf to our message that Christ is the answer to its most basic needs. It is dumb in that, though aware that much is tragically wrong, it cannot verbalize its problem or identify its malady. Moreover, the world cannot say, "Jesus is Lord," for that can only be the expression inspired by the Holy Spirit (1 Cor. 12:3). Quite as serious is the fact that, like the boy who threw himself into the fire and into the water, it seems bent on self-destructive acts, and it cannot seem to control these inclinations. Ecologically, the world is destroying the very environment upon which it depends. Politically, it is building the weapons to end its own existence. In more personal terms, there is a widespread tendency toward destructive addictions and enslaving habits from which there is no self-rescue. "This kind cannot be driven out by anything except prayer" (Mark 9:29). Powerless evangelism and ministry can only leave the world in worse shape than before.

They had to learn what we must learn. Last week's prayer will not suffice for this week's ministry. Neither these disciples nor today's are repositories of power which may be wielded at will. God's people are merely channels through whom God's power flows, and that is dependent upon a vital continuing relationship of prayer and spiritual discipline. Only then can witness be powerful and effective, and this is why personal evangelism—one of the greatest of all ministries—must begin in the prayer closet with an open Bible and a listening ear.

The Awareness of Power

Most servants of God can tell the difference between prayerfulness and prayerlessness in Christian service. Without prayer there is a lack of expectancy and a deficiency in earnestness. Warmth may be wanting and a certain perfunctory tone marks the activity. Even if the prospect or other Christians fail to detect it the prayerless witness knows, and a kind of hypocritical role play begins to emerge.

The simplest test of spiritual discipline for preachers who give invitations is the ease or nonease with which it is extended. Faithful prayer and study makes the invitation natural and fervent. Neglect, on the other hand, renders it difficult and unnatural. To extend an invitation after prayerless preaching creates an unmistakable dissonance well known to the ministry.

The same thing is experienced by the witness who invites people to make a decision without adequate prayer. It is a subjective matter, of course, but it is a phenomenon that is well known.

A Prominent Example

South Korea stands out today among the places in the world where powerful evangelism is taking place. Figures have been changing rapidly, but there is now 27.1 percent of the population embracing Christianity (*Working Together* 1983, 21) as against only 11 percent in 1966 (Wagner 1981, 136). "Evangelicals are growing five times faster than the population" (Nelson 1982, 175).

Americans who visit the churches are amazed at the prayer activity of the Koreans. In one church where I preached, two hundred persons came every morning at 5:00 to pray. In addition, there was all-night prayer every Friday night. In another church, members had covenanted together to spend four hundred nights in all-night prayer. Five members came every night at 10:00 and prayed until 6:00 the next morning. The vital relation between the prayer and the vigorous evangelistic missionary activity stands out in broad relief. South Korea today is a remarkable challenge to the devotional life of Christians all over the world.

Spiritual Discipline and Communication

Spiritual discipline has much to do with effective communication. As we have seen, communicating the gospel is what God had in mind for his church. It must take place if people are to hear and believe. We may expect that the rules of communication science will have large application to all that we do.

Importance of Credibility

Preaching, of course, is not the only way of communicating. Kraft feels that "life involvement" was the major method Jesus used. He means by this "a long-term association between communicator and receptor in a variety of life situations, many of which might be quite informal and not highly dependent upon verbalization as the only means of communication" (Kraft 1979, 46). That involved an impressively credible life. Perhaps no element in gospel communication is so important as credibility.

Spiritual discipline is a primary means of becoming what God has called us to be. It is in those exercises that we sense God's leadership and guidance. It is there that we confess and repent, reorient ourselves in spiritual concern, and renew our purpose to walk in the Spirit. It is spiritual discipline more than anything else that determines the kind of Christians we will be. It is only by spending time with God that we can become more like him. Here the inner self is nourished. That will determine to a great degree what other people see of the outer person, for the outer life is determined in large degree by the inner (Prov. 4:23).

A credible witness is simply one that can be believed. What a person is, always has much to do with the effectiveness of any encounter.

It is not possible for a witness to separate himself or herself from the message. The messenger is a message and a very important part of the whole.

The Credibility of Jesus

One of the reasons Jesus' words carried such authority was that he was absolutely credible. He did nothing to contradict what he taught. On one occasion when his enemies were so incensed that they "took up stones again to stone him" (John 10:31), Jesus challenged them on the basis of his own credibility. He said, "If I am not doing the works of my Father, then do not believe me; if I do them, even though you do not believe me, believe the works, that you may know and understand that the Father is in me and I am in the Father" (John 10:37-38).

Earlier Jesus had asked, "Which of you convicts me of sin? If I tell the truth, why do you not believe me?" (John 8:46). And when Jesus was tried, Pilate was compelled to say to the Jews, "I find no crime in this man" (Luke 23:4). This is precisely why he was so disturbing.

The cause of the unbelief of Jesus' enemies was to be found in them, not in him. He had been absolutely credible in the totality of his witness, and he was able to remind them of that. This, of course, is not true of witnesses today. Unfortunately, all too often the stumbling blocks are found in the messengers themselves. While human witnesses can achieve the credibility of Jesus only in degree, it is imperative that every witness be as credible as possible. We are epistles to be "known and read by all men" (2 Cor. 3:2); and it is still true that "he who says he abides in him ought to walk in the same way in which he walked" (1 John 2:6).

Paul's Concern for Credibility

Paul's credibility is a major concern in two epistles. In Galatians he takes great pains to reestablish his integrity. After Paul had visited Galatia on the first missionary journey, certain false teachers, whose exact identity is unknown, came preaching the necessity of keeping the law (Gal. 3:2). They apparently attacked Paul's apostleship and authority as well as his teaching. The urgent nature of the letter suggests that some were beginning to follow and believe them.

It is not hard to imagine the probable accusations against Paul. These teachers would have been quick to point out Paul's inferiority in comparison to the other apostles. Paul had not been with Jesus during his earthly ministry. The other apostles had. Almost without exception, they confined their ministry to Jews. Jesus also had ministered largely to Jews. The Old Testament said the law and covenant was forever (depending on their obedience); and when Jesus had sent out the twelve and the seventy he had sent them to Jews only (Matt. 10; Mark 6). Paul's ministry and message to Gentiles was to them a contradiction. These were plausible arguments to some, and Paul was not there to defend himself.

Chapters 1 and 2, therefore, are Paul's attempts to reestablish himself with the Galatians. He emphasized that he was an apostle by the will of God. Men had nothing to do with his call or appointment (1:17). His message was also from God (1:12). Men had no part in it (1:1). He had been a zealous Jew, even a persecutor of the church, but God had called him for a special ministry to the Gentiles (1:13-16). After conversion, he had gone into Arabia for an indefinite period, and he had not conferred with flesh and blood (1:17). When he had gone to Jerusalem three years later, it was only for fifteen days, and then he had seen only two apostles. In other words, the exposure was too brief to be seen as a means of getting his message from others (1:18-19).

When he did go to Jerusalem for an extended stay, he had laid his ministry to the Gentiles before those of repute: James, Cephas, and John. They gave their approval and extended to him the right hand of fellowship (2:1-10). Later Paul had had an encounter in Antioch with Peter. Under pressure from some Jerusalem Jews, Peter had withdrawn from table fellowship with the Gentile believers. Paul had rebuked Peter publicly and had won his point. Thus, it had been widely recognized, even by pillars of the church, that his message and ministry were of God. If that were not enough, Paul pointed out that he bore "on [his] body the marks of Jesus" (6:17), meaning the scars and wounds of his suffering. These were powerful proofs of his utter sincerity and commitment to the Lord, whose slave he was.

Why did Paul go to such lengths to defend his reputation against accusations by false teachers? It was because he knew that if the Galatians did not believe him, they would not believe his message. His credibility was the key to everything.

Paul did a similar thing in the last four chapters of 2 Corinthians. He had been attacked by false teachers who, once again, cannot be precisely identified. Paul used chapters 10—13 in an attempt to reestablish his credibility so damaged by these ruthless intruders. Among the things Paul pointed out was the fact that he had taken no money from them (2 Cor. 11:7). Instead, intense suffering had been his pay for spreading the message (11:23-33). He had performed the signs of a true apostle among them (12:12) and had not taken advantage of them in any way (12:16-18).

Since this church was greatly troubled, Paul planned another trip to see them. He wanted his visit to be as effective as possible. It was altogether important to reestablish his credibility, so they would believe him when he came.

As far as non-Christians were concerned, Paul was fully aware that he had to win them to himself before he could win them to Christ. This is reflected in his important statement about identity in 1 Corinthians 9:20-22: "While working with the Jews, I live like a Jew in order to win them; and even though I myself am not subject to the Law of Moses, I live as though I were when working with those who are, in order to win them. In the same way, when working with Gentiles, I live like a Gentile, outside the Jewish Law, in order to win Gentiles. This does not mean that I don't obey God's law; I am really under Christ's law. Among the weak in faith I become weak like one of them, in order to win them. So I become all things to all men, that I may save some of them by whatever means are possible" (GNB). In other words, Paul became as nearly like those to whom he witnessed as he could without compromise of Christian principle. Though a Jew, with his own culture precious to him, he was willing to live as a Gentile for the sake of credibility. He sought to see things from a Gentile point of view, state the gospel in Gentile terms of understanding, live as they lived, and feel as they felt. Paul said he did this "for the sake of the gospel" (9:23). He understood that it was necessary if he was to draw men to Christ.

Paul endeavored to show them the Christian life as well as tell them about it. His illustration other than Jesus was himself. More than once Paul dared to say, "Imitate me" (1 Cor. 4:16; 11:1; Phil. 3:17; 4:9; 2 Thess. 3:7-9). This was no arrogant statement. Paul knew the tremendous power of a credible example. Though he was not unaware of imperfections, he was confident that he was following the Lord (1 Cor. 11:1). This same emphasis and concern is no less necessary today.

The Pietists in Germany in the seventeenth and eighteenth centuries were known for their emphasis of spiritual discipline. Daily Bible study, earnest prayer, and small groups for growth were essential elements of this emphasis. One of their greatest leaders was August Francke. A paragraph about him by Earnest Stoeffler accents all that has been said.

> As a preacher he appears to have been eminently successful. Everywhere he went crowds strained to hear him. This seems the more remarkable, since the sermons which have come down to us appear to lack all sparkle and originality. They are hastily put together, insufferably repetitious discourses on a selection of themes which remain endlessly the same. There are few illustrations, no interesting turns in phraseology, no startling insights. In fact, they seem to be consciously following the model of Puritan sermons, which were designed not to be "witty." Thus, the appeal of Francke's sermonic effectiveness must be sought on the one hand, in his transparent sincerity, which gave everything he said an utterly authentic ring. His readers invariably felt that the message he brought them came directly from God. On the other hand, Francke was an uncommonly kind and gentle man, who seemed to be concerned personally about everybody's problem, without ever creating the impression of wanting to meddle in other people's business. For this reason the dirty alleys of Glaucha, with the accumulated filth of its 2000 inhabitants, suddenly seemed brighter when the "Pastor" passed by, while its many establishments for making whiskey, and its innumerable and ill-reputed taverns, seemed a little more like the portals of hell which Francke thought they were. Thus, to a most unusual degree the Pastor of Glaucha was his own message (Stoeffler 1973, 33-34).

The Power of Nonverbal Messages

Whatever a witness is, he must be a personal interactor and a communicator. In recent years many aspects of human interaction have been thoroughly investigated, and there has been a move away from the idea that communication is always verbal. In a face-to-face encounter, much communication is nonverbal, and, depending on what is communicated, it may be the most important part. One authority puts it as follows: "NV [nonverbal] signals for interpersonal attitudes are far more powerful than initially similar verbal ones.

. . . Usually the impact of words is weaker and less direct than the impact of nonverbal signals" (Argyle 1975, 362).

Nonverbal communication has to do with such things as facial expression, bodily movements, posture, gestures, eye contact, spatial distance between communicator and receptor, vocal quality, and intonation of voice. It is all that is left after the words are taken away, and, lest someone think this a fairly simple matter, we should know that there are many types of each of the classifications mentioned above.

Nonverbal communication is by its very nature far more limited in scope than verbal, but it is powerful to convey feelings of emotions, interpersonal attitudes, and even certain aspects of the communicator's personality. All of us convey feelings or attitudes of boredom, excitement, surprise, fear, interest, anger, pain, happiness, liking, esteem, guilt, doubt, lack of confidence or its opposite, and any number of other things without uttering a word. For example, a simple thing like leaning toward a person is a nonverbal indication of positive feeling as is looking at a person and smiling warmly. Even the degree of relaxation we assume can carry either a positive or a negative message.

There are at least two factors concerning this type of communication that makes it a matter of concern to the personal witness and that relate it to prayer and spiritual discipline. One is that it is powerful to either affirm or contradict what is said. People do not always tell the truth. They can send some very contradictory messages. For example, in response to a husband's question "What's the matter?" a wife may say, "Nothing is the matter!" but in such a way that the husband knows something is amiss indeed. Or a child who wants very much to continue swimming says, "I'm not cold," but chattering teeth and goose bumps tell quite a different story.

Many cases are far less obvious, but conflict is evidenced nevertheless. The contradictory message might be such a simple thing as a closed posture position which the receptor, though aware of some negative impact, cannot quite identify.

Second, while nonverbal signals can be conscious, they are more likely to be unconscious for most people

> do not know what they are doing with their bodies when they are talking and no one tells them. People learn to disregard the internal cues which are informative about their stream of body movements and facial expressions. Most interactive nonverbal behavior seems to be enacted with little conscious choice of registration, efforts to inhibit what is shown fail because the information about what is occuring is not customarily within awareness (Mortenson 1972, 212).

If, in our sharing effort, we are thoroughly in tune with God and earnestly compassionate and sincere, our nonverbal signals will reinforce and affirm everything we say. We will be much more apt to be convincing and to make a favorable impression on the person to whom we speak. If, on the other hand, our spiritual attitudes and fellowship with God are not what they should be, that may not be the result at all. It is possible for the nonverbal signals to altogether contradict what we say.

This is part of the reason nonverbal cues make such an impact. In that most of them are beyond our control because we are unaware of them, they are not apt to be faked or manipulated and thus are more believable. Therefore, when there is a conflict between verbal and nonverbal messages, it is probable that the nonverbal signals will be believed.

The importance of this is that God's servants are often called upon to bear witness to what may seem to be some very unlovable people. Some of them may bear the marks and wounds of wasted years. Others possess the habits, demeanor, and language of progressive disintegration. Some may be near the final limits of those destructive processes, and the evidence may be physical and moral filth, poverty, and a life situation that, from some viewpoints, is revolting. Sensitive Christians can quite unintentionally register shock or disapproval and, despite the best of intentions, find their encounter a distasteful task. Though the proper words may be spoken, their true feelings and emotions have unmistakably been communicated by nonverbal means. As those who have worked with deeply sinful people know, except a vital spiritual discipline regularly renews the flow of Christlike compassion and unless the ideals of selfless service are daily reaffirmed in prayer and commitment, it could be that some very bad situations will only be made worse.

Not only this, but some people to whom we attempt to share our witness may be quite skeptical to begin with. They may be convinced that Christians are not what they pretend at all. Certainly some of them will have heard or even spoken themselves of all the hypocrites in the churches.

To fail in prayer and vital spiritual exercise as the preparation and undergirding for effective witness may be to reveal unconsciously our inadequate and unprepared hearts and to confirm quite unintentionally the worst suspicions of the unbelieving. Hypocrites are, after all, those who send contradictory messages.

----

[1] Little is quoting John Stott at a Keswick Convention speaking engagement.

3
Theological Themes
for Witness

Every witness is a theologian. No one can explain God's salvation without expressing theology, nor will anyone be a consistent witness without some solid theological convictions. Some themes figure in every evangelistic encounter, and others continually give strength and zeal to the witness's endeavor. A number deserve our careful attention but space permits only those which are most basic.

The Seeking God

Evangelism is the human expression of the seeking nature of God. It is a manifestation of his action in the world through human instrumentality and an enterprise in which his Triune being is vitally involved. We may say that God's great redemptive plan was conceived by the Father, realized in the Son, and continues on by the Holy Spirit in and through human instrumentality. The operation in its entirety is firmly rooted in the love of God.

In the Old Testament

The first suggestion of God as the seeking God is seen at the very beginning of the human drama. Irrespective of the tragic failure of the first couple, and despite the fact that their disobedience was no secret to the omniscient God, the Father came seeking them in the garden (Gen. 3:9). He was not through with them despite their sin. God mercifully clothed them and set them outside the garden lest they "take also of the tree of life . . . and live forever" in a rebellious state (Hendricks 1977, 29).

Throughout the rest of the Old Testament, God attempted to seek out a people for himself, a people to bless and use in his redemptive purpose. All his sendings are related to this beneficent purpose. All of them speak clearly of the love of God.

In the New Testament

It is in the New Testament, however, where "the reality of God as seeking love" is seen in a new dimension. This is seen to be "at the very heart of our Lord's message and mission" (Ladd 1974, 82). In Christ, God takes the initiative in seeking out sinners. He was actively searching out "true worshipers" who would venerate him "in spirit and truth" for, as Jesus said, "such the Father seeks to worship him" (John 4:23).

Though no one was excluded, outcasts were prominent in his concern. Jesus especially identified with the lowly. While other religious leaders shunned them, Jesus sought them. He initiated the conversation with the woman of Sychar. He invited himself to Zacchaeus's house (Luke 19:5). He sent the twelve to the "lost sheep of the house of Israel" (Matt. 10:1-15). He constantly issued invitations, such as: "Come and see," "Follow me!" "Come unto me!" And to such people! The religious establishment recoiled from them. Jesus drew near them and walked by their side.

In Luke 15, Jesus, who came and showed us the Father (John 14:8-10), pictured God's seeking love most unforgettably. God was like a shepherd seeking his lost sheep, like a woman diligently seeking her lost coin, like a loving father longing after his prodigal son. Among his own statements of mission (to be discussed in chapter 4) was "the Son of Man came to seek and to save the lost" (Luke 19:10).

Other New Testament examples abound, which show that only unspeakable love would so seek out such undeserving creatures. No theological theme is more important in evangelism than this. Only infinite love would have devised such a plan.

Man Who Hides

Genesis tells us "they heard the sound of the Lord God walking in the garden . . . and the man and his wife hid themselves from the presence of the Lord God" (Gen. 3:8). Why would Adam and Eve hide from such a beneficent God? The answer is that they sensed the estrangement caused by their disobedience, and they were ashamed to encounter God. To this day all persons hide from God and avoid him for the same reason.

Man's Creation

The enormity of Adam's sin can only be seen against the background of creation. The Bible insists that man is a part of God's good creation (Gen. 1:31). Not only this, God distinguished man from every other created thing in that he made him in his own image (Gen. 1:27). This means that God endowed him with "the potentiality, ability, and responsibility to respond to God, the self, and others" (Hendricks 1977, 48). Additionally, he was a social being so created to experience completeness only in relation to others, hence the creation of Eve. Finally, God's human creations were free to make choices, a freedom necessary to moral beings. They were even free to rebel against their Maker. It was this "God-given freedom into which man was thrust that was the occasion but not the necessity for evil" (Stagg 1962, 19).

Man's Tragedy

In the context of this freedom—facing Satan's temptation—the couple exercised their privilege to choose in a most dreadful way. They chose against God. In simple terms a rebellion occured. Pride emerged, and Adam and Eve attempted to make themselves God. The empty promises of the adversary, "You will not die. . . . You will be like God," were too appealing. They sought to escape their dependence and be independent of their Creator (Gen. 3:4-5). They fell. Important for evangelism is the fact that this is the recurring experience of every person.

Far-reaching Results

The most obvious result of this tragic cosmic event was broken relationships. As sinful persons, the first couple could no longer enjoy their relationship with the holy God. They were no longer innocent. That is why they hid among the trees of the garden.

The relationship of Adam and Eve was also broken as Adam compounded his deed by blaming her. Their relationship with their environment was corrupted as they were no longer fit to live in the garden. They were now foreign to that surrounding. They must henceforth live outside in an environment that also bore the curse of their transgression.

Witnesses deal with many broken relationships today. The fall shows that a right relationship to God is basic to all other relationships. It is only when the broken vertical relationship to God is restored that horizontal human relationships can begin to achieve their full potential.

No one has escaped the effects of Adam's sin; for "as sin came into the world through one man and death through sin, and so death spread to all men because all men sinned" (Rom. 5:12). Adam's failure brought both death and sin into the world. However, persons become guilty not because Adam sinned, but as Romans 5:12 says, "because all men sinned." In other words it is personal sin, not Adam's sin that renders persons guilty before God.

Adam's sin did, however, result in "a state of sin in which there are tendencies that later lead to actual transgression" (Moody 1981, 290). Thus it is that "all men sinned," and evil and death became the universal experience.

It is against this background that theologians have often described man's problem as both "sins" and "sin." "Sins" include wrong acts and choices as well as improper attitudes and dispositions of mind. "Sin" is the inner principle against which persons struggle, "the nature and environment inclined toward sin" of which Paul wrote in Romans 7. "I do not do what I want, but I do the very thing I hate. . . . It is no longer I that do it, but sin which dwells within me" (7:15,17). All persons suffer the negative pressures of demonic forces that control and permeate the world that surrounds them.

Fisher Humphreys summarizes the problem succinctly: "Some of our problem is our own fault—we do wrong. And some of it is not our fault—things go wrong. For our sins we are guilty and need forgiveness; in our sin we are helpless and need liberation" (Humphreys 1974, 84).

What is abundantly clear is that man's predicament is utterly serious. The image is indeed marred. It is not strange, therefore, that, among other things, the Bible speaks of persons as lost, alienated, in darkness, blind, dead in trespasses and sins, children of wrath, transgressors, sons of disobedience, separated from Christ, strangers, far off, inhuman, unholy, haters of good, without hope, and without God.

The problem is of such magnitude that the only solution was divine intervention. Fortunately, though Adam and Eve hid themselves in the garden, they could still hear God's voice as he sought them. Part of the good news today is that sinful persons can hear the voice of the seeking God who has intervened to provide for their redemption.

Christ and His Redeeming Work

The Person of Christ

Since the Council of Chalcedon in AD 451, the church, both Catholic and Protestant, has agreed that Jesus was truly God and truly man. He was the divine Son of God who had become a man. These two natures were perfectly united in one personality. John declared, "The Word became flesh and dwelt among us, full of grace and truth; we have beheld his glory, glory as of the only Son from the Father" (John 1:14). "And the Word was God" (1:1). This was one apostolic testimony, among many, to the effect that one who was God assumed flesh and became also man to accomplish the redemption of lost humanity. Because that is true, millions have since echoed Thomas's confession, "My Lord and my God!" (John 20:28).

It is not enough that witnesses understand who Jesus is or to say that he died for our sins. Some prospective Christians will want to know more. What did such a death mean? Why did Jesus have to die to save mankind? Some understanding of the meaning of the atonement is therefore necessary.

The Bible does not give us a neatly packaged theory, nor did any of the early church councils attempt a definitive interpretation. Attempts by theologians since that time have been legion. Many of them have been helpful, but there is a consensus that no theory or combination of ideas has ever sufficiently explained this monumental event.

The central place of the atonement in the Scriptures is clear. A larger portion of the Gospels is given to that event than to any other. The cross was the central focus of apostolic preaching. While Paul did not view it in isolation from the resurrection, or the person and ministry of Jesus, his emphasis upon the cross was remarkable.

To the Corinthians, he could refer to his message as "the word of the cross" (1 Cor. 1:18); and he determined that amidst such wickedness, he would proclaim "nothing . . . except Jesus Christ and him crucified" (2:2). Paul could describe it thus because that was the central theme of all he proclaimed. It was the "word of the cross" that caused men to see their sin most clearly and led them to embrace the Savior most dearly.

While admitting inadequacy before this greatest of cosmic events, there are some understandings based on Scripture and long-standing attempts at interpretation that witnesses may pass on to their inquirers.

As Enabling Forgiveness

First, Christ bore our sins in such a way as to enable God to forgive us. Granted there are difficult questions, and our efforts must always end in mystery, but the Scriptures emphatically proclaim that this is true. Jesus understood his death in this way (Matt. 26:28), and the apostolic preaching trumpeted this truth as well (2 Cor. 5:21; Eph. 1:7; Col. 1:14; 1 Pet. 2:24; 3:18).

It was not, however, that God was merely a bystander who caused Jesus to die. "God was in Christ, reconciling the world unto himself" (2 Cor. 5:19, KJV). "The fullness of God is involved in Jesus' death, and the purpose for it and the plan it effects" (Hendricks 1980, 99).

Vincent Taylor has said, "Christ's passion is the kind of suffering which even men endure when they deeply love wrong doers, and it shows that forgiveness is not a light and easy thing" (1953, 45). At the cross, God in Christ accepted the pain and hurt of all our sin. The price was high. No man can do more than to lay himself down to die while praying for the forgiveness of his executioners. Because he so accepted the consequences sin caused, consequences that should have been ours, he can freely forgive us and enable us to have fellowship with God (compare Humphreys 1974, 114-118). Surely this is one aspect of the cross that is primary for evangelism.

As Enabling Victory

The cross means defeat for the forces of evil that enslave us. Jesus' whole life can be seen as a struggle with the forces of evil. Following baptism he was sorely tempted by Satan but emerged victorious. In Luke 10, when the seventy returned with their excited reports of demons being subject to the name of Christ, Jesus saw this as a great defeat for Satan (10:18). When Peter preached to Cornelius, he referred to Jesus as one who "went about doing good and healing all who were oppressed by the devil" (Acts 10:38). The cross was the grand climax of that struggle, and Jesus was the victor as confirmed unmistakably by the resurrection. Though evil forces are still active, the fatal blow has already been struck at Calvary. Because Christ won the victory over sin and death, we who are "in him" by faith can also experience victory. This means that, by the power of God's Holy Spirit we can live the overcoming life now and enjoy an eternal triumph over the grave later.

As Manifesting an Exacting Love

The cross is the supreme revelation of the love of God. Paul said, "God shows his love for us in that while we were yet sinners Christ died for us" (Rom. 5:8). John 3:16 has long been a primary passage that declared that love was responsible for the cross. The Scriptures declare also that it was a product of Christ's love (Gal. 2:20; Eph. 5:2,25). We have already seen that fullness of God was involved in the cross.

When an individual recognizes in a very personal way that Christ's death occurred in the process of rescuing perishing humanity, and when the momentous nature of that event begins to dawn, it awakens a corresponding love that will not permit that one to ever be the same again.

Others would doubtless emphasize other matters concerning the atonement, and there are other ideas and emphases that are of great importance. However, I believe these to be of greatest importance in evangelism. Christ's suffering enables God to forgive us. Christ's victory at Calvary enables us to live victorious lives now and to triumph later over the grave. It is the cross which kindles in us a Christlike love which we must manifest in the world.

Conversion

Years ago I paid a pastoral call on an elderly lady who was a new but zealous member of my church. I was reluctant to stop by. I had been there before, and the home was contentious. Two divorced daughters and their children also shared the small domicile, and they displayed their unhappiness like a badge. They made me feel that my visits were barely sufferable events and the cause of great inconvenience. Nevertheless, I went because of the mother.

Imagine my surprise when one daughter greeted me with "I don't know what that church has done to my mother, but she is a different person the last few months." She was obviously pleased about the change.

What had happened was that the mother had been converted. She was different—radically so, for as Paul said, "If anyone is in Christ, he is a new creation; the old has passed, behold, the new has come" (2 Cor. 5:17).

The Meaning of Conversion

A turning.—The word *conversion* is a translation of the Greek noun ἐπισ-τροφή. It occurs only once in the Greek New Testament (Acts 15:3). Some form of the verb ἐπιστρέφειν, "to turn," however, occurs some thirty-nine times. It is most frequently translated by the word *turn* or *return.* This is as it should be in that "the basic meaning of the word . . . is a turning round either in the physical or mental or spiritual sense of the term; and . . . when the word moves into the world of thought and religion it means a change of outlook and a new direction given to life and to action" (Barclay 1972, 20). Various forms of the word στρέφειν is used eighteen times, and its meaning is practically identical with ἐπιστρέφειν (ibid., 20).

A radical change.—It is clear that the "turn" the New Testament writers have in mind is a radical one. It is a "turn from darkness to light and from the power of Satan to God" (Acts 26:18). It is "from idols, to serve a living and true God" (1 Thess. 1:9), and a "turn from these vain things to a living God" (Acts 14:15). Often the word is used of those who simply turn to the Lord or to God (Acts 9:35; 15:29; 26:20; 1 Pet. 2:25), but they have turned away from unbelief and self-centeredness in order to do so. Such is the nature of the change called "conversion." It is a radical change and represents a reorientation and redirection of the whole person.

Repentance and conversion.—Occasionally the word *repent,* a form of μετανοεῖν, is used with a form of the verb for "be converted" or "turn." In Acts 3:19 Peter exhorted the Temple crowd to "Repent therefore, and turn again, that your sins may be blotted out" (also Acts 26:20). The two verbs are very similar in meaning though Stagg says, "The idea of conversion, which includes the whole man, more adequately represents the Greek noun μετανοία than does repentance" (ibid., 119). Haenchen remarks that both verbs can mean the "turning" to God, but when they "are found together, μετανοεῖν will express more the turning away from evil," and "ἐπιστρέφειν . . . the positive new direction" (Haenchen 1971, 208). Lenski says that the use of the latter "re-enforces" the former (1944, 141). The authorities obviously do not entirely agree, but one can conclude that the meaning of the two is very similar and generally express the same idea. There was no rigid, carefully defined way of expressing these things when the New Testament was written. The writers moved easily from one term to another to express this radical change in human experience. "Repentance to God and of faith in our Lord Jesus Christ" (Acts 20:21) is also the same thing as conversion. "Turning to

God" would be the equivalent of "trusting in God" when incipient Christian experience is meant. Confession or faith can be the equivalent of belief or trust. Many expressions therefore, more or less coincide (compare Humphreys 1974, 133-137).

A continuing phenomenon.—Although "the habitual use of the aorist tense in the oblique moods of the verb indicates" that conversion to Christ is a "once-for-all, unrepeatable event" (Packer 1962, 251), the Christian experiences further conversions. These have to do with concepts or practices that are inconsistent with the transformed life. For example, many believers have been converted from the racist views and harsh attitudes toward the poor in recent years. Some need to be converted from covetousness and greed to true stewardship and liberality. In that sense, conversions continue to take place throughout the Christian life.

Varied Conversion Experiences

Preliminary considerations.—The Bible shows no interest in classifying types of conversions. The long history of the efforts of human theorists to do so have produced vigorous debates and varied opinions.

In some evangelistic circles there has been a tendency to play up cases of dramatic conversion. Persons whose lives have been engulfed in blatant sin prior to their dramatic reclamation make attractive program material. Those who have come from the "guttermost to the uttermost" are indeed far less soporific in effect on tired audiences. We are, of course, sincerely glad for these marvelous examples of God's grace but sad for the misunderstanding they sometimes leave in their wake. The confusion is not the fault of those so converted. They have only told their story, which is what they should do. The fault is that of leadership which has failed to give a balanced picture of the variety of valid conversion experiences.

There is an old story of a large Saturday night evangelistic rally for young people where the ultra spectacular testimony was the rule. On succeeding Saturday nights they had heard from a converted alcoholic, a reformed drug addict, a convicted murderer, and a former gambling baron. A young Christian who had heard each one with spellbound awe was asked to lead in prayer. He prayed, "Lord, I have never been drunk, nor taken drugs, killed anyone, or gambled anywhere, but I pray that you can use me in spite of these handicaps."

We must understand that countless people have utterly undramatic conversion experiences. While there is no lack of sin in their lives, they are better off for not having tasted the sort that makes persons wary of the police and courts of law.

In that there is other information in this book on the decision-making process this part of the discussion will be brief, but conversion as an initial experience can occur quickly, or it may take a very long time. The probability is that most conversions take longer than is generally thought. The reasons why this is true will be in chapter 6; but suffice it to say for now that for most people, many different persons and experiences contribute to their conversion decision. Conviction for sin and sincere repentance usually take time, and for some, so does the understanding that God will forgive. Unconditional forgiveness is not easy for many to accept.

Three main types of conversion.—No two conversion experiences are exactly alike. They are as different and varied as the personalities and experiences of people. As Southard has said, "In the process of the new birth, the Spirit of God is as free as the wind" (Southard 1962, 18). For these reasons, it is somewhat perilous to try to classify the varieties of such a phenomenon. Some attempt at classification can be useful, however, and for that reason there have been many attempts to do so. While recognizing the difficulties, there seems to be a growing consensus that conversion experiences are of three main types: sudden, gradual, and unfocused.[1]

A sudden conversion is one that occurs in a very brief time span, a few hours or a day or so. Little or no serious thought has been given to religious matters prior to an intense recognition of personal need and the making of a life commitment to Christ. Sudden conversion is often quite dramatic and emotional. Many Christians expect to see this kind of conversion in mass evangelism campaigns. Testimonies from the mission fields of persons accepting Christ upon the first opportunity of hearing of him have also helped build expectations for sudden conversions.

Recent studies show that this type of conversion may be very rare. Some conversions long considered as sudden, upon careful investigation, turn out to be more gradual than supposed. The apostle Paul is an example. While he did experience a crisis that was dramatic and sudden, it is clear from Jesus' own words that Paul had been kicking "against the goads" (Acts 26:14). He apparently had had some serious misgivings over his activities for some time, and Jesus' statement to him (26:14) required no explanation.

Conversions that are truly sudden, as we have seen, are probably quite rare. I believe that every conversion involves a process in some way (compare Johnson and Malony 1982, 65). I think, however, the category should be retained, even if it means only that some rare individuals pass through the process at tremendous speed. Reports from mission fields and my own experience as pastor and missionary make me reluctant to surrender the classification.

I sat on the front pew one evening just before a service in a strange church. A lady tapped me on the shoulder and asked me if I wanted to hear something exciting. She said, "I'm a Christian now, but up until six months ago I had never in my life been inside a church, even for a funeral or wedding. I knew nothing about God, the Bible, Christians, or anything. I have a neighbor who is a Christian. She came to my house one day and told me about Jesus and her experience with him. I came to church the next Sunday and accepted

Christ as my Savior, and I haven't missed much since. I really am a new person in Christ."

We cannot know all the factors that may enter into preparing such people for ready response. The converts themselves may not be aware of all the factors. Yet it seems best to call this sudden conversion.

Gradual conversion involves a process which is described in detail in chapter 6. It is one of growing awareness and sensitivity in which a large number of people and events play a part. The process leads to a decision often less dramatic and emotional than in the case of sudden conversion. In fact, it may seem to lack those elements altogether. In other cases, the crisis can be quite dramatic.

I made first contact with one man when his Christian, but inactive, wife telephoned me. He had watched a Billy Graham telecast and had been quite disturbed by it. His wife asked me to talk to him, and I did. It was seven months and ten encounters later that he committed his life to Christ. Each time he seemed to move closer to a decision. He made it on his own, alone one day in his car, when he realized he had been running and hiding from God all his life. He was too tired to run anymore.

A lot of people had played a part in his conversion. There was his wife, her preacher father, a Christian or two along the way, Billy Graham, some friendly, warm church people, myself, and, doubtless, others we do not know. It also took a lot of time. He had been "turning" little by little, moving closer, running slower for several years, and especially so in those last months before the transforming afternoon. That was a gradual conversion experience.

An *unfocused conversion* is a kind of gradual experience in which the actual point of decision is unclear. Many believers who have no doubts that they have become Christians simply do not know when they "turned." These are usually people who grew up in godly homes under Christian tutelage from nursery days. Many seminary students fall into this category. They know they are trusting Christ alone for salvation. Their commitment is not mere intellectual ascent to basic truths about Christ. The decision time is simply unfocused. Johnson and Malony liken such experience to the tide. It can be observed to come in and go out, but the moment when it turns may be difficult to determine. Yet there is no doubt that it turns (1982, 38).

The point of decision.—It is important to say that in each of these cases there is a moment of conversion. Though some people may not know when it is, God does. This is widely affirmed (compare Southard 1962, 18; Barclay 1972, 95; Humphreys 1974, 131-32).

Regeneration is strictly the work of God (Titus 3:5). Conversion is the human response, however much enabled by divine grace. Thus from God's standpoint of regeneration, the turn is sudden and knowable. From the human standpoint of conversion the turn may be very gradual and unperceived, or it may be sudden and dramatic.

Stott likens the conversion experience to the birth of a baby. There is first a period of preparation, then the birth, followed by a considerable period of nurture and development (Stott 1959, 77-78). The prenatal period can be likened to the Holy Spirit's work of convicting the person of need, over a long or short period of time. Birth itself is sudden. The postnatal nurture is very akin to the maturation and development of the babe in Christ under the tutelage and care of the church. The Holy Spirit can compact the preparation process into a very brief period, or it may take a considerable number of months or years. It may be utterly void of dramatic experiences or unusual events, or it may have both.

False Conversions

It is no secret that the church has a serious problem with conversion. Some churches are full of unconverted people who have had no real experience with Christ. They are described by their pastors as present-day mission fields. Many church leaders acknowledge the problem and agree that there have been serious deficiencies in leading people to true spiritual transformation.

Culbert Rutenber has suggested that there are at least three forms of false conversion that all too often are supposed to be the real thing (Rutenber 1960, 160-65). One form is what he has called "doctrinal conversion." This he sees to be the substitution of one set of ideas for another. There is assent to and affirmation of these truths, but they remain only ideas or doctrines. There has been no experience of the person of Christ. Doctrines are only "means to an end." To know Christ is the important thing.

A second type of false experience is an "emotional conversion." Not a few have fallen victim of this aberration. Here tears or stirred emotions are sometimes mistaken for a deep conviction and commitment to Christ. There can be a spiritual experience and an awareness of God's presence without it becoming a salvation experience (ibid., 164). Consequently, there is no transformation of life, no inner experience of power and presence, and no outward change of ethics or conduct. Is this not what has happened to many children who later drop out?

The third type is a "moral conversion." This has to do with the adoption of a new set of ideals but not the acceptance of the ideal man as Savior and Lord. This may be very similar to what Johnson and Malony call "cultural conversion" (1982, 34). In themselves, doctrine, emotions, and morality are good things. It is just that they are not salvific things. Only Christ, who is a person, can save.

The witness must be aware of these possibilities and be on guard against them. True conversions alone can please God. Witnesses do God no service who are satisfied with superficial results.

The Church

From the standpoint of personal evangelism, the church can best be understood in relation to its mission. "Indeed the church is mission and where there is no mission there is no church" (Moody 1981, 427). God has called the church for the purpose of mission. Peter made this clear when writing to the dispersed Christians in North Asia Minor when he declared, "But you are a chosen race, a royal priesthood, a holy nation, God's own people, that you may declare the wonderful deeds of him who called you out of darkness into his marvelous light" (1 Pet. 2:9).

The People of God

The church is "God's own people." It is called to be his for the purpose of proclaiming the good news (1 Pet. 2:9). This passage, so nearly like Exodus 19:5, shows that the purpose of God formerly vested in Israel is now given to the new Israel, the church. Clearly, evangelism is the task of the church.

The people of God are a new humanity (Eph. 2:12). They are a new race of persons where all barriers that formerly divided and separated are broken down. No one is superior or inferior. All are a part of the household of God. All are "fellow-heirs, members of the same body and partakers of the promise in Christ Jesus through the gospel" (Col. 3:11; Eph. 2:19; 3:6).

It is important to see this equality in order to understand the centuries-old errors in regard to the status of laity and clergy. From the standpoint of Scripture the only difference between clergy and laity is one of function. Both are the people of God. The clergy simply have the task of training the laity so that they can perform their ministry (Eph. 4:11-12). The New Testament knows nothing of clergymen being paid to do the ministry of the church. Thus, the church is first the people of God. Each individual member is a minister of Jesus Christ, some having particular functions to enhance and enable the ministry of all.

The Body of Christ

The church is also the body of Christ (1 Cor. 12:29). This powerful metaphor shows the church to be the instrument of Christ in the world. It is the means by which he continues his work. This figure is powerful confirmation of all that was said concerning commands and commissions.

Paul used the metaphor to show believers the importance of living in harmony with each other and that this is possible despite great diversity. Every member is important to the other and necessary to the complete functioning of the whole. The church is like the human body. Just as each body part has its function, so does each member of the church (Rom. 12:4-5). The unity of the body and the functioning of each member according to design is essential to the health of the body and effectiveness in evangelism. Only a healthy body can measure up to the rigorous demands of New Testament evangelism.

The Fellowship of the Saints

The church is also a fellowship. Believers hold certain things in common, the new-birth experience being primary. This creates a bond "that is unique and which transcends all other human relationships" (Ladd, 543). Christian fellowship goes far deeper than the mere enjoyment of another's company. It is much more than pleasure of laughter or the joys of conviviality.

For one thing, Christian fellowship offers anyone loving acceptance and Christlike welcome. Barriers that shut people out are broken down. Distinctions of origin, nationality, social status, and sex no longer matter (Gal. 3:28). Christ is the all in all, and his Spirit enables every believer to offer his love to others.

Small-group interaction provides the opportunity to study and grow, to know others well, and be known by them. Further, there is the opportunity to join in pastoral concern and ministry. The church is the nurturing atmosphere God has provided. Believers both benefit from it and contribute to it.

John Stott has expressed the commonness of the fellowship relations as "what we share in together, . . . what we share out together," and "what we share with one another" (Stott 1971, 75-81). The first has to do with what we have jointly experienced and received in Christ. It includes all his blessings as well as any suffering we are called on to bear. The second has to do with the service, the commissions, commands, and challenges laid upon us by the Lord. The third has to do with a variety of things including material support, friendship, love, acceptance, encouragement, sympathy, testimony, and whatever else may be lovingly appropriate in particular situations.

The fact that the church can offer these things is no small factor in evangelism. It is no secret that many in our impersonal society are starved for just such fellowship. The more nearly the church can measure up to these ideals, the more powerful will be her evangelism.

The Evangelizing Church Today

God has done two momentous things to enable the church to do his work. He has poured out his Spirit on *all* flesh (Acts 2:17; compare Joel 2:28) and given gifts to men (Eph. 4:7). Perhaps the neglect of these truths has hindered the church more than anything else in carrying out God's purposes. Let us consider them in reverse order.

Gifts to the Church

Several passages indicate clearly that every believer is gifted (1 Cor. 12:7,11; Eph. 4:7; 1 Pet. 4:10; Rom. 12:5-6). There are no exceptions. "As each has received a gift, employ it for one another, as good stewards of God's varied grace" (1 Pet. 4:10). This does not mean that each believer has only one. Many are multigifted. Paul had, in addition to being an apostle, the gifts of pastor-teacher, evangelist, miracles, healing, and perhaps others. The same seems obvious today although the "gift mix" (Wagner 1979, 40) would be different than Paul's.

There are three locations where we see lists of gifts (1 Cor. 12:8-10,28-30; Rom. 12:3-8; Eph. 4:11-12), and other gifts appear elsewhere (for example, 1

Cor. 7:7; 13:1-3; Eph. 3:7; and 1 Pet. 4:10-11). There have been any number of attempts to classify the gifts into categories, but Murphy may be right when he says that all such efforts break down, and that when Paul wrote he had no thought of twentieth-century theologians "pigeon holing each gift into an airtight compartment" (Murphy 1975, 44). Most authors feel that these lists are only suggestive and not intended to be exhaustive.

It is important to see that the ultimate purpose of all gifts is for ministry. Some are clearly gifts to the church to equip the saints for ministry (Eph. 4:11-12), but, as Murphy points out, even gifts that seem designed primarily to strengthen the body or the individual do so with a further purpose in view. "So ultimately, every one of the spiritual endowments is meant to help the church in her outreach. Each moves her forward in her redemptive mission in fulfillment of the Great Commission" (ibid., XII) (compare Drummond 1972, 70).

Under no circumstance should a Christian find a reason here for failing to witness. One does not have to have the gift of evangelist in order to share. Those who possessed that gift were especially endowed with ability to communicate the Christian message and bring people to faith, but witness was certainly not restricted to them (compare Acts 8:1-4). Every believer must witness by means of and through the use of his or her gifts. All ministry to the unsaved in the name of Jesus is evangelistic ministry (Havlik 1980, 121-23). Every Christian at the same time is a witness and must bear witness.

The Laity in Evangelism

The great hope of our time.—There is no more important theological theme for evangelism than that of the role and responsibility of the laity. It is not new. Much has been spoken and written in recent years about the importance of this idea. It is simply that so much remains to be done. So few churches seem to have really grasped the idea despite all that has been said.

We have had almost two thousand years to prove beyond the shadow of a doubt that the professional clergy cannot win the world. If there is any real hope of winning the world, it lies in the implementation of the doctrine of the priesthood of the believer.

We have already seen that early believers assumed the responsibility for personal witness. Acts 8:4 records what may well be the greatest record of personal evangelism in the New Testament as the ordinary believers, not the apostles (8:1), scattered and preached the word. The hope of reaching the world in our time lies in our ability to reestablish that pattern.

Because of the prominence of the apostles—Peter and John in the early chapters and Paul in the latter—the extent to which God used and trusted the laity in Acts has often been overlooked. If we can see the full impact of their service in the early church, it may give fresh impetus to our implementation of it today.

Preliminary understandings.—To appreciate fully the impact of the laity in

Acts there are some necessary preliminary understandings. First, we should see that the most important theme of Acts is the breaking down of barriers, the most difficult being racial and cultural.[2]

A second matter concerns the ending of the book of Acts. It ends, strangely enough, in the adverb "unhinderedly." Scholars had long puzzled over the strange ending. Some felt Luke had not completed his book or that he intended to write more but did not. Frank Stagg concluded, however, that the ending was quite appropriate because it expressed this major theme of struggle to overcome barriers and enabled the gospel to be preached "unhinderedly" (Stagg 1955, 1-3, 266). In principle, at least, Luke has shown the gospel victorious over the obstacles that would have defeated God's purpose.

Third, we must reemphasize the meaning of Pentecost for the laity. Some said the strange speaking was drunkenness (2:13), but Peter stood with the other apostles to explain. What they were seeing was an actual fulfillment of the prophecy of Joel (2:28-32).

There are several major points here that are important for evangelism. A new age has dawned. The last days have begun. The Holy Spirit would be poured out upon "all flesh" (2:17). Persons of all races and all ages without regard to gender or social circumstances would experience this outpouring. Prophecy would be a privilege of both men and women. Leadership would fall to both young and old. In other words, God is going to use all kinds of "ordinary" people in the fullness of the Spirit. The Book of Acts shows that God did that.

Verses 19 and 20 are apocalyptic in nature. They are not to be interpreted literally. They testify to the momentous nature of what is taking place in the dawning of a new age and the pouring out of the Spirit.

This event ushers in a new era of mighty evangelism in which "whoever calls on the name of the Lord shall be saved" (2:21). The Spirit in this new era will break down old barriers of race and culture and allow Abraham's seed to bless all people. What happened in the following chapters shows that the first Christians took Peter's words seriously, perhaps more so than he himself.

The unfolding story.—In chapters 2—6 the apostles dominate the story. Nothing is said of Spirit-filled believers evangelizing others. What is said, however, is that much teaching and training was taking place (Acts 2:42; 5:42). Just as Jesus had poured himself into the apostles to prepare them for service, the apostles were pouring themselves into their converts for the same purpose.

The story of their fruitful service begins to unfold in chapter 6 as a fellowship problem arose over the fairness of the distribution of alms to Hebrew and Hellenist widows. The apostles announced that it was not the sort of problem that should take their time. The brethren should "pick out . . . seven men of good repute, full of the Spirit, and of wisdom," who could be appointed to that duty (6:3). The apostles would continue to devote themselves "to prayer and to the ministry of the word" (6:4). It is important to notice that the seven were chosen from among the "ordinary" members of the church although they stood out as having excellent spiritual qualities.

Powerful lay witness.[3]—The problem was soon eliminated (6:7), and Stephen, one of the seven, went beyond serving tables. He did "great wonders and signs" (6:8) and spoke with "wisdom and the Spirit" (6:10) so much so that certain Jews instigated accusers who charged him with speaking "against this holy place and the law" (6:13), saying that Jesus would "destroy this place," and "change the customs which Moses delivered to us" (6:14). Of Stephen's ministry and arrest Stagg remarks: "Stephen, so far as the records go, was the first of all the disciples to see Christianity in its relationship to the world. . . . He recognized that Jew and Gentile were to be united as brothers in Christ. He dared to see; he dared to speak. In so doing, he gave his life but inaugurated a new era in Christian history" (Stagg 1955, 96).

Stephen defended himself by reviewing Hebrew history. As for the "holy place," he showed that God had never limited his activities to one nation or Temple. Many of the great spiritual events in which they took such pride had happened far from Palestine. Many of them happened prior to the law and the Temple. Holy ground was wherever God spoke to men (7:33), not one place, or one building in one nation. God's presence was universal (7:2-50).

Moreover, the Temple stood because God condescended to the request of David who wanted to build one. After Solomon erected it, it was made clear that God does not dwell in man-made edifices, nor could he ever be limited to them. Stephen saw it to be temporary. The tabernacle that moved with the people, which God himself instructed them to build, much better pictured the universal presence of God (7:44-50).

Finally, Stephen pointed out the perversity of Israel in resisting the Holy Spirit. They were repeating the mistakes of their fathers, the killing of Jesus being the supreme expression of their wickedness (7:51-53).

The remarkable thing is that Stephen, with such courageous and pioneering insight, was not an apostle but one of the "ordinary" members of the church. God used this faithful layperson to challenge the erudite religious establishment to see their narrow, myopic outlook, and inexcusable perversity. He died for his creative defense, but such costly proclamation had far-reaching results as we shall see.

The next phase of the story unfolded immediately. Stephen's death precipitated a persecution causing the church to be scattered all through Judea and Samaria (8:1). For some unknown reason, the apostles did not leave Jerusalem (8:1). Thus when we read "Now those who were scattered went about preaching the word" (8:4), we know that they were the laity, the nonprofessionals of the church. The first postresurrection evangelizing venture outside Jerusalem was conducted, not by apostles, but by the ordinary members of the church.

Some were scattered into Samaria, an area which Jewish prejudice rendered largely off limits (John 4:9). The intense animosity between the two nations was well known. The preaching of the word in Samaria represented a significant racial-cultural breakthrough.

One of those who preached and did wonders and signs in Samaria was Philip, one of the seven (6:5). Many believed Philip's message and were baptized (8:12). When Peter and John came from Jerusalem to investigate, they saw that it was a work of the Spirit and joined in and preached in many Samaritan villages on the way home (8:25).

Once again we see a layperson leading the way and breaking barriers. This was a case of the apostles following the laity rather than vice versa which we might have expected.

This same Philip was then sent by the angel of the Lord to the road that goes from Jerusalem to Gaza (8:26). There he met an Ethiopian, a eunuch, an official of the queen of his land. In that he was returning from worship in Jerusalem and reading a scroll of Isaiah, he was doubtless one of many God-fearers of those times (8:27-28). This means that he had been drawn to Judaism and lived as a Jew except that he had not actually become a proselyte. That would have required several things, including offering of sacrifices, baptism, circumcision, and embracing the nation as well as the religion (Stagg 1955, 107). The latter two were barriers that left many as God-fearers instead of proselytes.

He was also a eunuch, and, in all probability, this was an even greater hindrance to his becoming a proselyte (Deut. 23:1). This man was no stranger to religious barriers and hindrances. Thus when Philip preached to him about Jesus (8:35) and brought him to the point of desiring baptism, it was quite natural for him to ask, "What is to prevent [hinder] my being baptized?" Some ancient manuscripts have "If thou believest with all thine heart, thou mayest" (8:37, KJV), which is omitted in the Revised Standard Version. While the latter version is no doubt correct, Philip said this in effect when he took him into the water and "baptized him" (8:38).

Once again it is most remarkable that the removal of hindrances for God-fearers and eunuchs was first understood and announced by a layperson. Two more great barriers were, in principle, done away. The church was on the way to an "unhindered" gospel.

It is true that Peter also won a God-fearer Cornelius, his friends, and household, to Christ. As Stagg points out, however, God had to give him a special vision repeated twice to get him to go, and his reluctance is quite in contrast to the eagerness of Philip (8:30) (1955, 107). Even when Peter arrived at Cornelius's house, he asked why he had been sent for (10:29). Stagg remarks, "Such evangelism! And yet, there are those who continue to say that Peter opened the door to the Gentiles; it would be closer to the truth to say that the Gentiles opened a door to a larger world for Peter!" (ibid., 119).

The most significant step of all is once again accomplished by laypersons. Luke testified to the far-reaching effects of Stephen's defense when some of the persecuted believers from Jerusalem "traveled as far as Phoenicia Cyprus and

Antioch." Thus far, these had only preached to Jews (11:19). But "some of them, men of Cyprus and Cyrene . . . spoke to the Greeks also" in the city of Antioch, and "a great number . . . turned to the Lord" (11:20-21). For the first time utter pagans heard the word and believed. It is true that both Cornelius and the eunuch had been Gentiles, but they were God-fearers greatly influenced by Judaism. What seems to be intended here are purely pagan Gentiles. It should be noted that not all agree at that point. The text is uncertain here. Some authorities have the word *Greeks* while others have the word that could be translated "Hellenists" meaning Grecian Jews. Neil points out, however, that even if the latter texts are correct, it must be used here in the sense of Greek-speaking Gentiles, not Greek-speaking Jews (Neil 1973, 143-44). Most agree that the translation "Greeks," meaning pagans, is necessary to contrast with "Jews" (11:19) and make sense of the account.

For the first time, the pagan world was penetrated, and a church of far-reaching significance established at Antioch. In the light of the Jewish attitude encountered by Paul and others, this was another remarkable breakthrough. Most significant is the fact that it was done by laypersons.

Each of these was a crucial, pivotal event opening new vistas for the gospel. There were steps requiring deep courage, strong convictions, and keen spiritual insight. It is most remarkable that God's instruments of achievement were "ordinary" Christians. Yet Joel's prophecy had predicted just such things (Acts 2:17-21). The Spirit was poured out on "ordinary" believers, and great things took place, ushering in a new day of evangelism.

If God used laypersons for such significant service in the early church, it is reasonable to think that such is his intention today. In fact, this is the primary thrust of the theme of the priesthood of the believer. Not only can every believer go to God for himself, but every believer has a ministry which must be carried out in the power of the Holy Spirit. Here is the present hope of moving the world for Christ. Any theology of evangelism today must leave a large place for this indispensable work of the laity.

---

[1] I am indebted to Dr. Craig Skinner, professor of preaching at Golden Gate Baptist Theological Seminary for this term.

[2] For a full explanation of this and other themes see Stagg, 1955, 4-18.

[3] It was in Stagg's book on Acts (1955) that I first saw the significance of the ministry of the laity in Acts. I am indebted to him for pointing out this series of breakthroughs.

4
Biblical Basis
of Personal Evangelism

If Christians are to engage in personal evangelism, it is not strange that they want to see it in the Bible. When we look for its scriptural basis, it is no surprise to find it in some form throughout the book. That is thoroughly in accord with the biblical declaration that God's concern for persons began before the foundation of the world (Matt. 25:34; Eph. 1:4; Rev. 13:8).

Old Testament Emphases

Universal Concern

While we look principally to the New Testament for direction in evangelism, it is well to see that the Old Testament is not void of this interest. From the beginning, God's concern for persons was universal. This did not cease with Abraham's call. Though the focus was narrowed to one nation consisting of Abraham's descendents, this particularization was with universal benefits in mind, for God purposed to bless and use Israel as a means of blessing all nations (Gen. 12:3; 18:18; 22:18; 26:3; 28:13-15). This nation was appointed to a royal priesthood in the world (Ex. 19:5), an assignment later given to the church (1 Pet. 2:9). While the covenant effectively set Israel apart from other nations, others were not excluded from participation in its blessings. Foreigners could become Jews by circumcision (Ex. 12:48), and sympathy and kindness toward foreigners was enjoined in several passages (Ex. 12:49; 22:21; Lev. 19:33-34; Deut. 10:19). While all Israelites probably did not observe these merciful injunctions, it is true that, from the time of the Exodus, Israel was accompanied by a mixed multitude (Ex. 12:38; Num. 11:4).

God's concern for the nations is expressed repeatedly. It is especially prominent in Solomon's prayer at the Temple dedication (1 Kings 8:41-45), and in the Psalms and Prophets (Ps. 22:27-28; 47:6-8; 68:28-32; 72:8-17; 86:9-10; 102:15-22; Isa. 2:2-4; 11:1-9; 19:23-25; 56:6-7; 66:18-24; Jer. 3:17; Hab. 2:14, 20; Zeph. 3:9-10; Zech. 9:9-10). Clearly, Israel was the intended means of drawing other nations to God.

Unfortunately, Israel was far too susceptible to evil foreign influence to be of much positive attraction for others. During most of her history she was more influenced than influential and more prone to be led than to lead.

Centripetal in Nature

It is important to see that Israel's intended impact was to be centripetal rather than centrifugal. Her role was not one of vigorous missionary outreach as seen in the New Testament but one of magnetic attraction. Israel was to be a holy people (Lev. 19:2) and enjoy God's consequent blessings (compare Peters 1972, 21). This would not go unnoticed by the nations. A number of Old Testament passages show the expectation that the nations would be drawn to Jerusalem to be instructed in the way of the Lord, so appealing would this nation be (Isa. 2:2-4*a*; Micah 4:1-3*a*; Isa. 66:18-19). The coming of the queen of Sheba to "inquire of Solomon" (1 Kings 10:1-13) and the eunuch who was returning to Ethiopia from Jerusalem (Acts 8:27-28) may well illustrate response to this principle (ibid., 21).

Generally speaking, Israel's witness, such as it was, was national and corporate rather than personal and individual. There are only occasional instances where individuals spoke to non-Jews about the power and glory of Israel's God. Daniel, for example, witnessed to the kings of Babylon and to Darius the Mede. While this resulted in an acknowledgment of Israel's God and tolerance and respect for Jewish worship, it was not to the exclusion of the gods they had always served (Dan. 3—6). A little Jewish maid made known to a Syrian army captain that there was a mighty prophet in Samaria who could show him how to benefit from the power of their God. The nature of Naaman's commitment is somewhat in doubt in that he mentioned his need to continue accompanying his master to the house of Rimmon (2 Kings 5:18). He did say to Elijah, however, "Behold, I know that there is no God in all the earth but in

Israel, . . . henceforth your servant will not offer burnt offering or sacrifice to any god but the Lord" (2 Kings 5:15-17).

Jonah's preaching to sinful Nineveh is an additional example of centrifugalism and of pagan response to Israel's God. The latter may be the most centrifugal model in the Old Testament. Jonah's reluctant obedience and uncompassionate attitude was a parable of the nation in relationship to the world. There are others as well, but they are largely isolated instances, the overwhelming thrust being centripetal.

Despite Israel's continual failures and consequent judgment, the centripetal forces were not entirely unfruitful. Recent scholarship finds considerable evidence for the fact that there were numbers of people attracted to Judaism, in varying degrees, in both the preexilic and postexilic periods of Jewish history. This was also true in the Greco-Roman period, and the large number of God-fearers at the advent of Christian preaching proved fertile soil for gospel seed (Pope 1962, 921-31).

New Testament Concerns

The Broad Basis

The biblical basis for personal evangelism does not depend upon a few proof texts of the New Testament. It is rooted in the Scriptures as a whole and demonstrated by the Spirit and model of Jesus, the apostles, and the early church. Evangelism is the warp and woof of the New Testament. It is, therefore, not strange that Skevington Wood has called the New Testament the "incidental literature of evangelism" (Wood 1966, 11).

We find the biblical foundation also in the missionary nature of Christianity itself, for personal evangelism is a primary means of communicating the Christian message. It is, nevertheless, good to see that there also are some direct New Testament commands from the lips of Jesus that relate directly to personal evangelistic encounter.

Centrifugal in Nature

While the essential thrust in the Old Testament was centripetal, in the New Testament it is centrifugal. The conduct of God's people is no less important; for the Christian life of worship, sacrificial service, and obedience continues as a powerful attractive force (Matt. 5:14-16; 1 Pet. 3:1); but the emphasis is on the new outward thrust.

The Commands of Christ

Among the passages which enjoin personal evangelistic responsibility are some direct commands. These were given both during the days of Jesus' earthly ministry prior to his death and during the forty day postresurrection ministry.

Precrucifixion Directives

One of these commands is found near the beginning of Jesus' ministry. He addressed two fishermen and said, "Follow me and I will make you become fishers of men" (Mark 1:17). The words translated "follow" is actually an adverb meaning "hither" or "come hither," but it is used as a kind of imperative. In combination with the adverb that follows, it means "come with me" in the sense of becoming a disciple. It was a demanding summons in the nature of a military order (Turlington 1969, 273). Two others, James and John, were also called, and they responded as did the earlier two (Mark 1:19-20).

While these men had met Jesus before (John 1:35-37,40-42) the fact remains, however, that these men "left their nets and followed him" (Mark 1:18) after only limited exposure. The tenses indicate a decisive once-for-all act. They intended to leave the fishing behind and follow the Master. This speaks of the power and authority of Jesus. He addressed them as one who had the right to make radical demands and to issue such a summons.

If they had already answered his call to salvation, which seems likely, they were now called to learn to reproduce themselves. To follow him was to respond to a call to evangelism. Jesus' purpose was crystal clear; they would learn to fish for persons.

This passage is more than a historical account of the call of four disciples. It is a key to the central thrust of Jesus' ministry. He was beginning the training of a group to carry on his work after his departure. He was demonstrating his method, a strategy for evangelism, and not for just then but for now as well. Every believer was to be a priest and minister of Christ (1 Pet. 2:9-10). Evangelism was to be the concern of every Christian. Each follower would have centrifugal responsibilities. To follow Jesus in any generation would mean fishing for persons.

Matthew's account of the sending of the twelve contains a series of powerful imperatives (10:5-8). Jesus commanded them to "go rather to the lost sheep of the house of Israel" (10:6), and "preach . . . saying, 'The Kingdom of heaven is at hand' " (10:7). In addition they were to "Heal the sick, raise the dead, cleanse lepers," and "cast out demons" (10:8). This is best seen as a training mission and as something they would keep on doing.

The assignment to the "lost sheep of the house of Israel" was temporary. The responsibility was later broadened to include the world (Matt. 28:19-20). Jesus was simply sending them to sow in prepared soil. With some exceptions, this was Jesus' own practice. It did not mean the Gentiles would be forgotten.

Note that the twelve were to do just what Jesus had been doing. They would go as he had gone, preach an identical message, and minister to people in the same way. The mighty works would demonstrate that the very kingdom they preached was breaking in upon them. Not only would they meet crushing needs; they would be fishing for men. This too was more than a training mission for the twelve. It was a part of Jesus' evangelism design for the church.

Luke makes this even more obvious by providing an account of the sending of the seventy (10:1-12). The commands and instructions are very similar. So is the strategy. Only the area was different as they worked in Judea rather than Galilee. Also, they were to preceed him into the towns along the way in the capacity of forerunners (10:1).

The joyous reports to Jesus at the end of the mission indicate that they had been empowered to minister in the same manner as the twelve. They exclaimed, "Lord, even the demons are subject to us in your name" (10:17).

The seventy were also commanded to pray for more laborers, so great was the need. Jesus had given the same instruction to his disciples in Galilee (Matt. 9:37-38). Here is another imperative vitally related to personal evangelism. It expresses Jesus' permanent intention. Evangelistic effort is to be both continuous and intensified. Additional laborers were to be thrust out as a result of prayer.

Each aspect of the sending is significant. The sending two by two, the preaching of the message, meeting human needs through ministry, praying for laborers, the complete dependence upon God, (Luke 10:3-7), and even the joyful sharing of results (10:17) are patterns for New Testament churches today.

Personal evangelism was intermingled with all these activities. No better methods for winning people have been found. The fruitful church will embrace these commands of Jesus as applicable to the present day and binding upon all followers of Christ.

Postresurrection Commissions

The word *commission* causes most Christians to think automatically of the Great Commission. There is, however, besides the one in Matthew, one in Mark, Luke, and John, and another in Acts (see Matt. 28:18-20; Mark 16:15; Luke 24:47-49; John 20:21; and Acts 1:8). We can safely assume that during the various postresurrection sessions with his disciples, Jesus delineated the future task many times. That each evangelist records his Spirit-inspired remembrance of those instructions is testimony to their importance amid the teaching materials of those days. When considered as a composite, there are at least four major thrusts that can be seen as core material, each one of particular importance for personal evangelism. Each evangelist either states these in some way or, as is especially the case with John, implies them. (All of these are implied by John in that they are all modeled by Jesus.)

1. Human instruments must take up the task.
2. The gospel message must be shared (assumed in Matthew as an integral part of making disciples).
3. It must be shared in all the world. ("Go," commanded in Matthew and Mark, is implied in each.)
4. It is to be shared in the power of God. (This is seen in the larger contexts

of Mark [16:16-18], Luke [24:49], and John [assumed if they are sent
as Jesus was sent].)

Besides these core matters, there are additional aspects or emphases on the part of the individual evangelists, or some basic idea is taken further or accented in a special way. It is for that reason that Matthew and John will receive special attention.

There are only two imperative verbal forms in the commissions. One is "make disciples" in Matthew although his "go," a participle, can have an imperatival force (Moule 1953, 179-80). The other is "preach" in Mark. It is clear, in all, however, that Jesus is giving instructions. These are the things his followers are to do, and they may be taken as commands, though other grammatical moods are used. The next paragraphs will help us to see why.

The Great Commission.—Matthew's Commission has been of primary influence in evangelism, for it is doubtless the best-known missionary passage in the New Testament. Despite that fact, the churches have been less than faithful to its major thrust. Personal evangelism is clearly a part of an appropriate obedience, but it must be of particular kind and quality. It is a passage worthy of careful perusal.

The setting is an unnamed mountain in Galilee to which Jesus had directed them. Though Matthew mentions only the eleven, some find grounds for including a much larger group (Coleman 1963, 91; Lenski 1943, 1166-67). Regardless of the number, however, it is clearly a mandate designed to reach far beyond the eleven. It is a task that must involve the whole church. Only a totally mobilized constituency could hope to accomplish so comprehensive a mission.

Johannes Blauw sees this commission the "great turning point" in the direction of their labors. Up until the resurrection there had been no call to mission. There had been teaching, training missions, modeling with observation and learning; but, for the disciples' part, all was restricted to "the lost sheep of the house of Israel" (Matt. 10:5). Here the mission is directed to the whole world (1962, 83-84).

Peculiar to Matthew is Jesus' statement of his supreme *authority* over the whole universe. There were at least two reasons for this expression. First, there was a need to affirm plainly what his resurrection so clearly implied. Jesus had both stated and demonstrated his authority on many occasions prior to the crucifixion. He said, "All things have been delivered to me by my Father" (Matt. 11:27). "He taught . . . as one who had authority" (Matt. 7:29). His disciples were amazed that "even winds and sea obey him" (Matt. 8:27), and that "with authority and power he commands the unclean spirits, and they come out" (Luke 4:36). Jesus demonstrated authority to raise the dead when he cried, "Lazarus, come out," and "The dead man came out" (John 11:43-44). Thus, it was no new claim. It was only that the crucifixion had taken place. The one in whom they had placed all their hopes had been so humiliated and abused that it was not strange that questions remained in the hearts of some. Matthew states plainly that "some doubted" (28:17). Jesus helped clear the air with this forthright claim.

Second, the *assignment* was so staggering in scope that it needed to come from the highest authority. As supreme Lord of the universe he had the right to send his ambassadors across every boundary—cultural, racial, social, or geographic—with the good news he had brought them. The command to evangelize, therefore, for the disciples and for us comes with an authority no one can supercede. Surely that authority had come home to the disciples as they heard his assignment.

Evangelism is clearly the central thrust of Luke's commission ("repentance and forgiveness of sins should be preached in his name," 24:47), but Matthew carried his further. He assigned the weight to the verb translated "make disciples" (28:19). It is extremely important to understand his meaning, for it is here that the church has so often failed. The verbal form denotes a sharp command of a military kind, and it comes from the one holding supreme authority in the universe. For the Christian the matter of making "followers" or "learners" is not a matter of choice. It is imperative.

Evangelism is foundational to all Christian discipleship for it begins with conversion. It must be an evangelism that insists upon a sufficient basis of understanding. It will abhor "easy believism." It must be thoroughgoing and responsible, for this kind of evangelism is unfinished until the convert is firmly planted in discipleship activity and able to reproduce himself. Neither can it conceal the hard sayings of the gospel. Potential converts must understand all that is required, and everything it may cost. Matthew has thus centered on a thoroughgoing evangelism in which the work of the evangelist goes far beyond the point of conversion. He is concerned to have responsible members for the church (compare definition, chapter 1). Of course others may help with the process, but the evangelist will be responsible to see that it does not fail to take place.

Notice that the word *disciple* is used in a number of ways. Jesus was not the only one who had disciples. John the Baptist had them as did Moses. The Pharisees had them also, along with many itinerant teachers or philosophers of the day. Any follower of a teacher could be called a "disciple." In the New Testament the term is used most frequently for the twelve but also for many others. On one occasion, when Jesus had uttered some hard sayings, we read, "After this many of his disciples drew back and no longer went about with him" (John 6:66). Thus was it used of some who had made extremely shallow commitments. In Antioch, the term became a synonym for a Christian (Acts 11:26) (compare *Discipler* 1978, 4:1).

When Jesus used the term, however, he gave it new depth and content, for he enunciated some weighty requisites for discipleship. John Havlik's outline of Luke 14:25-33 illustrates the high demand content of Jesus' view. A disciple cannot be possessed by others (14:26); self (14:27; 9:23); or things (14:33).[1]

I was a small boy during the depression in the early 1930s. Among other things toys were short in supply, so boys my age played follow the leader. Whatever the leader did, we tried to do. We played seriously. It was a terrible blow to boyish pride not to be able to do what the leader did. I know now that that was just a game small boys play.

In the Christian realm, discipleship means following the leader and doing what he did. It is utterly serious. Here one cannot play games. It is the very heart of the Great Commission. It is a matter of life or death.

The participle translated "go" clearly indicates the centrifugal nature of the commission. All the commissions imply it, and Matthew and Mark state it. It can be carried out only by moving boldly into pagan circles with the gospel message.

The making of disciples is not simply a matter of going, however. There are the important activities of baptizing and teaching. Baptism is an act of obedience symbolizing death, burial, and resurrection. It is an open declaration of faith in Christ and commitment to his cause. It marks publicly the break with the past and the beginning of the new life in Christ. Teaching involves conveying all Christ taught during his earthly ministry. This involves hard work and a process that requires time—a lifetime. It is an absolute essential in making disciples of the sort that Jesus envisioned, and it is also a requisite to effective reproduction. To teach all that Jesus commanded means teaching holistically. Love of neighbor, concern for injustice and oppression, and a burden for the poor must get attention. Teaching the second and great commandment (Mark 12:31) becomes a part of the Great Commission. Such training has an obvious and important bearing on the future of personal evangelism.

It is already obvious how the church has often failed to fulfill the commission, for far too few disciples in the fullest sense have been made. Too often the church has been satisfied to offer cheap grace. All too frequently it has failed to carry out seriously the teaching aspect of the commission. The result is that millions of members cannot be found. Among millions more, knowledge of the Christian faith is negligible at best. Such followers seldom win others or seriously try to meet human needs. Consequently, their light is dim or nonexistent. Their centrifugal force is nil. Stagnant churches that repel rather than attract are the sad result.

There is one other major aspect of the commission, the *assurance* of divine presence and power. Matthew expresses it as "Lo, I am with you always, to the close of the age." Luke gives this aspect special importance in his Acts' commission putting it first and making the witness dependent upon the empowerment by the Holy Spirit. He makes it clear that they weren't to do anything until the fulfillment of the promise, that is, the experience of the Holy Spirit at Pentecost. The assurance of the commission was that Jesus would continue his work through them by the power of the Holy Spirit.

John's Commission.—John's commission is the shortest but the most comprehensive. One commentator suggests that, despite this, it has been neglected because it is so demanding (Stott 1975, 23). It is a sentence laden with content. "As the Father has sent me, even so I send you" (20:21). There are, of course, things Jesus did that we cannot do. We cannot call a Lazarus from the grave, live sinless lives, or turn water into wine among other things. Yet, insofar as it is humanly possible, we are to do what Jesus did. It is again the case of following the leader, but we must be careful to note all that Jesus did. Jesus ministered to the total person. He met needs as he found them. His works spoke with the same unobscured clarity as his words. The result was powerful evangelism/ministry which resulted in thoroughgoing discipleship. This leads us logically to an investigation of Jesus' own example.

The Model of Jesus

Centrality of Personal Evangelism

The most powerful biblical impetus to personal evangelism is Jesus' own model. As a personal evangelist, he has no peer. He is the supreme teacher and example. His model is the pattern and design every Christian must strive to imitate. He was not simply "a" model; he is "the" model. If the Johannine commission is obligatory upon us, his activity is that which we must reproduce.

Jesus said he would make his followers fishers of men. He did not simply tell them; he showed them. He not only commanded them to "make disciples" but also made some himself and demonstrated the discipleship process in the lives of the twelve. Before he sent them out, he went out and allowed them to watch and learn by observation.

Jesus' ministry was person centered. He was deeply involved with people in the most vulnerable sort of way. Personal work was basic to all else he did. What we see Jesus saying and doing in personal evangelism is of paramount importance for our perspective.

We are not so much concerned here for his technique and methodology. That will come later. What we must see is the central place that personal evangelism held in his training activity and ministry, his deep concern for the present and eternal welfare of persons, and the relevance of these for our own service in the light of the commissions.

His Concept of His Mission

We can see these concerns in Jesus' concept of his mission (compare Havlik 1980, 87-100)[2]. Several times Jesus made some plain statements about why he came. These tell us much about his mission and, consequently, ours.

When Zacchaeus expressed his new life by declaring his intention to make restitution to his victims and to share liberally with the poor, Jesus said, "Today salvation has come to this house. . . . For the Son of man came to seek and to save the lost" (Luke 19:9-10). Zacchaeus had certainly been lost. He was lost in greed, selfishness, extortion, and callous unconcern for others. He had traded the respect of his fellows for monetary reward and self-esteem for an accumulation of things. He was lost to himself and lost to others, for whom he had been only a serious liability. Most of all, he was lost in sin and estrangement from God. In his encounter he was found by Jesus and, consequently, found himself, values, concern for others, and new purposes in life. He was saved from sin and for a new kind of existence. He was a new man in Christ. Jesus looked at the changed Zacchaeus and said in effect, "This is why I came."

When Jesus sat eating with tax collectors and sinners (Matt. 9:10-13), the shocked Pharisees asked the disciples why he did such a thing. Jesus' answer was, "Those who are well have no need of a physician, but those who are sick. Go and learn what this means. 'I desire mercy, and not sacrifice.' For I came not to call the righteous, but sinners." In effect Jesus was saying that showing mercy was far more important than religious observance by men of unrepentant hearts. He came to help those who obviously needed him. Everywhere Jesus showed himself the friend of sinners.

When the mother of James and John came to request kingdom positions of power and authority for her sons, Jesus gave a revolutionary lesson about greatness. In his kingdom such would not be measured by authority exercised but by lowly service. It would come by following in the footsteps of the Son of man who "came not to be served but to serve, and to give his life a ransom for many" (Matt. 20:28). Jesus' whole life was one of humble service, the peak of that ministry being his own sacrificial death. In other words, he came to serve persons and finally to offer the supreme service—his own life—that many (a Semitic expression for all) might be saved.

On another occasion Jesus said, "I came that they may have life, and have it abundantly" (John 10:10). Quite in contrast to some earlier false leaders who were insurrectionists and insurgents and whose ill-conceived directives brought only empty promises and much trouble, Jesus had come to bring abundant life. In John, the word *life* means eternal life, but possessing that life has a transforming effect on the present also. Jesus came to enrich every dimension of human existence. While this does not mean freedom from difficulties and trials, it does mean a new quality of being, characterized by peace, loving fellowship, victorious living, sacrificial concern for others, meaningful purpose, and confidence in a glorious future. Jesus intended to transform earthly existence as well as provide for future salvation.

There are other "I came" statements as well. When Jesus said, "Think not that I have come to abolish the law and the prophets; I have come . . . to fulfill them" (Matt. 5:17), he was doubtless answering the Pharisee's charge to that effect. The passages which follow (Matt. 5:21-48) show what Jesus meant. He had come to accomplish the intention of the law and bring it to its full expression. He brought out its true meaning and lived in demonstration of its purpose. He removed the sham of Pharisaic interpretation. He elevated the ethical demands and emphasized the priority of the personal above the ceremonial. He came to show the way to true morality and the meaning of the redeemed life.

This life that Jesus came to make possible made the most rigorous demands. It might result in divided households and enmity between family members (Matt. 10:34-36). Kinship is actually spiritual rather than physical, and allegiance to Christ could lead to martyrdom (10:39). Yet it is in such commitment and sacrifice that one truly finds life. To lose life is to find it, and to find it, as Jesus intended it, is the all important matter.

These statements show the central place that persons, in the totality of their existence, occupied in the mind of Jesus. No price was too high, no sacrifice too great, and no demand too stringent to enable persons to experience and know his saving presence. When seen in all their implications, this meant that no aspect of life was to be exempted from his transforming power. It was not just man's relationship to God that needed transformation but man in all his relationships. All hatred, poverty, selfishness, cruelty, uncaringness, injustice, oppression, immorality, greed—in short, sin in every form must come under the judgment of Christ. The new community demonstrated its redemption by manifesting an entirely new morality in the world.

Jesus came to bring a radically new life to human beings, a life that begins with evangelism. This concern Jesus fixed at the very center of his life.

His Compassion and Concern

We can also see Jesus' focus on evangelism in his compassion and concern. *Compassion* is a Jesus word. Barclay says that, except for the fact that it is used in three parables which Jesus told, it is used exclusively of him (1964, 276-80). It is a powerful word used of "an emotion which moves a man to the very depths of his being" (ibid., 276). Barclay says there were three human situations which so moved Jesus: human sorrow (the widow of Nain, Luke 7:12); the hunger and hurt of persons (the thoughtless crowd which followed him to a desert place, Matt. 14:14; 15:32; Mark 3:7, and the plight of the leper, Mark 1:41); and the lostness of persons (as when he saw a crowd like shepherdless sheep, Matt. 9:36) (ibid., 277-78). It was compassion that enabled the Father to welcome the prodigal son (Luke 15:20). It was situations such as these that moved Jesus to the very depths and led him to reach out in loving words and deeds that constituted evangelism.

Jesus expressed his deep salvific concern in various ways. Sometimes he did it with thought-provoking questions. "For what will it profit a man, if he gains the whole world and forfeits his life? Or what shall a man give in return for his life?" (Matt. 16:26; Mark 8:37).

Often it was by hortatory statements. "Do not fear those who kill the body but cannot kill the soul; rather fear him who can destroy both soul and body in hell" (Matt. 10:28). "But seek first his kingdom and his righteousness, and all these things shall be yours as well" (Matt. 6:33).

Sometimes his concern was found in the thrust of his parabolic teaching.

"Fool! This night your soul is required of you; and the things you have prepared, whose will they be?" (Luke 12:20). Such was the question asked of the man who lived for things and had forgotten God. In the parable of the pearl of great price, the pearl is the kingdom of God. It is of inestimable value. Though it may cost a person everything to possess, it is worth it. The Kingdom is something that must not be missed whatever the cost. It was out of such expressed concern that Jesus' evangelism sprang.

His Conduct of Ministry

Finally, we see the deep concern of Jesus for evangelism in the conduct of his ministry. We find him powerfully sharing the gospel with all kinds of people in every sort of situation. He often spoke to groups, but much of his public ministry was personal. Even with great crowds pressing in on him, he seemed always to have time for individuals. Leighton Ford says there are thirty-five personal evangelism interviews in the Gospels (Ford 1966, 67), and according to John, "there are also many other things which Jesus did" which he did not record (John 21:25). He dealt with fishermen, tax collectors, seizure people, lepers, and others with unclean diseases, cripples, the blind, government officials, prostitutes, thieves, religious leaders, mendicants, and the demon possessed. Dirt, disease, body odor, festering sores, lesions, and blood did not repel him. In fact he was especially drawn to the suffering, the poor, and the unfortunate. At the same time he did his best to win the rich young ruler and prominent Nicodemus, who seems to have become a disciple (John 19:39). Jesus shared in the synagogue, the Temple, in numerous private houses, at the seaside, on a mountain, in the judgment hall, and on the cross. At any place, to any person, in any situation Jesus seized opportunities to proclaim his message.

Not only this, but all the while he was training his group to carry on this work following his death and ascension. While they profited much from the public ministry, there were many private sessions where Jesus gave them his undivided attention.

In that we are sent to do all the Father sent him to do (John 20:21), each aspect of his model is indispensable for our study. Our evangelism must as nearly as possible follow his, for our mission is determined by his mission.

The Apostolic Model

It is also important to see how the eyewitnesses responded to his commissions, commands, and personal example after the resurrection. The ministry of those closest to Jesus has much to say about how they understood their evangelistic responsibility, and how present-day believers must understand theirs.

Happily, we find them vigorously repeating the ministry patterns of Jesus. Acts is replete with courageous ministry/evangelism. Great numbers believed, and the church became a force to be reckoned with.

Peter and John

Pentecost was a mighty demonstration of the continuing work of Christ by the power of the Holy Spirit. Much personal witnessing is implied prior to Peter's great sermon (Acts 2:4-8,11). Certainly they were carrying out the commands of Christ, for beginning at Jerusalem they were witnessing (Acts 1:8; compare 2:14,37), baptizing, and teaching (Matt. 28:19-20; compare Acts 2:41-42).

Peter and John healed a paralyzed man at the Gate Beautiful, and Peter preached a stirring evangelistic sermon to the crowd with marvelous results (3:11-26; 4:4). They were arrested by the authorities, but when brought before the elders, scribes, and high priest and family, they testified boldly of the Christ the authorities had crucified and whom God had raised. Though warned against further preaching, they answered, "We cannot but speak of what we have seen and heard" (4:18-19).

Following prayer and a refilling of the Spirit, they "spoke the word of God with boldness" (4:31) and continued doing what Jesus had done by performing signs and wonders (5:12). Great numbers believed (5:15). Though arrested, they were miraculously freed by an angel and followed his directions by preaching in the Temple where discovery was certain. They were summoned again by the authorities, but boldly stated, "We must obey God rather than men" and gave further powerful testimony (5:29-32). Though beaten and charged again not to speak in Christ's name, they rejoiced over their suffering and immediately went back to preaching and teaching (5:40-42). They had obviously taken seriously Jesus' words, "as the Father has sent me, even so I send you" (John 20:21).

All the apostles seem to be included in most of the above activities, but Peter and John were dominant. We can assume that amid this powerful activity, there was much personal witness. Although it does not say so specifically, there was bound to be dialogue and questions. Those who said, "We are witnesses to these things" (5:32) were sure to have powerful answers for whoever expressed a need.

Somewhat later, Peter and John went to Samaria as emissaries of the Jerusalem church to investigate reports of wide response. Upon seeing it to be of the Spirit of God, they joined in the work (Acts 8:14-17). On the way home they preached "the gospel to many villages of the Samaritans" (8:25) thus showing obedience to another aspect of the Acts commission (1:8). Luke showed Peter enjoying a great evangelistic response at Lydia following his healing of a paralyzed man (9:32-34), and also at Joppa after raising Dorcas from the dead (9:36-42).

Peter was extremely reluctant to go to Cornelius's house. God had to give him a special vision to overcome his Jewish scruples. Cornelius was a God-fearer, a devout but uncircumcised Gentile adherent to the Jewish religion (10:1-2). When Peter preached to Cornelius's household, kinsmen, and close friends, Peter and his companions were amazed to see the Holy Spirit fall on them just as he had upon the Jews (10:44). Despite Peter's Jewish reluctance, he had taken another significant step outside the bounds of rigid Judaism in taking the message to the wider world.

Paul revealed that when Peter came to Antioch to investigate the evangelization of the Gentiles, Peter withdrew from table fellowship apparently under pressure of men "from James" (Gal. 2:12). Unfortunately, we have no record of Peter's explanation of his strange conduct. In the light of his experiences of seeing genuine converts in Samaria (Acts 8:14-17,25), and in that he lodged with Simon the tanner whose occupation was unclean (9:43), and in that he had seen God's work among the God-fearers in Joppa (10:44-48), it may be that Peter was not quite as fickle as most have supposed. Even though it was a wrong decision, he may have withdrawn from the Galatian Gentiles because Jewish evangelism was being adversely affected in Jerusalem. His action may have been more out of concern for the lost Jews in Jerusalem than for the negative effects on Gentile believers in Antioch.[3]

Whether the above suggestion is valid or not, Luke's account of the apostles in the days following Jesus' ascension is one of fearless, determined evangelism in which the personal aspects were pronounced. It is a picture of disciples doing what Jesus did while he was among them.

Paul

Paul's model is a most vigorous one. He began preaching immediately after his dramatic conversion (Acts 9:20-22). Often it was amid persecution and, not infrequently, in peril of his life (9:28-29; 13:50; 14:5-6,19; 16:22-24; 17:5-7,10,14; 18:6; 19:25 to 20:1; 21:27-36; 22:22-28,30).

After the conversion of Gentiles at Antioch, Barnabas brought Paul from Tarsus to lead the new work. There the Holy Spirit directed that Paul and Barnabas be set aside for special missionary labors. The rest of Paul's life was spent in activity much like that of Jesus. He preached and testified, met physical needs by miraculous works of healing and exorcism, relieved poverty and famine-stricken saints, trained helpers, strengthened converts, and planted churches in various provinces of Asia and Europe.

As in the case of the other apostles, it is necessary to make some assumption about his personal evangelism in many of the places where he labored. They are safe assumptions, however, because in some instances Luke told of definite personal encounters. At Paphos, Paul won the pronconsul Sergius Paulus (13:7-12). At Philippi, he won Lydia and her household (16:14-15) and, later, the Philippian jailer and his household (16:25-33). When Paul paid a final visit to the Ephesian elders at Miletus, he reminded them that while he had been among them, he taught and testified "in public and from house to house" (20:20-21). This he did "night and day" admonishing "everyone with tears" (20:31).

Paul witnessed to Governor Felix and his wife Drusilla (24:24) and to King

Agrippa and his sister Bernice (26:27-29). Later in Rome Paul was in his own hired house, though chained to a guard, and he "welcomed all who came to him preaching the kingdom of God and teaching about the Lord Jesus Christ" (28:30-31). In Philippians Paul mentioned that the "whole praetorian guard" and "all the rest" had come to know that his imprisonment was for Christ (Phil. 1:13), and he closed the letter with the words, "All the saints greet you, especially those of Caesar's household" (4:22). All these suggest an abundance of personal encounters and that Paul's witness was faithful, powerful, and patterned after that of his Lord before him.

The Early Church

As we have seen, one of the most exciting aspects of early church life was the vital witness of ordinary Christians. It is abundantly clear in Acts and from the previous chapter that the people of God considered personal witnessing their responsibility (8:1-4). Evangelism was exceedingly powerful as laypersons refused to leave this task to the apostles and elders. Suffice it to say here that the hope of the modern church lies in the mobilization, training, and launching of the laity in this same biblical pattern of personal witness.

---

[1] From a sermon delivered at Alaska State Evangelistic Conference, 1976.

[2] I am indebted to John Havlik's great chapter on "Mission into Danger" in his book *Where in the World Is Jesus Christ?* (Nashville: Broadman Press, 1980), pp. 87-100.

[3] I owe this idea to a lecture by Dr. F. F. Bruce delivered at Wycliff Hall, Oxford in November, 1982.

5
Tools, Methods, and Principles

Every witness needs some tools. Just as craftsmen and professionals have appropriate tools, so does the Christian who would share the faith.

Tools are important. Often for the want of a particular tool, a job remains undone. It takes a scalpel to perform an operation, a syringe to give an injection, a pipe wrench to loosen a joint, and a saw to cut a board. Without those specific tools, the tasks are most difficult or impossible to accomplish. The witness needs specific tools. Without them, the sharing task too would be very difficult to do.

These tools are simple but effective. A witness can use them almost immediately, and Christians are often amazed at their power.

There are also some productive methods of sharing the faith and using the tools. Certain principles are also observable in the evangelism of Jesus that are applicable as witnesses use the tools and methods. This chapter will attempt to highlight some of the most important of these.

Tools

The Testimony

A testimony is an account of what someone experiences or sees. People give them in the courtroom every day. A witnessing testimony is a verbal or written account of one's experience. This is what John did in writing his first letter.

He was recording "that which was from the beginning, which we have heard, which we have seen with our eyes, which we have looked upon and touched with our hands, concerning the word of life" (1 John 1:1).

The testimony can be an awesome tool. Advertising experts discovered this long ago. Television stations broadcast dozens of testimonies everyday at tremendous expense. One minute of advertising time during peak hours can cost staggering sums, but the power of the testimonial makes it worthwhile. People relate their satisfying experiences with such things as soap, beauty aids, cars, hygiene products, underwear, diet aids, food, and almost anything people use. Madison Avenue people are not dumb. They know an effective tool when they see one.

Robert Camargo, a Christian advertising executive says that people listen to testimonies for two reasons:

> 1. Someone else has already incurred whatever risk may be involved with using the product (even if the risk is only the loss of money), so their fears are greatly reduced.
> 2. More importantly, they listen because a testimonial is far more believable concerning the product's value, than a slick advertising campaign that is capable of making a yard full of weeds sound like an acre of gold (Camargo 1982, 13).

The testimony is biblical. Andrew bore testimony to his brother Simon, saying, "We have found the Messiah" (John 1:41). Later, Philip found Nathanael and said, "We have found him of whom Moses in the Law and also the prophets wrote, Jesus of Nazareth, the son of Joseph" (John 1:45). After an encounter with Jesus, the Samaritan woman went into the city saying, "Come, see a man who told me all that I ever did" (John 4:29). Then John wrote, "Many Samaritans from that city believed in him because of the woman's testimony" (John 4:39).

Luke recorded three accounts of Paul's testimony, in Acts. In chapter 9, Luke gave his own account. In chapter 22, he showed Paul using it as a part of his defense before a threatening Jewish mob. Later, Paul gave his testimony passionately before King Agrippa (26:2-29). The fact that Paul told it differently in chapters 22 and 26 shows that he adapted it to his audience. This strongly suggests also that Paul used it constantly. Since the apostle is one of our best models for Christian activity, it would likely enhance our effectiveness to place far more emphasis on personal testimony than we do.

With testimony ready, a new Christian can witness immediately. As in the case of the woman of Sychar, some of the most effective sharing takes place in the fresh enthusiasm following the saving encounter.

In a church where I spoke recently, a youthful convert excitedly phoned her brother and two sisters long distance to tell them what had happened to her. Much earlier, on the mission field, a young woman invited forty of her friends to her public testimony of baptism. And why not? Indeed, why anything else?

A Christian can testify with authority. No one else has had that exact experience, though many have had a similar one. Life-changing experience, supported by Scripture, is interesting and compelling when told humbly and sincerely. Popular talk shows are little more than people telling about what has happened to them, and they maintain their appeal for years. People are interested in what has happened to others, particularly when it is of transforming significance.

There are at least three parts to a good evangelistic testimony. First, there should be a word about the pre-Christian life. What was it like in realistic terms before the encounter with Christ? Second, the conversion itself must be shared. How did the change come about? And finally, there should be a positive word about the new Christian life. What difference has the experience made in specific terms?

The first part is important from the standpoint of identity. If the prospect is concerned at all, he or she can identify with this pre-Christian existence. That is where the prospect is. The better the witness knows the person the more he or she can include aspects that relate well to that individual. This must always be done, however, in perfect honesty. God does not bless untruth.

The second phase is equally important, particularly if the prospect is reluctant to listen. Here the focus is upon Christ, and how he has brought about forgiveness and transformation in response to repentance and faith. Finally, the difference between the old life and the new should be stated in concrete ways. "Formerly I carried a terrible burden of guilt, but now I am enjoying the very peace that God promised," or, "Before I was a Christian, I had no real goal or purpose in life, but now I know God has given me something to live for" (compare Kennedy 1977, 74).

This is not a day for the "language of Zion." Take pains to use simple speech understandable to secular people. Write it out. Go over it and polish it and commit it largely to memory so it can be ready whenever there is an opportunity to use it. Be flexible enough to add matters pertinent to the prospect's situation or to leave out things that seem irrelevant. Don't memorize to the point of repeating it mechanically. Relive it as you tell it, and relate it naturally in whatever words come to mind. Let it be fresh and alive. Be sure it is honest and without exaggerations or embellishments. God blesses truth. The Holy Spirit is "the Spirit of truth."

It is important to avoid extraneous matters. Many testimonies seem to "ride off in all directions" and cover things unrelated to the purpose. Try it on some knowledgeable Christians and get their feedback. Ask them to be honest and accept their criticisms graciously.

It is generally best to avoid the spectacular. Though many people do have unusual spiritual experiences that are real to them, matters such as visions, dreams, and most miracles are best left out of a simple witnessing testimony. This may not always be the case, however. The witness will have to be very sensitive here. In no case should prospects be led to believe that they must have a spectacular experience. It is usually best to present the kind of experience with which the typical prospect can readily identify.

It is also wise to eliminate terminology like "God spoke to me," or "God said this." It might lead some to expect God to speak in an audible voice.

People who were converted as small children often feel their testimony has little dramatic appeal. Nevertheless, since there is only one way to be converted, the testimony can emphasize the repentance and faith that took place, however undramatically, and that even children of sufficient age and understanding can become Christians.

This is a good opportunity to emphasize the simplicity of God's plan while not neglecting its demands. There is a sense in which everyone who wants to be a Christian must become childlike in trust and commitment. Jesus did say, "Unless you turn and become like children, you will never enter the kingdom of heaven" (Matt. 18:3). The witness should also show how much that experience has shaped and molded his or her life even though it occured at a tender age. Kennedy suggests using someone else's testimony such as one's pastor (1977, 73).

It is well to remember, however, that everyone who is a Christian has a testimony. It is usable beyond what most would suspect.

Memorized Scripture

It is best to let the Bible tell some of the good news in its own words. It is no secret that the Scriptures are powerful. Jeremiah found it to be like "a fire" in his mouth and "like a hammer which breaks the rock in pieces" (Jer. 5:14; 23:29). The writer of the Book of Hebrews said it "is living and active, sharper than any two-edged sword, piercing to the division of soul and spirit, of joints and marrow, and discerning the thoughts and intentions of the heart" (4:12). For Paul, it was one of his spiritual weapons with "divine power to destroy strongholds . . . and take every thought captive to obey Christ" (2 Cor. 10:4-5). That is why, incidentally, many people will not read it. It is too powerful and discomfiting. They have to lay it aside. This does not mean the gospel loses its power when we tell it in our words, but many people have a special respect for the Bible. When some of our presentation is directly from the Bible, it adds to the authority of our effort.

The more Scriptures memorized, the higher the probability that we will have available just the passage needed. This also lessens the likelihood that we will suffer embarrassment over hunting for a passage without success.

This does not mean that we are to use the memorized portions like a cowboy with a six-shooter who fires at the slightest provocation. Rather, those passages provide a reservoir of truth out of which we may draw the appropriate word at the most opportune time. Sometimes we will quote a brief passage. Other times we will convey the truth in our own words. Occasionally, we will have the prospect read the passage. Knowing the passage and its location is essential in any case.

Everyone can memorize despite protests to the contrary. It is the rare person that does not know his or her name, address, telephone number, social security number, available television channels along with a few favorite programs, and even a verse or two of a best-loved song. People do memorize and, if real effort is extended, improvement takes place.

The human memory has enormous capacity. Prior to the days of the printing press, people memorized the equivalent of hundreds of pages of printed material, and the memory still has such capacity today though quite latent in most people.

Not least, what is required can be memorized in time otherwise wasted. There are all sorts of situations in which we waste time waiting or in which we can do two things at once. We wait in line at the supermarket, in the doctor's or dentist's office, at school picking up the kids, on husbands or wives, or at stoplights. Shaving, washing dishes, walking, or even jogging are activities during which one can memorize. Put the Scriptures on flash cards, and go over them at every spare opportunity. In fact, four sessions of five minutes are far more productive than one session of twenty minutes.

Albert Schweitzer had the secret. When someone asked him how he had been able to earn four doctor's degrees by age thirty, he reportedly replied; "I learned to use the minutes because the hours never came."[1] Anyone who learns that secret, even partially, can accomplish much. They can certainly memorize Scripture.

Moreover, there are concommitant blessings. Such memorization does more than help prepare a witness. Spiritual strength flows into one's life. Did not Jesus fend off Satan's temptations by replying with Scripture? The Word is a defense against the contaminating power of the world (Ps. 119:9). It is a chief means of spiritual growth (1 Pet. 2:2), and it greatly enriches teaching, devotionalizing, and preaching. Some of the greatest sermons come from extended meditation upon a memorized passage. Thus Scripture memorization should become not merely a brief exercise for the earnest witness but a lifelong habit which continually enriches one's life.

Booklets and Bibles

Small booklets containing a presentation of the gospel are in widespread use today. They have been both highly praised and roundly condemned. A number of parachurch organizations have published their version as have some denominational agencies and local churches. Since they are much in use, a brief consideration of their merits is in order.

They do have some advantages. First, they aid in overcoming the greatest enemy, fear. A part of that fear is not knowing what to say. Since an ordered, easily read presentation is on each successive page, that obstacle is largely removed. Second, in that there is no need to worry about what comes next, the witness can listen carefully to any question or feedback from the prospect. Third, since such booklets usually have symbols and pictures in addition to printed material, and since the booklet is usually held so the listener can see it, communication can take place through both eye and ear gates. Fourth, the booklets do present an outline of the gospel; and finally, it is something to leave behind for the prospect to read. That is always a good idea. People who are sold on using booklets would doubtless add that thousands of people have been won through their use, and that would be true.

These materials, however, are not without drawbacks. Some people, both witnesses and prospects, sense something of a saleman's "pitch" in a prepared and packaged presentation. If the same presentation is used repeatedly with all sorts of people, it can become mechanical and stale. More serious is the fact that some presentations fail to give sufficient emphasis to the demands or expectations of the gospel. While there is usually some reference to Christ's lordship, there is little explanation of it; and seldom does one find reference to counting the cost or the requirements of self-denial and cross bearing (Luke 9:23; 14:25-33). Such materials can thus be too simplistic and make the decision sound too easy. Perhaps the greatest liability is the possibility of leading people to premature decisions or even of manipulation. The next chapter explains why this is so, but most booklets lead right to an invitation and a prayer, sometimes irrespective of the prospect's response. There is good evidence to show that not a few false commitments have been made.

To use slavishly a prepared tract may rob the witness of the spiritual adventure of depending upon the Holy Spirit for appropriate responses and emphases and, consequently, some of the best of Christian experience. Few events are more memorable than those in which one senses the powerful guidance of the Spirit in selecting and saying just the appropriate word to meet the particular needs of a lost individual.

A quick perusal of the evangelistic encounters of Jesus are enough to show that Jesus used no stereotyped approach. He began with people where they were and spoke to their needs as he saw them. Since he is our supreme model, more will be said of this later.

Nevertheless, there may well be a good way to use booklets, taking advantages of their pluses while avoiding most of their drawbacks. Most laypersons who begin to witness need some structure in order to begin. Since the real hope of reaching large numbers of people rests with the laity, it may be best to begin with tools that will get them started. If the tract can be used as an *adaptable guide* around which to present the message, while at the same time maintaining awareness of particular individual needs, it can be a helpful means of launching hesitant servants into their work. The demands of the gospel must not be omitted, however, and witnesses must be sure that prospects understand enough to make a valid decision. Chapter 6 will add to our understanding of the matter.

Such tools furnish valuable aid to beginners although the adaptable guide, with certain qualifications, can continue to be used as a summation of the salvation message.

Presenting Christ from the New Testament, in the light of uncovered needs, is probably the superior way. The respect accorded the Bible by many people is an advantage lost with other materials. It is the best gift to leave behind. Certain helpful passages and verses can be marked without the suggestion of a stereotyped presentation. If they need more time and deeper understanding, paperback New Testaments are inexpensive enough that most churches can afford to use them and give them away.

Illustrations

Good illustrations have great appeal because they are interesting. People will listen. Jesus, the great teacher, was the master of illustration, and his discourses are filled with them. Jesus used the sower, the fishnet, a grain of wheat, weeds, children, leaven, sheep, pearls, hidden treasure, and many other things to make his points. He was a master at relating the known to the unknown. People hung on his words. They understood him. He could take abstract ideas like love, hope, and faith and relate them to everyday phenomena.

Every witness ought to have an arsenal of simple illustrations that help people understand the meaning of faith. If one can draw them from personal experience, they can be especially powerful, and there is less danger of relating something the prospect has heard before. We can use other sources as well, but one or two of a personal nature will probably be the most effective.

The following are two from my own experience which can serve as examples. The first helps to show what saving faith is. The second shows how the exercise of faith is an everyday matter for all people and that the same sort of trust must be directed toward God through Christ. They are written as a person might use them in a witnessing encounter.

> I was a young boy in the midst of the great depression. Though my father had a job, there were weeks when his factory only operated three or four days. Our neighbors were pretty much in the same situation, although some were less fortunate. Though the youngsters on my street played baseball, we were hard up for equipment. Our bat was a piece of wood taken from an old barn on the back of our property. It had been whittled down to look like a bat, but it was unbalanced and entirely unsatisfactory. Our softballs were not much better. All of us had asked our parents to buy us a bat, but, the depression being what it was, none had.
>
> One week a huge breakdown of machinery occured at my father's factory. He worked seven days in a row. That meant overtime and a larger check. One night toward the end of that time I renewed my request for a bat. My father said, "Well, I know how bad you boys have wanted a bat. I'll just get you one on Saturday when I receive my pay." I ran out on the street and called everyone together and announced, "We've got a bat!" Everybody cheered. Then they said, "Well, where is it?" I replied, "It won't be here till Saturday night, but my father said he would buy us one." We lived the rest of the week in happy anticipation and talked about our bat every day till Saturday when my father brought it home.

We experienced that euphoria because we took my father at his word. We actually believed he would give us the promised bat. That is a fair illustration of what faith is. It is taking the Father at his word and believing his promises based on the work of his Son.

Of course, every illustration has some imperfections and falls short of divine truth. In this case, once faith is placed in Christ there is a down payment, a guarantee, that comes to the believer in the person of the Holy Spirit who lives within (Eph. 1:12-14; Rom. 8:16). The illustration did not show this, but it does illustrate faith.

> When my wife and I were serving in a Third World country as missionaries, we took a journey from our language school location to see the city and institution where we would eventually serve. It was our first trip of any distance by car, and we had only begun to use the language with any fluency. To our surprise we came to a bridge over a large river that was obviously restricted to one-lane traffic. A substantial sign with warning symbols was in an obvious location. As we read it we could hardly believe our translation. It read, "We are very worried about this bridge!" I did not know exactly what to do. I couldn't remember ever having crossed a bridge in which the highway department did not have confidence. Fortunately, while we contemplated what we should do, a loaded truck came by and crossed safely, thus encouraging us to proceed in our tiny foreign car.

> I realized for the first time how much faith I had been exercising in the highway departments of the world. How many bridges had I crossed in my years of driving, trusting quite unconsciously in the designers, engineers, and contractors responsible for the structures? Then I thought of all the other areas of life where I also exercise faith. When I buy a can of food off the supermarket shelf, I am trusting the expertise of the canners who produced it. Each time I bend toward a drinking fountain, I trust the water purification people to have done their work. Whenever I get an injection, I am exercising faith in the skills of numerous medical people. Having lived in several highrise areas, I am amazed at the amount of faith I place in the elevator companies. The point is that we exercise faith in many ways every day.

We constantly place our trust in the work of others. Saving faith is trust exercised toward Jesus Christ and his finished work at Calvary. Seeing we cannot rescue ourselves from our human predicament, we trust him to save us. That is saving faith.

These serve to make an abstract term like faith understandable. It is always best to clothe such terms with human flesh. Then they are reasonable and comprehensible. Almost everyone has had some experience that can illustrate various aspects of the salvation experience. This can be put to good use in the interests of understanding.

It is a good idea to get a notebook in which to save good material. Usable illustrations are readily available in Christian books, sermons, newspapers, and everyday experience. Save them and use them before you lose them.

Suitable Questions

A difficult matter for many witnesses is shifting the conversation from everyday concerns to spiritual matters. Not a few disappointed Christians have reported, "I just couldn't get into spiritual things." Even if the encounter is in the framework of church visitation night when people expect the caller to talk about church, the visitor may not get beyond, "we missed you in Sunday School. Do come next Sunday."

No two situations are the same, and no collection of possible questions will offer the right approach for every situation. If some are readily available, however; and, if one knows what to ask, they can be most helpful.

Some will see prepared questions as another version of a stereotyped approach and a possible obstacle to the work of the Holy Spirit. Once again, however, having worked with laypersons, I regard some previously thought-out questions as an indispensable aid in the beginning. When a person becomes skilled he or she may not need them, but let us not forget how difficult it is for many to begin. The majority of laypersons need some structure in order to launch out.

One should avoid questions that can be answered with yes or no unless there is a logical follow-up inquiry that requires explanation. For example, "Have you experienced the new birth? If the answer is yes, follow with "Would you mind sharing your experience with me?" If the answer is no, one can ask, "Would you allow me to share my experience?" If there is no logical follow-up that leads to conversation, one can end up in an awkward situation with nowhere to go. One should never ask a question and then fail to listen attentively to the answer.

Questions that ask how a person feels about something are better than those that ask for facts. The latter may embarrass the prospect who does not possess the facts, but no one is void of feelings. Questions that begin with "How do you feel about . . ., What is your opinion of . . ., or Why do you think . . ." are calculated to produce the best results (compare Landry 77:4, 557).

Two of the most widely used questions today are "Have you come to the place in your spiritual experience where you know that you have eternal life?" and "If you were to die today and God should ask you why he should allow you to enter heaven what would you say?" (compare Kennedy 1977, 17-18).

Edwards suggests several shift questions in his book *How to Have a Soul Winning Church*. His question, "Since you moved here, have you and your wife given much thought to spiritual things?" is less abrupt than the two above (1962, 121). The question will vary with the particular person or persons addressed. Though this question can be answered yes or no, it has value in that it mentions spiritual things. The subject has been opened. Of course, the witness will have found out in casual conversation that the prospects have moved in the last few years as a high percentage of people have.

The question, "In the light of our current situation, what, in your opinion, is our greatest spiritual need?" can either follow the proceeding one or stand on its own (compare ibid., 121). Most people are somewhat concerned about the general deterioration of the moral situation, however much they may be contributing to it. They are often alarmed at what other people are doing and probably have an opinion, which is what has been asked for. Hopefully the witness can agree with some part of the answer and move on into scriptural material.

"In your opinion, what is required for one to call himself or herself a Christian?" is another good question (compare ibid., 124). This will reveal whether the prospect is a Christian or not. Once again, agree with some part of the answer, if possible, and move on to share the gospel.

Another approach might be, "In recent years, not a few very prominent people have stated publically that they have been born again." Mention can be made of one or two examples, and then ask if they have had that experience. If yes, ask them to share it. If no, ask permission to share your experience or to show from Scripture how it can happen to anyone.

A student in seminary class recently shared a question he uses: "On a scale of one to ten, where would you place yourself from the standpoint of a fulfilling and happy life?" Irrespective of their answer, he uses Colossians 2:9 to show that real fullness or completeness of life is found in Christ and then quotes the well-known aphorism, "there is a God-shaped vaccuum in every life that only Christ can fill."

The point of these questions is to help persons get started in a spiritual conversation. Anyone can devise others, following the guidelines given. A little practice at using them will help immeasurably. They may not be needed. Spiritual matters may come up naturally. They are helpful to have in mind, however, just in case.

Methods and Principles

Jesus and Personal Evangelism

Jesus cannot be associated with one stereotyped method. He approached each person on an individual basis and dealt with no two people in the same way.

In one sense we could say that Jesus was a method. Incarnation was God's means of bringing the good news to the world, and Jesus was the fulfillment of the Father's design. E. M. Bounds said years ago that "men are God's methods" (Bounds 1907, 5), and there is much truth in that assertion. In today's world, however, both persons and methods are necessary, but persons are always more important than methods.

It is important to observe certain patterns and principles in the evangelism of Jesus. His evangelism has certain discernible characteristics worthy of meticulous contemplation. He is the evangelist without peer. He is the supreme teacher. While our human limitations preclude doing much that Jesus did, he nevertheless modeled a style and a spirit that can teach us much.

Many of these principles are seen elsewhere in this book. Jesus' example is so important, however, that it is well to make brief mention of the most salient features of his evangelism here.[2]

First, he was reverent and respectful toward persons. Jesus' attitude was in stark contrast to that of the religious leaders of the day who made so much of form and ceremonial cleanness. The adulterous woman in John 8 whom others accused, Jesus treated with profound respect. His gentleness and graciousness with such people was beyond the understanding of his self-righteous opponents.

Second, he was compassionate and sympathetic. Perhaps the encounter with the leper best demonstrates these qualities. "Moved with pity, he stretched out his hand and touched him" (Mark 1:41). Jesus touched the untouchables and included the excluded.

Third, he was self-sacrificial. He was heaven's best for earth's worst. He gave himself to people, so much so that, on occasion, there was no time to eat (Mark 6:31). At other times, the work was so satisfying he did not want to eat (John 4:32). The one from heaven stooped to share in human hurt, sweat, poverty, injustice, disappointment, pain, and death in his efforts to redeem humankind.

Fourth, he was dialogical (compare Borg 1981, 31). He listened as well as spoke. He was a master at asking questions, drawing others out, listening between the lines, and penetrating to the heart of problems. He was superb at two-way communication.

Fifth, he was demanding and challenging. Jesus offered no easy way. He warned of the costly nature of discipleship. He called for decisions. "Follow me" (Mark 1:17); "Go, sell what you have, and give to the poor" (Mark 10:21); "You must be born anew" (John 3:7); "Enter by the narrow gate" (Matt. 7:13); these were characteristic of his ministry.

Sixth, he was spontaneous and opportunistic. There was a "whenever, wherever" character to his evangelism. Anyplace, anytime was appropriate to meet human need, including publican's houses and sabbath days (compare chapter 4, "His Conduct of Ministry").

Seventh, he was holistic. Jesus was concerned for the whole person. All human concerns were his. He attended afflicted bodies as well as sick minds. He was concerned about this life as well as the afterlife.

Eighth, he was personal and vulnerable. He mixed and mingled with the crowd. Conversation ensued with every sort. He was in their midst. Fingertips and elbows jostled him incessantly. Finally, ridicule, mockery, stripes, blows, thorns, and nails verified the extent of his selfless exposure.

Last, he was prayerful Jesus demonstrated constantly his dependence upon the Holy Spirit and his vital relationship with the Father. His ministry began in prayer, for he prayed at his baptism; and his final words were a prayer from the cross, lifted to the Father.

Not only did Jesus model these principles, but some justification for most methods used today can be found in his example. What follows is a brief discussion of the most popular and fruitful means of personal evangelism at the present time.

Inductive and Deductive Approaches

The nearest thing to method in Jesus' evangelism was what Hunter labels the inductive model (Hunter 1979, 45). It is an approach that moves from the particular to the general. In the process of relating to a given prospect, some specific need surfaces, for example, a lack of peace or fulfillment. The witness shows the relevance of the gospel to that particular need. If the surfaced problem is lack of peace, the witness can turn to Jesus' great promise of "the peace of God, which passes all understanding" (Phil. 4:7). The next step would be to show that Christ alone is the source of these things, and one must know him by personal faith to enjoy them.

If there is leadership of the Spirit to do so, the witness may move on to show how Christ meets the more basic needs regarding human estrangement and redemption (compare ibid.; Aldrich 1981, 87-89). Considerable explanation of the gospel may be needed before the prospect has sufficient knowledge for making a valid decision to accept Christ as Savior and Lord.

This method is very similar to what is known as "Friendship Evangelism," for it implies spending time with the person and building a relationship of credibility and confidence in which needs can be expressed (see McPhee 1978; McDill 1979).

The deductive approach is that which has been popularized by many current training schemes. It moves from the general to the particular. The prepared booklet which we have already discussed, which offers to all alike a general summary of the gospel and invites the prospect to pray and accept Christ, epitomizes this approach. Both Hunter, who is the source of the term (1979, 38), and Aldrich (1981, 84), who also uses it, feel that the inductive method is more usable and practical for today in view of widespread secularism and pluralism. Many other current writers agree, and some are quite negative toward anything that smacks of a "canned approach."

I agree that the inductive method is best, and it is a goal toward which witnesses should work. The next chapter will point out further limitations of the deductive approach. Even so, the latter method is not without value. As mentioned before, it can be helpful when used as a flexible guide and as a means of proclamation.

I belong to a denomination whose evangelism program is essentially deductive. Many churches teaching it to their laypersons are experiencing impressive results, particularly in areas where the gospel is better known. My guess is that where the attitude and spirit of the witness is truly Christlike, and where he or she is careful to see that the prospect understands the gospel, God can use almost any method. This does not mean, of course, that some methods are not better than others or that we should not work toward the best means.

The deductive approach, while inferior to the inductive, recognizes human limitations and enables new Christians and some decidedly reticent persons to share their faith in an effective way. Growth and experience will lead them toward a more inductive approach.

Using Relational Webs

In 1979, Win Arn published the results of an investigative survey involving 8000 persons designed to see why people joined the church of which they were a member. He found that the overwhelming number (70-90%) did so because of the influence of a friend or relative in that church (Arn 1979, 11). Since that time, many have built upon his finding and emphasized the importance of evangelism among the friends, relatives, and associates of Christians. This emphasis now goes under many names, but I have borrowed the term *web evangelism* from Miles (1981, 127) who in turn credits it to Donald McGavran.

Every person has relationships with family, close personal friends, and other associates through the workplace, the school, clubs, and other membership groups and organizations. These are now seen to be the most natural persons to receive our witness. Wolf makes an excellent case for this as a biblical method (1979, 110-16). This is an important discovery which should be regularly emphasized in evangelistic teaching.

These relationships offer distinct advantages. They overcome the difficulty of receiving a message from a stranger discussed elsewhere in this book. They provide bridges of friendship across which the message can move and offer a Christian presence which is altogether essential to vital evangelization.

This is the place for all witnesses to begin. The church's most fruitful field for evangelism lies here. On the other hand, web evangelism has some limitations and will not by any means win all persons who need to be won. In our secular society there are many unsaved people who have no witnessing Christian in their relational web. Moreover, if they have Christians in their web, they may be of a sort to exert a negative rather than a positive influence. While we acknowledge the power of this method and the urgency of its use, other methods must be used as well if we are sincere in our attempt to reach all who are lost.

Witnessing Through Ministries

Launching ministries is an extremely important means of opening doors to personal evangelism. They were certainly blended and mingled with the evangelism of Jesus. The possibilities are wide indeed, and those ministries undertaken should be related directly to discovered needs. Day care, literacy classes, tutoring, employment assistance, emergency shelter, medical care, counseling services, food distribution, clothes closets, and interpreting services may serve as examples.

These ministries are more than a means to evangelism. They stand on their own feet as the response of a good neighbor (Luke 10:29-37) and as obedience to the great commandment (Lev. 19:18). If done in Christlike spirit, they manifest the love and concern of God and preach without words. They establish a necessary credibility and provide the bridge of friendship across which natural faith sharing can move.

In an urbanized, secular/pluralistic setting, ministries are a necessary and significant aspect of evangelism strategy. The personal evangelist cannot afford to overlook their positive impact and decisive role.

Using Small Groups

One of the most productive methods involving personal evangelism is the small-group approach. Churches that train leaders in this method are often experiencing amazing results. The explosive movement in Korea today has much to do with the power of small groups.

There is nothing new about small groups. They are found among the Hebrews during the Exile (Bangham 1974, 13). One was gathered around Jesus. Many early Christian congregations were small-group house churches, sometimes gathering secretly to escape persecution.

Dissenting groups used them during the Middle Ages, and it was a method of the Pietists after the Reformation. One of the most effective users of small groups was John Wesley who directed people into weekly classes. Largely by that means, thousands were converted; and his movement is credited with vastly influencing the moral climate and, ultimately, the history of England.

Small groups have been rediscovered in our time. Two major factors account for their powerful appeal: the loss of community in our highly mobile society and the consequent loneliness and rootlessness of so many (ibid., 18).

Not all small groups are evangelistic. A small group that has an evangelistic purpose has certain distinct characteristics. Considerable experience has produced helpful principles and guidelines, and anyone wishing to use this method should take the opportunity to study first. This can preclude many an error and pitfall.

Aldrich suggests that the only Christians who should be at an evangelistic home Bible study, other than the leaders, are those who bring unsaved (1981, 190). The discussion must be dominated by the non-Christians, and an atmosphere of warmth conducive to acceptance and free expression must prevail (ibid., 190).

Any personal evangelism is best done in a gentle, low-key manner during the informal discussion after Bible study or during refreshment time. It will come in response to questions asked. It may be in the form of a simple testimony. Extreme care should be taken not to drive away the unsaved who come to study and discuss Scripture. They must be given time for the Bible study to speak and the Holy Spirit to convict. The personal evangelist must be extremely sensitive at this point. On the other hand, if a person clearly desires to accept Christ, it is time to help.

I have attempted to discuss briefly the major methods and approaches used in personal evangelism today. There are many others. Methods change constantly though the core message remains the same. There is a continuing need for thought and innovation in finding better and more effective methods. This is especially true in view of the task of evangelizing the vast urban centers.

---

[1] Source unknown.

[2] For the principles and terms, I am indebted to Miles 1982A, 11-86; Drummond 1972, 54-56; Lischer 1982, 8-11.

6
The Journey into Responsible Christianity

Shortly after I had committed myself to the preaching ministry, I had an opportunity to supply a small-town pulpit for a number of Sundays. I was eager to share my faith and make some visits in the community. On one weekend a zealous Christian friend, several years my senior, accompanied me to the field. He was especially eager to make some visits. He was a "graduate" of the "don't-take-no-for-an-answer" school of evangelism, and he regarded himself as a skilled witness.

When he heard about a young farm wife with an unsaved husband, he was determined to go win him that day. We found him in the barn busy at chores. We introduced ourselves, but he was obviously not glad to see us. My friend seized control of the encounter immediately and began a simple stereotyped presentation of the gospel. Despite negative responses from the farmer and numerous signals that he was merely tolerating us, my friend pressed him until he bowed his head for prayer. Following that, as best I remember, my friend got him to shake hands as a symbol of agreeing to accept Christ. We pumped his arm in congratulatory joy and, having urged him to come to church for baptism and membership, we went on our way.

I was uneasy, and I showed it. My friend noticed and said, "Now you just leave him to the Lord. For all we know he is down on his knees in the barn right now asking God for mercy." As I look back on it thirty-five years later, I think perhaps he was on his knees—looking for a big rock to throw at us.

He never came to the church. The congregation called a pastor, but I continued to ask about him. The reports were always disappointing. I sensed that my friend and I had done him in a disservice. Yet no one had wronged him intentionally. My witnessing companion that day was an utterly sincere Christian. We had done only what we had thought we should do, if perhaps a little too vigorously.

A cardinal rule of medical school is "do no harm." A doctor's treatment should never leave the patient worse than it found him. Neither should the ministry of a Christian witness serve to erect new walls between the prospect and God.

This chapter might seem negative about evangelism to some. It is important to read it through, however, for it is my intention to be wholly positive about *responsible* evangelism.

I do not forget that at the same time the above incident was taking place, others were being won by somewhat similar methods. It is a fact that a gracious and loving God overrules some of our well-meant blunders. Delos Miles tells of one overeager visitor who was so determined to see his prospect that he barged into the man's bathroom and witnessed to him even though he was bathing. Despite such callous effrontery, the man later became a Christian and joined the church (Miles 1982A, 17). But God should not have to overrule such insensitive actions.

Wide Misunderstanding

False Assumptions

We have already seen that while conversion does involve a moment of decision, most people go through a preparatory process that leads to it. It is extremely important that witnesses understand the nature of that process.

Some personal evangelism programs and witness styles used extensively in the past, and some in use today, are based on false assumptions about unsaved people. One false assumption is that unsaved people are just waiting to hear the gospel. We might call this "the myth of the waiting heathen." There has been a good bit of preaching to the effect that our neighbor is just waiting for us to share the gospel or that lost people in mission lands are just waiting for a missionary to come.

There is a sense, of course, in which that is true, but while there are exceptions, the vast majority simply do not know they are waiting, either at home or abroad. Many are satisfied as they are. While people can be won, it ordinarily requires much prayer and hard work. The overemphasis upon sudden conversion has obscured the fact that most people pass through a process of gradually increasing awareness that leads to decision. While some people may pass through the process quite rapidly, a witness must not run ahead of the Holy Spirit.

A much more serious, erroneous assumption is that anyone to whom we witness is ready to be persuaded to accept Christ. This supposes that they have sufficient understanding of the gospel to make a valid, life-changing decision. While some are ready or nearly ready to decide, many are not. Premature persuasion has the potential of erecting new barriers between the prospect and God.

What must be understood is that the conversion decision is always based on certain cognitive understanding. While the precise minimum understanding for Christian conversion is not possible to determine (Ferm 1959, 50), there is, nevertheless, an understanding without which a valid conversion cannot take place (see ch. 1).

Intellectual understanding is not all that is required. There is still the all-important work of the Spirit in convicting of sin and bringing a person to the point of life commitment. The gospel, however, is the factual basis of our faith.

Inadequate Materials

Further compounding the problem of false assumptions is the fact that many of the materials people are trained to use are based on the same false assumptions (compare Engel 1979, 78). Most of the booklets and tracts used today assume that the prospective Christian already understands enough of the gospel to be saved or that they can understand enough through a brief presentation or review. Some, of course, do have sufficient knowledge and are ready to believe. Many, however, are far from being prepared to make a decision after a quick reading and explanation of a tract.

Moving toward a decision involves changes in the beliefs or presuppositions which the non-Christian holds. For this to occur the person must feel a sense of need and want to change. Creating awareness of need in the lives of people who say they feel satisfied as they are is the primary challenge to evangelistic efforts today (compare Engel 1979, 74). That will be a major concern of the next chapter.

Abbreviated Methods

An additional element of the problem is that, as the world has become increasingly more secular, our methods of dealing with inquirers have been sharply abbreviated. Samuel Southard has documented this development in his study of evangelism from the standpoint of pastoral care. In his concern for a better record of preserving converts among Southern Baptists, he decries "manipulative attitudes and techniques of some evangelists" and the "coersion of children." He says, "A ten second questioning by the pastor has replaced the month-long agonizing of Puritan New England and the congregational examinations of frontier Kentucky." He asks, "How can church membership mean anything when a walk down the aisle of a church is the only visible requirement of conversion?" (Southard 1981, 25).

Southard points out that when "instant" evangelism made its appearance in the camp meetings about 1800, those who answered the call for decision were not immediately considered to be saved. Their response was regarded merely as one important step, and it was the practice to examine each of them carefully. Some groups like Methodists put them in instruction classes prior to membership. Other groups encouraged conversations with elders, and some required candidates to give public account of their conversion experience prior to baptism. In addition to these safeguards, Baptists took disciplinary action when the conduct of converts denied their profession. Southard summarizes by showing that such elements as inquiry, private or public examination by a pastor or church, public recounting of experience, prebaptismal probation/ instruction periods, and discipline have often been replaced by a brief conversation with a candidate at the front of the auditorium (Southard 1981, 27-31). Obviously these accusations do not apply to every church, and it does not mean that churches today should go back to the methods of the frontier. It does help to awaken us to a very serious problem that needs immediate and careful attention.

Unhappy Results

A few years ago, a troubled student sat dejectedly in my office. He was working in a telephone campaign wherein he read an evangelistic tract over the phone, asking for certain responses and then for a Christian decision. His assigned area was populated by many professional people and persons of wealth and position. All was not well. He said something like this, "I feel myself invading their private space without having earned the right, and their responses are not positive at all." I felt for him. His experience was a pertinent illustration of the problem before us.

A combination of wrong assumptions, shallow methods and materials, and abbreviated methods have had a number of untoward results. For one thing, not a few persons have reacted negatively like those my student friend phoned or like the man cited at the beginning of the chapter. Some want nothing more to do with us. Such methods, despite our best intentions, have earned their hostility and avoidance, and new barriers may now exist between them and the seeking God.

Another consequence of such methods is the loss of a large percentage of those who make public decisions, both in evangelistic campaigns and regular services. After a few weeks, many of them cannot be found. "From 40 to 50 percent of those who join a church each year fail to follow through and develop as disciples" (Edgemon 1980, 542).

Needless to say, persons who have joined a church but who never participate in spiritual worship, growth, or service are a poor advertisement for the

Christian faith. They represent a major embarrassment for the church as well as a tragic loss of person, power, and talent.

This is a pertinent concern for every church family. Many children each year suffer the same malpractice. Since these are the methods often modeled and taught, many parents do little to remedy these deficiencies in the home. Thus, an alarming percentage of church children become teenage dropouts and spiritual delinquents.

The Postive Side

There is a positive side that must not be overlooked. In the midst of these activities about which there must be concern, many have also been genuinely won. Great numbers of our members decided for Christ in evangelistic meetings and found their way to a deep and lasting commitment despite the prevalent superficial methods of dealing with converts. Others have been won in their homes during a brief visit where the witness made only a minimal presentation of the gospel. Some have joined churches with little or no followup program and have survived and grown despite all. For that we can only be glad, and yet sad for others turned away by those same methods.

Many who have participated in the above have only done faithfully what they were trained to do. Most have never intentionally manipulated anyone. All of us have superior hindsight. What we must do is understand as clearly as possible what has occurred and resolve to do our work as responsibly as possible using the best methods available.

Essential Understandings

The Engel Scale

One of those who has seen and analyzed the problem with the most clarity is James Engel. Engel was for many years a professor of marketing at Ohio State University where he specialized in analyzing audiences for effective advertising strategy.

After his conversion, while retaining his university position, he served for several years in student evangelism and then blended his skills in the analytical approach to problem solving with his deep concern for responsible, productive evangelism. As a professor and director of the School of Communications at Wheaton Graduate School, Dr. Engel has focused on the problem of wrong assumptions and the process which preceeds and follows the Christian conversion decision. His analysis has lent itself to a graph which is now widely used and known as the "Engel Scale" or the "Engel Model" (Engel 1979, 83).

The model has been subject to various modifications (Engel 1975, 44-45 footnote) and some would change it slightly based on theological preferences (Ford 1977, 87), but the essential thrust is clear. I have made one addition. I have added the word *Ministry* to "Proclamation" under the "communicator's role" to reflect my definition of evangelism in chapter 1.[1] What follows is a brief description of the scale. I am greatly indebted to Dr. Engel for the ideas which follow.

Overview.—The scale really tells its own story. The essential point for our discussion is that persons who are converted pass through a process of increasing awareness and understanding of the gospel and of their responsibility towards God. Three principals are involved in the process: God, the human communicator, and the prospective believer. The art of communicating the gospel to the non-Christian is seen as a task in which the Holy Spirit uses persons as his instruments while he, at the same time, does his convicting work.

The model represents a pattern which we may *usually* expect to see, allowing for the vast variation in individual personality and experience. The sovereign God remains free to work as he may please.

God's role.—God's activity is first seen in terms of "general revelation." This refers to God's disclosure of himself in nature and in conscience (Rom. 1:18 to 2:16). According to Paul, God has revealed "his invisible nature, namely, his eternal power and deity." These have "been clearly perceived in the things that have been made" (Rom. 1:19-20). This is God's revelation of himself in the created world.

This is so real that no person shall have an excuse for failing to honor him as God and offering him thanks (Rom. 1:20). To do so is to reject the basic knowledge God made available to everyone (Barrett 1957, 36).

Paul added that while the Jews have the written law, the Gentiles "show that what the law requires is written on their hearts" (Rom. 2:12-15). This knowledge is the possession of every person, though the blinding effects of evil may cause some to deny that it is so (2 Cor. 4:4). This is God's revelation in conscience, and people are responsible for it. The witness may count on that much truth residing in every heart.

God further works by his Holy Spirit to bring conviction to the human heart (John 16:7-11). While the communicator proclaims the gospel, the Holy Spirit makes it effective. When a person responds to the call for decision by repentance and faith, the Holy Spirit carries out his work of regeneration (Titus 3:5).

Immediately following conversion, the Holy Spirit begins his sanctifying work guiding the new believer into the church and in Christian growth (Phil. 2:12-13). As the new believer responds to his leading, further changes in beliefs and behavior take place as depicted by +2, +3, and beyond on the scale.

Role of the communicator.—The witness is the instrument of the Holy Spirit to incarnate the gospel and proclaim it in word and deed. Here the role of proclamation and ministry aims toward providing the necessary understanding of the gospel. As needs surface, the communicator and the church will do all in their power to minister in the name of Christ.

Role of the prospective believer.—The stages numbered −8 to −1 are arbitrary designations intended to show various stages at which unbelievers may be found and the progressive steps toward decision. Persons at −8 have only the benefits of general revelation. This would be especially true of people in

Engel Model [2]

GOD'S ROLE	COMMUNICATOR'S ROLE		MAN'S RESPONSE
General Revelation		−8	Awareness of Supreme Being
Conviction	Proclamation & (Ministry)	−7	Some Knowledge of Gospel
		−6	Knowledge of Fundamentals of Gospel
		−5	Grasp of Personal Implications of Gospel
		−4	Positive Attitude Toward Act of Becoming a Christian
	Call for Decision	−3	Problem Recognition and Intention to Act
		−2	Decision to Act
		−1	Repentance and Faith in Christ

REGENERATION   **NEW CREATURE**

Sanctification	Follow-Up	+1	Post Decision Evaluation
		+2	Incorporation Into Church
	Cultivation	+3	Conceptual and Behavioral Growth
		•	• Communion with God
			• Stewardship
			• Internal Reproduction
		•	• External Reproduction
		•	
		Eternity	

non-Christian nations, but they are found where Christianity has wide influence also. Levels −7 and −6 represent growing awareness of the gospel.

The next phase, −5, is extremely important. Here the prospective believer grasps what the gospel would mean to him or her personally. A partial understanding, at least, of what becoming a Christian might entail, and a growing inclination towards it marks this stage. A "positive attitude" towards taking this all important step, −4, easily leads to −3. Here the powerful conviction of the Holy Spirit makes estrangement from God and the need of his forgiveness most real, so real that, unless rejection occurs, the prospective Christian is led to repent and become a new creature in Christ.

I believe every witness should study this model. The understanding of its thrusts and implications could change substantially the way many Christians do evangelism.

The Neighbour Model

Ralph Neighbour has served as a creative and resourceful pastor in the Southern Baptist Convention for many years. In 1969 he launched an experimental church in Houston, Texas, with the purpose of reaching secular people. He has worked over the years to develop a method of equipping laypersons to contact, cultivate, and win the more difficult people so often neglected by the typical church. He has served as consultant to a number of mission fields and tested and developed his methods in various parts of the world. His is perhaps the best "how-to" manual for training laypersons in relational evangelism in print today.

Neighbour has also pictured the process leading to and beyond decision in a very helpful way (Neighbour 1982, 11). His "Response Pyramid" shows persons moving through five levels of progression.

Level five is simple "Awareness" that comes about through contact with a caring Christian or through observing the activity of a serving church.

"Receptivity" is the fourth level marked by attempts to help prospects with distorted ideas which have grown out of past experiences. The prospect no longer avoids the gospel, but begins to respond to both the messenger and the message (tracts) so as to take a "new look" at the Lord.

At level three, "Body Relationship" affords exposure to the witness's life, reveals needs, and leads to reevaluation. The friendship of prospect and witness and share-group sessions with other Christians affords further comparisons. The Word is pictured to the prospect through relationships and creates a desire for more information.

"Bible Content" at level two helps the prospect understand the Christian message. The pattern moves from personal testimony, to one-on-one instruction, to group study in Sunday School and church services. The Word is proclaimed through Bible content.

At level one, "Commitment," the prospect hears a detailed presentation of the gospel. An invitation leads to acceptance of Christ as Lord and Savior.

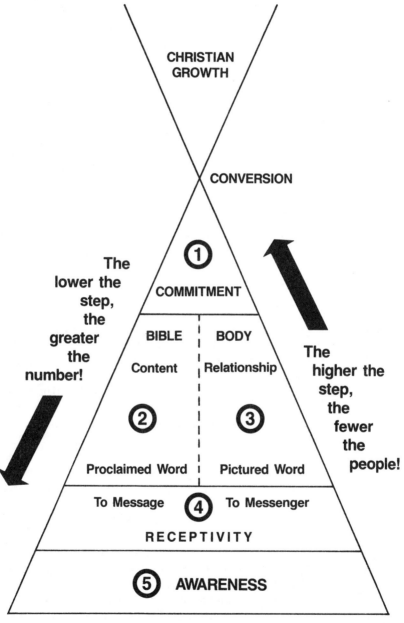

Neighbour's Model [3]

The Way People Come to Christ...

CHRISTIAN GROWTH

CONVERSION

The lower the step, the greater the number!

① COMMITMENT

BIBLE | BODY

Content | Relationship

② | ③

Proclaimed Word | Pictured Word

To Message ④ To Messenger

RECEPTIVITY

⑤ AWARENESS

The higher the step, the fewer the people!

We must work with people at ALL levels!

This is followed by Christian growth through the study of prepared materials which Neighbour calls "Survival Kit." The believer is integrated into a church and trained for productive service.

Neighbour emphasizes also that witnesses "must work with people at all levels" (1982, 11). One of the most attractive features of his method is the strong emphasis on personal relationships and serving people in the light of their needs. He sees this as a vital part of evangelistic ministry which is also an emphasis of this book.

Neighbour's model is similar to Engel's. The latter appears in a text on Christian communication theory. Neighbour's is found in a manual which provides "how-to" training materials for Christian witnesses. The serious student will want to read both Engel and Neighbour as well as other similar models such as those in Alan Tippett (1977, 203-221) and Charles Kraft (1983, 105-108). The idea that nonbelievers move through different levels of awareness, understanding, and incorporation is well established and is extremely important.

Meaning for Personal Evangelism

The central thrusts of this chapter point to some implications of major importance for personal evangelism. To miss them or to ignore them would mean a continuation of false assumptions and repetition of old errors that have potentially negative effects.

Meeting People Where They Are

Witnesses must begin with people where they are and not where we might prefer them to be. Many strong voices are saying this, and we must hear them. This will usually mean spending the time to establish a relationship of confidence, sometimes a great deal of time, for we often have to earn the right to ask the questions that reveal where people are. The non-Christian must be convinced of the witness's credibility and concern. We have to realize that in secular society it is not always appropriate to begin with a persuasive presentation of the gospel.

Requisites for a Valid Decision

No one is ready to be confronted with a decision until two things occur: the prospective believer has an understanding of the basic facts and demands of the gospel, and the Holy Spirit has obviously moved the person to the point of understanding their problem with God. To do otherwise is to run ahead of the Holy Spirit and to possibly cause negative reactions.

In sharing the gospel, the communicator must proclaim its demands as well as its blessings and benefits. The requirements of discipleship (Luke 14:25-33) and the meaning of Christ's lordship must be clear along with the promise of a meaningful life and an eternity with God. The nonbeliever must count the cost as well as weigh the gain (Luke 14:28-30). When the Holy Spirit and the communicator have obviously led the prospect to sufficient knowledge and deep conviction, then the witness invites him or her to make a decision (compare Acts 2:38-40; 3:19; 16:31).

Witnessing in Word and Deed

Cultivation of the non-Christian will often involve ministries to meet revealed needs. Christian witness is one of word and deed by credible persons, and we cannot ignore what was so obviously the pattern of Jesus' own ministry and that of apostles.

Allowing Necessary Time

Thoroughly responsible evangelism usually requires time. This does not mean that decision is not a most urgent matter. We can let our prospects know of the urgency of the gospel while at the same time respecting their needs as to time. This is responsible urgency. Change of attitudes and beliefs, thorough repentance, and the understanding of unconditional forgiveness take time with most people. Evangelism done in this way will seem slower; it will take extra work and ministry, but it will be more fruitful and lasting. If such effort can reduce the large number who are lost to the churches after making initial decisions, it will be worth whatever energy it requires.

Moving Persons Toward Decision

If by our witness we have only been able to move persons closer to a decision, that can be considered significant service (Engel 1975, 48). The process which leads to conversion can be a very long one for many people, and any progress is important. A keen sensitivity to the Spirit's leadership will determine the proper moment for gentle persuasion towards a decision.

Completing the Task

The work of the witness is not complete at the point of conversion. The work of aiding and encouraging the believer in growth and development is of extreme importance, beginning with assistance in evaluating their decision.

All too often communicators have left converts to struggle for themselves, assuming that once a decision is made their work is finished. In a sense, this neglect is so serious that it parallels the ancient Greek practice of exposure in which unwanted new babies were left outside to the mercy of the elements. If they survived such neglect and were found by others willing to take them in, people assumed the gods had willed that they live. The application is an obvious and serious one. To leave new converts without care and nurture is spiritual exposure.

The time immediately following decision is crucial. While many converts experience joy and relief, communications research has shown that dissonance also follows important decisions. If a person has had a real struggle letting go of his or her previous life patterns, the dissonance may be strong indeed

(Zimbargo, Ebbeson, and Maslach 1977, 238). The new convert needs the help of the communicator to affirm the decision and to help reduce the dissonance. The crucial nature of this postdecision period is accented by the large numbers that seem to disappear very soon after the initial commitment, a matter already discussed in this chapter.

Assimilation into a local church is absolutely essential. The church is part of the good news in that it is the fellowship of Christ's true family (Mark 3:34-35). Worship, nurture, inspiration, instruction, and growth are fostered by the church in the power of the Holy Spirit. Note that the process is unending. The believer has become a disciple but also continues becoming a disciple. Growth to the point of being able to assume the role of witness should be one of the early goals of Christian growth. Christians must be able to reproduce themselves.

Gathering the Ready Harvest

None of this changes the fact that we will still meet people whom the Holy Spirit has prepared to hear a forthright presentation of the gospel and be converted. God is at work in his world, and persons are to be found at all levels described by Engel and Neighbour. There are indeed some who are ready to believe, and we should waste no time in helping such persons become Christians.

This chapter is an effort to point out some abuses and misunderstanding of the past that have resulted in abortive decisions and heavy losses of potential believers. It is intended to point to a process that witnesses must respect. Failure to understand these principles has caused the loss of many potential friends of evangelism. The teaching of this material, along with that concerning conversion in chapter 3, should help correct abuses and contribute substantially to responsible witnessing.

---

[1] I do not imply that Dr. Engel overlooks this. His worthy illustration about ministry to Quichua Indians says otherwise (1979, 84).

[2] Adapted from (Engel 1979, 83).

[3] 1982, TOUCH Ministries Seminar, 11.

7
Winning the Satisfied

It is already clear that most non-Christian people are not just waiting for our message. Many of them feel quite satisfied the way they are. Such assertations are not idle speculation. Carefully executed investigations have made it quite apparent.

In David A. Roozen's study, *The Churched and the Unchurched in America,* published in 1978, he found that 32 percent of the population in America were unchurched (Roozen 1978, 5). He counted anyone as unchurched who attended less than once a year, and all others as churched except for those expressing a Jewish preference or preference for another religion. The latter two were excluded from the study.

While Roozen did find a higher satisfaction level among the churched than the unchurched when one adds his "very happy" category to the "pretty happy," the percentage totals are not very different. Among those expressing no religious preference, the total who said they had found life exciting was 5 percent higher than the churched Protestants. The surprising thing was the relative satisfaction and happiness reported by the unchurched. Most of them clearly did not see themselves as persons in great spiritual need (ibid., 28).

Similar results are seen in the Gallup organization's later study although the differences between the churched and unchurched were more marked. Church attendance, high commitment, and the spiritual life made a real difference. It is just that the people in the opposite categories did not see themselves as being very unhappy or dissatisfied (P.R.R.C. and Gallup 1982, 58-59,128-29). A majority of unchurched people are satisfied with their lives as they are and sense no great need for what the gospel has to offer.

Bishop Stephen Neill said, "When we talk about evangelism, what we really mean is church extension, working out from the Christian ghetto to the fringes of the Christian ghetto. But how to emerge into the de-Christianized world we just don't know" (*E & E Newsletter,* 1983 special edition). Indeed, the great problem before us today is vital evangelism among the multitudes who do not think that the church has anything worthwhile to offer. This chapter is an attempt to make suggestions as to how this might be done.

Harry Emerson Fosdick used to say, "Every man is an island. You row around him until you find a place to land. It may take minutes; it may take years" (Seamands 1981, 81). Bengel, the German Pietist remarked, "No one . . . is so coarse-haired, that he does not have a spot where he can be reached" (Stoeffler 1973, 104).[1] Such is the spirit of this material. It represents that "rowing around" in the belief that the churches can find "a place to land." It is written in faith that those sensitive "spots" are there, and that they can open the way to reaching the satisfied.

Identifying the Satisfied

Fashioned by the World's Mold

Many attempts have been made to analyze the negative influences and forces that separate people from God. Many movements, philosophies, and attitudes are blamed or incriminated in mankind's oblivious disregard of God.

Secularism, humanism, atheistic existentialism, scientism, relativism, materialism, depersonalization, alienation, the drive for self-fulfillment, "me firstism," and others are regularly blamed. I am impressed, however, that Louis Drummond is right when he suggests that even though all these forces have exerted some influence on the average person, "few have thought out in a systematic way their life-style—they just live it. Most people are just pragmatists. If a thing or thought works, they uncritically utilize it. The results are that the bulk of people live a practical, secular life" (Drummond 1972, 16). Most people are influenced by these things subconsciously and subliminally (Watson 1976, 14). Most simply absorb their life-style from their surroundings: their friends, groups, the media, the prevailing norms and conventions of the times, in short, from all the voices clamoring to be heard except, perhaps, that of the church. This is part of the reason it is so evil. People are being spiritually maimed and disfigured by forces and movements of which they are largely unaware.

The Unreached Undereducated

Another increasingly important factor often overlooked is that Americans do not really constitute the literate, erudite society our space probes and computer hardware suggest. For adults twenty-five years of age or more, the average educational level is one semester of college. Only about 17 percent have four years or more beyond high school (US Department of Commerce 1982-83, 143). "A staggering 23 million Americans—1 in 5 adults lack the reading and writing abilities needed to handle the minimal demands of daily living. An additional 30 million are only marginally capable of being productive workers. . . . More than one third of adults have not completed high school" (Wellborn 1982, 53). Consequently, many of these lack the skills for employment and live at poverty level.

This means that, if we are serious about reaching the poor, there are some obvious ministries to be carried out, and the message must be conveyed in simple and understandable terms. It may be that many leaders have been overly concerned about fashioning the message for "modern man," usually meaning the erudite person, and missing the level where so many of today's people are to be found.

The Misled Better Educated

An interesting thing has taken place among the better educated. They have been schooled in the scientific method. This means that hypotheses are formulated, then tested, reformulated, and retested to establish what is true. It is a generation taught to investigate. In regard to Christianity, however, the majority seem to have rejected it without bothering to investigate its claims or test a single aspect of its proclamation. What is even worse, many have a very distorted idea of Christianity and have "unscientifically" rejected what they *think* it is (compare Barry 1965, 8).

The Task of the Witnessing Community

Changing Attitudes

If the "satisfied" are to be moved toward Christ, it means that their attitudes will have to change. Of course, this is true of anyone who would be moved toward Christ, but the "satisfied" have little or no inclination to change. Many non-Christians who begin to attend a church or who respond positively to our witness have some inclination in that direction, and that is important, however slight it may be.

An attitude may be defined as "a general and enduring positive or negative feeling about some person, object or issue" (Petty and Cacioppo 1981, 7). Attitudes are generally seen to be internal, and they vary in intensity and importance. They are not directly observable and therefore must be inferred from behavioral evidence.

Attitudes are "summaries of our beliefs." They assist other people "to know what to expect from us," and may "express some important aspects of an individual's personality" (ibid., 8).

Some theorists emphasize three components of attitudes when studying attitude change: the cognitive, what one thinks or believes; the affective, how one feels; and the behavioral, how one acts (Zimbardo, Ebbesen, and Maslach 1977, 20). Thus, a person's attitude conceptualized in that way would include his or her beliefs, feelings, and actions.

When we think of changing the attitude of a non-Christian who is satisfied as is, we must think in terms of all three dimensions; for they are vitally related one to another. Since attitudes are "enduring" feelings, such change may not come easily. Indeed it may prove quite difficult. Nevertheless, this is the work of the Holy Spirit using human instrumentality, a fact that must be kept constantly in mind lest the task seem impossible or improbable.

Changing Beliefs and Behavior

It is important to understand that all people, Christians and non-Christians, have beliefs or presuppositions by which they live. Many of them that have to do with God and life in general are distorted. For example, many believe that money is everything and that most of the really satisfying things in life are related to it. Others believe that God, if he exists, is not at all what Christians proclaim him to be. Some think that churches are just after people's money and that, underneath, preachers are like Sinclair Lewis's *Elmer Gantry*, perhaps allowing for an occasional exception. Still others believe Christianity is appropriate only for elderly ladies and small children. Strong people, they think, should be able to stand on their own feet and cope without it. There are many more, but these may serve as examples of how the cognitive dimension must change if persons come to Christ. Feelings and behavioral intentions must also alter along with beliefs.

Unfortunately, the desired behavior change does not always follow changed beliefs and feelings. Other factors can interfere. When I was a missionary in a Muslim land, supposed converts did not always follow through with baptism, church membership, and service because of family pressure or even actual fear of consequences. Social pressure or other factors can frustrate the best hopes and efforts of the witness. Sometimes they work the other way as well. Factors that either impede or encourage the expected behavior following attitude change are sometimes called "situational pressures" (Simons 1976, 90). There can be many of them and some are quite powerful.

Resistance to Change

Every person has a built-in resistance to change. "All the forces which contribute to stability in personality or in social systems can be perceived as resisting change" (Watson 1969, 488). Anyone who has worked with people and proposed change knows this truth from experience. "Since many people interpret any proposal for change as bad news, it is not surprising that they tend to express hostile feelings not only toward the proposal, but also toward the person who is responsible for introducing the proposal" (Schaller 1972, 71). While this is not true in every case, Schaller's principle can help us understand some of the resistance encountered when individual change is the issue, and the person involved is generally satisfied as he or she is.

Where resistance may become especially pronounced is in the case of a witness who instigates an agressive "head-on" confrontation attempt to win a satisfied person. This response can be understood partially in the light of the theory of psychological reactance as formulated by Jack Brehm in 1966.

The theory has to do with the threat to free choice. Whenever our freedom of behavior is restricted, or even threatened, we react. Free behavior is whatever is open to us to do, including how or when it might be done. The intensity of the resistance will vary with the importance and amount of the free behavior being eliminated or threatened. The more important it is and the greater the amount in jeopardy, the stronger the reaction. If possible, the person so affected will try to regain the lost or threatened freedom. There will be a strong desire to engage in it and perhaps an attempt to do so (Brehm 1966, 1-16).

Once when I was an overseas missionary, the government decreed that citizens and residents could no longer listen to certain foreign radio broadcasts. I had *never* listened to some of them. The moment my freedom to do so was restricted, however, I had a sudden urge to see what they had to say, so I listened. As government officials intensified their campaign, I even listened to some I had never bothered to tune in before. Most people have experienced very similar things, and I can appreciate what may happen when a witness approaches a "satisfied" non-Christian in such a way that he or she senses that freedom of choice is being threatened (compare Griffin 1976, 50-52).

Thus, the witness must be very sensitive in approaching the "satisfied." To be "wise as serpents and innocent as doves" is essential (Matt. 10:16). Gentleness and patience, showing evidence of sincere love and concern, is necessary as an attitudinal approach. Showing Christianity to be a great new opportunity will usually be better than to back the prospect into a corner where he or she may focus on the loss of supposed freedoms.

Obviously, we cannot all become accomplished psychologists or experts in communications or persuasion. Understanding some typical human response, however, can make us more sensitive to people's feelings and help us to cooperate with the Holy Spirit as he works in and through human processes.

A New Look at Some Traditional Approaches

Contact with Non-Christians

It goes without saying that if we are to win unsaved people, we must have contact with them. Many Christians have largely isolated themselves from non-Christian people. Despite the fact that this problem has been carefully described and deplored by able writers and leaders, in some ways, the narrowing of contacts has continued. The proliferation of Christian schools and the listing of Christian business guides are two ready examples. The blessings and benefits of Christian schools are well known, and everyone likes to trade with merchants who are honest and reputable; but considered strictly from the standpoint of contact, each of these reduces the number of associations with non-Christians that would otherwise occur.

There is doubtless now a wider understanding of the problem than previously, but a large educational task remains. Contact with the unsaved must be intentional, and Christians must be trained to do it. As Paul Little has said, "If everyone who has the disease is quarantined, the disease won't spread" (Little 1966, 28). Separation of church and state does not mean separation of church and society.

The Corinthian church had suffered this same misunderstanding. Apparently the Christians there had interpreted a previous Pauline letter to mean that they should not associate with sinners. Paul explained that he did not mean that at all. Any isolation must be from the unrepentants who call themselves "brothers" (and that as a last resort) but not from nonbelievers whom we must win (1 Cor. 5:9-11). We have only to look to the example of Jesus who became known as "friend of sinners," and who associated freely with tax collectors, prostitutes, and outcasts. He was a master of contact without compromise and of association without alteration of his conduct or character.

Cultivation of the Unsaved

As secularization and pluralization have increased, cultivation has taken on proportionate new importance. Credibility, as previously emphasized, is absolutely essential. Recipients of the message must feel that the cultivator is believable. This is crucial for several reasons.

Children are conditioned from earliest days to be wary of strangers. They cannot accept candy, rides, or favors from them. Strangers who "hang around" or who try to "butter up" children are to be reported immediately. A bit later it becomes common knowledge that there are "a lot of 'odd' religious persons around." Everyone knows that "people don't give things away. There will be a catch somewhere." Add "don't let anyone put something over on you," as we are told hundreds of times, and the suspicion level becomes very high.

All this makes it very difficult for people to receive a message from a stranger. Increasingly, important communications must come from one believed to be a credible messenger. Of course, there are exceptions, and we must respond to them, but the cultivative efforts that build friendship and credibility represent time well spent. This is all the more essential when trying to help the "satisfied."

Sowing the Seed

Jesus said, "If you continue in my word, you are truly my disciples, and you will know the truth, and the truth will make you free" (John 8:31-32). If people are to experience New Testament liberation, they must know the truth, the very thing that most "satisfied" people do not know.

My first pastoral responsibility was in an agricultural community. Farmers there were very careful about sowing. They spent a lot of time and money preparing the soil before planting. Plowing, discing or harrowing, and fertilizing usually preceeded sowing. Many of them felt there were propitious times for sowing as well, and most homes had a copy of *The Farmer's Almanac*. Each of these is suggestive for wise sowing among the hard to reach.

To one who thinks he or she is "satisfied" the witness may have to say, "I know that you feel that you are not interested now, and I wouldn't think of pressuring you in any way, but let me tell you briefly what happened to me and how it happened. One day, sooner than you think, it could be helpful and seem more needful than it does right now."

Find some gentle, nonconfrontational way to sow the seed. It has amazing power to take root and grow, even after a long interval of time.

The Role of Guilt

Traditionally, evangelists and personal witnesses have relied on guilt as a powerful motivator of attitude change. Typical Bible passages about sin, read or quoted and empowered by the Holy Spirit, have been the heavy artillery in many an encounter that led to sincere commitment to Christ. Ask any prayer meeting crowd for salvation testimonies, and some are sure to speak of the intolerable guilt that caused them to seek God's forgiveness. Guilt will continue to be an impetus fostered by the Holy Spirit to move people toward Christ.

What we seldom hear, however, is the experience of those who have reacted negatively to what may have been an overemphasis on guilt. Social psychologists have been interested in the role of guilt on compliance for some time. Some of their experiments can help us see some possible consequences of too much emphasis in this area.

Researchers have reported tests in which subjects were caused to do or to think they were doing something mildly harmful to someone else (Freedman, Wallington, and Bless 1967, 117-24; Carlesmith and Gross 1969, 232-39). For example, subjects in the experiments were induced to tell a lie or to knock carefully arranged index cards of a graduate student on the floor or to supposedly give electric shocks to another person who gave wrong answers. The subjects who did these things, or thought they did, demonstrated their guilt, as compared to others who had not done them, by their greater willingness to help carry out a somewhat unpleasant, time-consuming task to assist the victim. Thus, guilt, as expected, was shown to be a powerful factor in securing compliance, but two interesting side effects were observed that can be of significance to witnesses. One was the tendency of the guilt-laden subjects to want to avoid meeting the victim of their injurious act (Freedman, Wallington, and Bless 1967, 122; Carlesmith and Gross 1969, 238). The other was that some subjects showed disdain for the confederate who made the unpleasant request on behalf of the victim. One said, "I didn't like that guy. He knew he had me in a situation where I owed him something and he took advantage of it by asking me to make all those phone calls for him" (Carlesmith and Gross 1969, 238). Other experiments have confirmed this finding (ibid.). In other words, the person who causes the guilt feelings tends to be avoided and disliked.

The implications for evangelism are clear. First, if there is an overemphasis on guilt, it may cause the prospect to avoid the witness. Even worse, it may cause him to avoid God. Second, if there is a tendency to dislike the person who causes guilt, such an emphasis can destroy the bridges of confidence and friendship so often necessary to effective witness (compare Griffin 1976, 63).

Anyone can test these ideas in his or her own experience. I once forgot a wedding. I felt guilty. Fortunately, it was an informal, home ceremony and not an elaborate, all-church affair; and they waited for me. I need not tell you how I would have preferred to avoid having to face that couple. When I did, they were exceedingly gracious, but the recall of that situation affirms for me the truth of this assertion about avoidance.

Many a pastor has been shocked to discover that someone violently dislikes him simply because he heightened that person's guilt by his witness and preaching. While a certain amount of this is probably expected, the more positive presentation of Christ should render such the exception rather than the rule.

Third, it is important also to notice the hollow compliance on the part of the subject who expressed his dislike of the confederate. This is hardly the kind of response the Christian witness seeks. Yet, guilt can produce a superficial outward response while the inner man remains untouched (Griffin 1976, 64).

Fourth, overemphasis on guilt can have negative emotional effects. Not a few persons are institutionalized today due to their inability to handle guilt. This doesn't mean that we cannot share the gospel. It simply means that a balanced presentation of the good news is the healthiest approach, leaving the matter of conviction to the Holy Spirit (John 16:7-11). He is the one who can do it safely and well (ibid., 64-66).

Finally, one searches in vain for much emphasis on guilt in the ministry of Jesus. No one could accuse him of overemphasis at this point.

Certainly, the realization of one's guilt is necessary, and in some cases a real emphasis upon it may be needful. These findings, however, should help witnesses be cautious about unnecessary emphasis. In cases where the pastor or witness feels it necessary to especially focus on guilt, a corresponding emphasis on God's forgiveness and cleansing would be wise.

The Role of Fear

Witnesses have looked to fear of judgment and eternal punishment as a vital element in changing attitudes and bringing persons to salvation. While due to increased longevity and better health death may not now be the primary anxiety for most, it is still a potent motivator of persons toward salvific faith. Plenty of people will testify that fear of judgment was the primary concern that brought them to Christ. Others, however, seem not to have been moved by fear at all.

Jesus certainly used fear as a stimulus toward salvation (Matt. 10:28; 6:30). For that reason alone, one cannot reject fear as a valid motivation to be used by the Spirit.

Simple observation tells us that some high fear messages are effective. As I write this a wave of fear has swept the homosexual communities in the major urban centers because of an outbreak of a new and thus far incurable disease named AIDS. It has already led to attitude change. The media reports the closing of homosexual bathhouses, reduced patronage in the bars, and a good bit less promiscuity. Some police have demanded and received protective gear for use in answering calls in the homosexual community.

In recent years, social psychologists have investigated fear as a means of encouraging people to stop smoking, brush their teeth, drive safely, use safety belts, build fallout shelters, avoid venereal disease, and many other things. Solid conclusions which do not call for further study, however, are quite limited. Questions can be raised about most of their results thus far, but there are a few things about which some consensus seems to be forming.

While fear as a powerful motivator is recognized, the old assumption that the higher the level of fear the more persuasive the communication is no longer supported by many investigators. The relationship between fear and persuasion is seen to be complicated by a number of variables such as personality characteristics, source credibility, the specificity and validity of the recommendations for those made fearful, and a few others (Higbee 1961, 428-32). In general, high threat messages seem to be more productive than low threat in persuasion (ibid., 441; Simons 1976, 13).

Despite that, however, it is clear that high fear messages do not always work, and Griffin argues convincingly for a more moderate fear level as the most productive way of presenting the gospel. For one thing, there is some evidence that up to a certain level, increasing fear enhances the effectiveness of the message in changing attitudes. Past that point, however, other factors such as avoidance and aggression enter in and make added fear counterproductive (Griffin 1976, 70; Beck and Davis 1978, 82; Higbee 1969, 439-41).

Griffin gives three reasons why this is so applicable to Christian witnessing. First, there is the possibility that if the fear level is too high, an avoidance reaction will set in (Griffin 1976, 71-73; also Higbee 1969, 430; Mewborn and Rogers 1979, 251). The message and messenger are simply shut out as something too fearful to contemplate. This might be particularly true of those who cannot cope with threats and also of persons of low self-esteem (Higbee 1979, 430).

Second, the recipient may respond to the extreme threat by concluding that the possibility of it happening is very unlikely (Griffin 1976, 73-74; compare Higbee 1969, 440). Apparently, people find this easy to do. After all, many are in the same boat, and few of them seem to be overly concerned, so they argue. People are not very concerned about what seems unlikely to take place.

Third, if the threat is too severe, the solution may not seem adequate to remedy it. In other words the remedy must be as potent as the predicament (Griffin 1970, 74-76; compare Higbee 1969, 441).

Few consistent witnesses have not heard some prospect say, "It all sounds too easy." What has probably happened is that the person has perceived something of the magnitude of his problem, and the gospel as offered has not seemed commensurate with the need. Perhaps, if Jesus' warning about counting the cost and his themes of cross bearing and self-denial had been included, it would have seemed different.

Not all will agree with these suggestions, but such findings deserve serious consideration. Fear will remain a part of the gospel message, for "It is a fearful thing to fall into the hands of the living God" (Heb. 10:31), but just what level of fear can best be used by the Holy Spirit for most people in today's world is a question worthy of sensitive concern. At least, these findings should cause us to pray for careful guidance as we present the fear aspect of the message.

Some Newer Concepts

Changing Behavior to Change Attitudes

We have already seen how changing attitudes can often result in a changed behavior. It is also a fact that a change in behavior can help in changing attitudes.

We attribute certain characteristics to people whom we see acting in certain ways (Zimbardo, Ebberson, and Maslach 1977, 73). For example, I have a friend who likes to get to the airport or anyplace else he is going far earlier than necessary. Because that is true, I describe him as an extremely punctual person. We make judgments like this all the time. Based on observed behavior, we attribute positive or negative characteristics to people and think of them in that way.

What is important to see is that we do the same thing to ourselves. Based on what we do or how we see ourselves act, we attribute certain characteristics to ourselves and tend to perceive ourselves as persons who do not that sort of thing (ibid., 78-79). For example, I jog quite regularly, so I think of myself as a person who exercises discipline in regard to trying to keep in shape. I didn't always do that. I used to eat far too much and exercise far too little. I only began to think of myself as a disciplined exerciser after I began my new behavior. Of course, this does not apply if there is pressure or compulsion to speak or act in a certain way. Such perception occurs only where the action takes place without significant outside manipulation (Simons 1976, 117).

This can be very important in personal evangelism. If we can get a person to carry out some specific behavior that is characteristic of a Christian, the non-Christian may begin to perceive of himself or herself as the sort of a person who would do that kind of a thing. That can be very important in helping to bring about the necessary attitude change.

In the first church I pastored after seminary, the congregation built an education building and the members did much of the work. One of the deacons had a tough-talking, antichurch neighbor who was restless on Saturdays and liked to work with his hands. The deacon persuaded him to come one day and help him work on the church. This man became a Christian a short while later and is an active deacon today. What happened was this: once he had done a service for the church, he began to think of himself as a person who would do that sort of thing. He soon did some other work also and later attended worship. He began to change his attitude toward the church, church people, and finally, toward Christ. His changed attitude followed his changed behavior.

Charitable acts of service towards unfortunate people in the name of Christ might be a likely place to start. For example, helping with a clothes or food closet for the poor, tutoring children, helping new immigrants with the language or immigration papers, singing in a special concert, or assisting the elderly are things some non-Christians will do.

According to the theory, if people will agree to do a small thing, then they are more likely to do a significantly larger thing than those who have not done the small thing (Petty and Cacioppo 1981, 167).

Unfortunately, it works both ways. If persons are asked to do something of this sort and they refuse, then they see themselves to be the kind of persons who would not do that kind of thing; and their negative relationship toward spiritual things may be intensified (ibid., 168). Thus it is important to ask them to do something they are most likely to do.

It goes without saying that such responses should be voluntary. No pressure or manipulation of any sort should ever be used. A person must always be free to say yes or no and still retain the esteem of the one who asked.

Discovering and Ministering to Needs

"Satisfied" people will not ordinarily become interested in Christianity unless they sense that it can meet some perceived personal need. As we saw in the previous chapter, we must begin with people where they are, and that is where they are.

Many have written helpful material in this regard (compare Miller 1977,

64-80; Hunter 1979, 35-63). The point of much of this material is that the witness must discover some need or needs the nonbeliever has and show how the gospel is relevant to that need, as well as to ultimate needs. If the nonbeliever is to be attracted to the gospel, that is the way he or she will come.

This often involves dealing with felt needs that are not nearly so important as ultimate needs. The latter have to do with repentance and faith followed by growth and service and losing oneself in the life of God. Felt needs may be more nearly for food and clothing, help with an out-of-control teenager, loneliness, domestic strife, moral problems in the home, depression, and despair. Felt needs are not to be taken lightly (Jas. 1:15). We are to meet them as nearly as we can and then move, as Jesus did, to ultimate needs.

Responsive Periods

The first person to whom I witnessed following my own conversion responded as follows: "You know, if you had caught me eight or nine months ago, I would have been glad to listen. I wondered a lot about Christianity then, and I would have considered it seriously, but I have since met a professor at the university who teaches comparitive religion. I now believe all religions have merit, and a person should not restrict himself to one."

Nothing I said evoked any interest in the gospel, and I felt disappointed. Nine months earlier, I needed help myself and could have offered him none. I did not know at the time what I had encountered, but I understand now that my friend had gone through what we may call a period of openness and questioning. Unfortunately, no Christian had been there to help him.

Such times of receptivity are well established. One can perhaps see it to some extent in his or her own life, depending on the age at conversion. I was not receptive at all when I was eighteen, but when I was twenty I was so ready to hear the gospel I did not wait for a witness to find me. I hunted up a Christian who could help me give my life to Christ.

Donald McGavran devotes a whole chapter in *Understanding Church Growth* (1970, 216-32) to varying receptivity of individuals and groups. He discusses the causes and the bearing of such fluctuation on missions. He sees these receptive times as extremely important for strategy in evangelism.

He feels that these times of receptivity flow like the tide. They may remain much longer than a high tide, but they eventually recede, and it is not absolutely certain that they will come again (McGavran 1970, 218). Sometimes these occur on mission fields after long years of almost imperceptible results. So it is in the lives of individuals, and these opportunities must be used. As Paul said, we must redeem the time (see Col. 4:5, KJV).

Even more recently, considerable research has been done concerning adult development and the various stages or patterns through which they pass. The most significant work is that of Daniel J. Levinson and his associates.

Though Levinson's study was confined to men from late teens to late forties, he suggests that, allowing for certain biological and social differences, the developmental periods through which women pass may be similar. One limited study has already pointed in that direction (Levinson 1978, 9).

Most significant for evangelism are the transition years marking the end of one era of the life cycle and the beginning of another. These are the "early adult, 17-22" (ibid., 19,56-57); the "mid-life, 40-45" (ibid., 60,191-95); and the "late adult, 60-65" (ibid., 34-38,62) transitions. In addition, Levinson finds an "age thirty 28-33" (ibid., 58,84-89) and an "age fifty, 50-55" (ibid., 62) transition, each of which occur in the midst of their eras. In the cross era transitions the very "fabric of one's life" undergoes change (ibid., 19), while in all five, intense questioning about life may occur. While people can become Christians at any age, understanding these periods, the fact that serious questioning takes place, and the kinds of questions raised should be of invaluable help to the witness. After all, many of these questions are those to which Christianity provides an answer.

Various factors influence the intensity and significance of these periods for different people, but times of transition and change, when persons reflect, make reappraisals, rethink values, and project new patterns can be fruitful opportunities for evangelism. "Christianity is a pilgrimage and it makes the most sense to people when they are ready to make some journey into life space" (Southard 1981, 62).

Thus, we do not give up on those who seem satisfied. In the case of some, we wait prayerfully for a time of openness to come.

Times of Crisis

Crisis ministry is another great opportunity for the sincere witness. Crises come into the lives of all people. As Eliphaz, Job's friend said, "Man is born to trouble as the sparks fly upward" (Job 5:7). Second, it is during these times of crisis that the presuppositions by which a person has lived are most likely to be seen as inadequate. It is a time when many people recognize the need of help from beyond themselves.

When Robert Ferm was preparing *The Psychology of Christian Conversion,* he took surveys, mostly among Christian college students and faculty. He found that 40 percent of his respondents had had some sort of critical experience prior to conversion which had caused them to think seriously about spiritual things. They listed death, natural disturbances, illness, a stirring sermon, and the misadventure of friends as major stimuli (Ferm 1959, 140-43).

Southard reported the outcome of a 1965 survey of persons converted as adults in six Texas presbyteries. Results suggested "the need for a savior was most vivid when personal security was shaken by some change in social circumstances or self-esteem was challenged by a new role as husband, father or manager" (Southard 1981, 61).

The witnesses must be alert to these times that constitute major or minor crises. From the spiritual standpoint these can be disguised blessings which clearly reveal needs.

Tender love and the utmost sensitivity are called for here. There can be no obtrusiveness in the presence of grief or trouble. To show sympathetically that "the Lord is near to the brokenhearted" (Ps. 34:18) and that "he heals the brokenhearted and binds up their wounds" (Ps. 147:3), or that God is "a very present help in trouble" (Ps. 46:1), combined with a personal testimony of God's care and concern is not offensive.

I know a fine deacon today who, thirty years ago, accepted the Lord only two days after his father's untimely death. I had thought he would be mad at God. The Holy Spirit, however, used the grief to open his heart to faith and commitment. Sensitive ministry combined with sympathetic witness may be one of our best means to reach the "satisfied."

Offering a Cause

The chapter on cause hunger in James Jauncey's book has always intrigued me (1972, 45-54 also 1978, 51-60). He contends that people have a basic need to identify with a great cause, some all-consuming purpose to which they can dedicate their lives.

Jauncey maintains that through much of history most people have had to expend all their energies to provide food, shelter, and basic necessities. Only in recent times has economic prosperity in the Western world freed a large number of people for other things. As a consequence, cause hunger has manifested itself in all sorts of campaigns, marches, protests, and demonstrations.

He sees Christianity as God's provision to perfectly satisfy this need. It is not simply *a* cause, it is *the* cause. Nothing is better suited for giving persons an all-consuming purpose in life and an exciting reason for living.

If it is true that meaning is now man's primary anxiety, then we truly have something to offer in the kingdom service aspect of the Christian life using God-given gifts and abilities. Jauncey says that, in his youth, he attended missionary meetings in which furloughing missionaries gave testimonies and told of unmet needs. When the invitation was given for persons to dedicate themselves to Christian service and to the meeting of those needs, he was surprised at the non-Christians who volunteered. He later concluded that they were cause-hungry people who saw a great life purpose to which they could wholly give themselves. They had not been moved by the evangelistic efforts of the church, but they were greatly touched by the opportunity to identify with a great cause (Jauncey 1978, 51-52).

Some might object that this is out of order and that people should become believers prior to trying to serve Christ. There are no rules, however, that dictate how one must be attracted to the gospel. Every person is different, and we must expect that all sorts of appeals will be used to lead people to the Master.

What I am saying is that we must not forget the satisfied simply because that is the way they feel at the moment. God is at work in his world. Each person's circumstances are changing every day. The person who was impossible yesterday may be far more receptive today. We cannot think of abandoning the satisfied any more than we would abandon a mission field because the work is hard. We must constantly work with old and new methods to convey the truth and win the lost.

---

[1] Citing Claus, W., Von Bengel bis Burk, in Wuttembergische Vater, vol. 1, 1887.

8
Mass Media
and Personal Evangelism

The word *media* is, of course, plural; and there are all kinds of the mass variety used in evangelism. Books, films, magazines, tracts, secular and religious newspapers, radio, and television all come under this heading. The fact is, however, that in evangelism in America television and—to a much lesser extent—radio so overshadow the others, and such large claims are made for them, that the discussion will largely be confined to that type media.

Some may wonder why television is even discussed in a book on personal evangelism. The reason is that some of those involved in religious television are, consciously or unconsciously, claiming to be able to do much of the work of evangelism for the local churches. This discussion should alert us to the need to weigh carefully some claims being made and, more importantly, help us see the indispensable nature of personal evangelism through the local church.

Hopefully, all unfounded dreams of some easy, shortcut, lightening-quick method of world evangelism can be laid to rest.

The electric church or electronic church has become a popular term used by friend and foe to refer to an amazing phenomenon of our time. I think Jeffrey Hadden's definition is a correct one: "All electronic communication that is generally perceived by senders and receivers alike as religious in intent and content" (Hadden 1980, 2). Likely, however, when most people hear the term, they tend to think of six to ten national religious television personalities and the large followings they command and, to a lesser extent, some well-known radio personalities and their constituencies. That is the way it will be used in this chapter to refer to persons and programs whose names have become household words.

Not everything to be said, however, can be applied equally to each situation. There is so much variety in the electronic church, and it is increasing so rapidly with the proliferation of cable that much will have to be applied with discretion and careful discernment.

Electronic media influence us enormously. Ninety-eight percent of American homes have television, and there are far more radios than people, the average household having 5.5 sets (US Department of Commerce 1982-83, 555). While figures vary, William Fore estimates that the average person over eighteen spends 26.4 hours before the television screen and 21.3 hours listening to radio each week. This totals 47.7 hours equaling two full days and nights every week. This means that more time is spent doing that than at any other activity except sleeping, to which it runs a very close second. By comparison, reading books, something of no small significance from the Christian discipleship point of view, consumes a mere twelve minutes per week (Fore 1979, 4).

Something which occupies so large a segment of our lives cannot help but be of tremendous influence. One authority has pointed out that it represents the third major communications revolution: the invention of writing being the first and the invention of movable type, the second (Hadden 1980, 5-6). It is small wonder that communications experts feel that one must understand something of these media if one is to understand life as it is today.

This power of electronic media has not been overlooked by those with Christian concerns. Coincident with the growth of these media has been the use of them by various Christian groups and individual personalities. Recent years, especially 1970-75, have seen a tremendous surge in the use of television as a means of religious communication. It is now an enterprise so large as to be called "big business" by *The Wall Street Journal* (Montgomery 1978, 1).

One major concern is to see just how effective this revolutionary development is in the area of evangelism. Are thousands really won at home and abroad? Is this, at last, the major means of carrying out the worldwide scope of the New Testament commissions as some seem to think?

Great Claims

God's Means to Reach the World

Not a few proponents of the electronic church make some large claims concerning its abilities that either directly or indirectly relate to evangelism. Ben Armstrong, executive director of National Religious Broadcasters, claims that the electronic church, as he defines it, reaches more people each week than all the local churches put together. According to his calculations while 42 percent of the population attends church each week, 47 percent sees or hears some religious program. He goes on to say, "I believe that God has raised up this powerful technology of radio and television expressly to reach every man, woman, boy or girl on earth with the even more powerful message of the gospel" (Armstrong 1979, 7).

Fulfillment of Prophecy

Furthermore, he sees these media as having eschatological implications. He calls attention to the passage, the "gospel of the kingdom shall be preached in all the world for a witness unto all nations; and then shall the end come," and states, "certainly for the first time in human history we are in the midst of fulfilling the conditions of Matthew 24:14" (ibid., 172).

Armstrong also reports a meeting which David DuPlessis, a well-known Pentecostal apologist, had with Karl Barth in which Barth asked, "If you are so sure the Bible predicts the future why aren't radio and TV there?" DuPlessis answered, "They are!" and referred him to Revelation 14:6-7, a passage which reads: "I saw another angel fly in the midst of heaven, having the everlasting gospel to preach unto them that dwell on earth, and to every nation, and kindred, and tongue, and people" (KJV). Revelation 14:7-9 mentions two other angels, one announcing the fall of Babylon and another warning of the consequences of receiving the mark of the beast. These three angels, Armstrong thinks, may stand for three satellites, each capable of covering one third of the earth, thus making possible preaching the gospel to every nation in the world (ibid., 172-3). Even though the technological means for doing this is available and even if such an interpretation of that passage were plausible, it seems to me that there would be some significant political, sociological, and religious reasons to negate such a possibility.

The point, however, is that many of those involved in electronic media promote it as the great hope of worldwide gospel proclamation and as a means of quickly winning thousands of people—"of claiming the whole world for Jesus." That many Christians and Christian leaders hold these same hopes is evidenced by the amazing ease with which charismatic personalities raise huge sums based on this appeal.

That is by no means the only appeal. Promises of powerful prayer for personal problems or those of loved ones, offers of books, gifts, Bibles, trinkets, lapel pins, travel opportunities with program personalities, the possibility of miracles, and other personal blessings are all there. Yet the bottom line that legitimizes most of the offers and appeals is what can be done for others through the ministry, particularly evangelistically. That they simply cannot do what they suggest seems obvious for several reasons.

Obvious Powers

This is not to say, of course, that television is not a powerful medium, for it is indeed. From a religious standpoint, television has shown tremendous power in connection with charismatic personality to build empires. Like a giant electronic vacuum sweeper, it sucks up ordinary people, students, faculty, and especially money to build colleges, medical and specialized schools, headquarters—sometimes complete with hotel, restaurants, studios, and even camping and recreation facilities.

Furthermore, it can inform. It is a potent reinforcer in regard to affirming people in what they believe. It can plant seed. It can even persuade to a limited degree. Neither is there any doubt about the affection with which Americans regard this medium. It has become the chief source of entertainment for the majority, and, in fact, the relationship has gone beyond mere affection. Marie Winn, in her book *The Plug-in Drug,* sees television as "a narcotic on which millions are hopelessly hooked. They simply can no longer cope without it" (1977, 11).

Others point out that it transcends the literacy barrier, already seen as important even in the United States. And, indeed, some nonchurchgoers are reached, particularly the shut-ins and elderly. Great Christian personalities are exposed to potentially large audiences that otherwise might remain relatively unknown. It can even be an instrument of change, especially when one is predisposed to it, and can alter or influence attitudes when the mind is not already made up. In truth, it has brought about a communications revolution of great proportions as indicated earlier.

For the power of this medium and for the good it is able to do, we can be truly thankful. Indeed, it would be a shame for the gospel not to be heard and seen via such a means. And especially for those helped toward a Christian commitment or strengthened in their spiritual resolve, we can only praise God.

What the Christian must realize, however, is that, strange as it may seem and powerful as it is, television is not the great instrument of evangelism that people think it is. There is an increasing number of sobering voices concerning the claims about evangelism that, up to now, have been little heard or, if heard, ignored by the large army of supporters both within and without the local churches.

Counterclaims

Christian Communication Experts

Viggo Sogaard, communications specialist at Tollose School in Denmark and training coordinator of Asia Christian Fellowship, has pointed out that "Communication theory . . . is now quite refined and applies to Christian communication." He then says rather bluntly that: "Media are often viewed with awe as if they are able to communicate messages by themselves. . . . Radio and TV . . . are not effective for decision making" (Sogaard 1980, 6). Later, but in connection with the previous statement, Sogaard adds: "Evangelism must be centered in the local church and not in some outside organization. The cutting edge of a church is where its members meet society—embodied in neighbors, colleagues, friends and family" (ibid., 7).

He is not alone in that conviction. Hear Charles Swann, General Manager of Station WRFK-FM, Union Theological Seminary, Richmond, Virginia: "Mass media in American Society are probably inefficient at changing people's minds. In fact, only in the absence of previously held opinion are they effective at creating opinion. (I submit that religion is a subject on which nobody in America does not have an opinion already closely held)" (Swann 1980, 2, parentheses his).

Robert Don Hughes, assistant professor of Mass Media at Southern Baptist Theological Seminary writes, "Christians must use the media to make the audience aware of the gospel's existence. Changing the minds of members of that audience—'winning' them—will remain a responsibility of individual Christians through personal encounters" (1984, 33).

Other Authorities

Joseph Klapper, a long recognized authority in the field of communications, has written: "In general, mass communication reinforces the existing attitudes, tastes, predispositions, and behavioral tendencies of its audience members, including tendencies toward change. Rarely, if ever, does it serve alone to create metamorphoses" (1973, 191). Or note this more recent and slightly different appraisal by Emmert and Donaghy: "The mass media may directly persuade us to choose a particular brand of cheese or a particular deodorant, but they seldom persuade us to vote for a candidate or to make a major financial investment" (1981, 364). In other words, the mass media may influence persons regarding minor matters; but, when it comes to major decisions such as a life commitment to Christ, there are other elements that must enter in which will be discussed later.

Considerations

Audience Sovereignty

What these researchers say about the weakness of mass media in regard to influencing major decisions is true for several reasons. First, there is the obvious but often overlooked fact that the audience is sovereign. This means that the individual decides whether or not to view or listen to a program. Evangelism cannot take place at a given hour, regardless of how many Christian programs are offered, if a person has decided to watch secular entertainment, which a large majority apparently do.

Not a few have supposed that if they just sponsor a Christian television program, they will have a large number of viewers. That is a patently false assumption. A vast number of viewers will no more tune in a religious program than they will go to a stadium to hear a great evangelist preach.

Selective Reception, Retention, and Perception

This leads to a second explanatory principle. People practice selective reception, selective retention, and selective perception. Research has revealed some very interesting things about people's attitudes and the communications they receive. First, they often tend to read, watch, or listen to communications that are in sympathy with views they already hold, and they avoid those of a different hue. Second, they remember longer those communications which support their position while forgetting easily their antitheses. Finally, people commonly distort or reinterpret unsympathetic views in such a way that they end up using them to support their own previously held opinions. An example might be communications about monogamy. According to occasional news reports, there are a few die-hard polygamists left in the country. They are sometimes discovered and arrested. These would not only be less likely to read interpretations of the Bible that affirm monogamy, but also they would be less likely to remember them. They may also distort and reinterpret what they do read so as to use it to support their own view. Joseph T. Klapper sums it up this way:

> Now it is obvious that if people tend to expose themselves mainly to mass communications in accord with their existing views and interests and to avoid other material, and if, in addition, they tend to forget such other material as they see, and if, finally, they tend to distort such other material as they remember, then clearly mass communication is not very likely to change their views. It is far, far more likely to support and reinforce their existing views (Klapper 1973, 185).

The word *tend* is an important one here. Earlier I used the word *often.* I did so because there are some exceptions to Klapper's dictum as one might suspect. It has been discovered that there might be some reasons why a person would watch a program that did not support his or her existing views. For example, someone might do so in order to seek usable information because of interest in a particular topic or even to be entertained by listening to a person with an opposite view or views (Severin and Tankard 1979, 250). Or suppose a confirmed non-Christian is spending the night in a town where only two channels can be received, and both have a religious program. If the non-

Christian watches at all, he or she will have to watch something counter to his views.

According to Severin and Tankard,

> The three selective processes can be thought of as three rings of defenses, with selective exposure being the outermost ring, selective perception coming in the middle and selective retention being the innermost ring. Undesirable information can sometimes be headed off at the outermost ring. A person can avoid those publications and programs that might contain contrary information. If this fails, the person can then exercise selective perception in decoding the message. If this fails, the person can then exercise selective retention, and just not retain the contrary information (ibid., 137).

Not everyone agrees about selective exposure. It has been called into question and subjected to debate (compare McGuire 1968, 797-800; Sears 1968, 777-87). For that reason, some would have less confidence in selective exposure than in selective perception and selective retention (Severin and Tankard 1979, 137). At the same time, it is clear that other experts consider it valid despite questions raised (Katz 1968, 788-96; Emmert and Donaghy 1981, 96-98) and applicable also in regard to mass media evangelism (Engel 1979, 53; Griffin 1976, 150-56).

To the layperson unacquainted with the intricacies of social psychology, the commonsense logic of the idea seems obvious enough. Most are aware of exercising selective exposure themselves. It is also obvious that there are exceptions. The electronic church does have non-Christian viewers and also some genuine conversions. At the same time, most of the nonbelieving world does not watch, and selective exposure is a large factor in their decision.

The work of the Holy Spirit has not been forgotten, nor is he limited in any way by these ideas. He is "free as the wind," and the non-Christian viewer of the electronic church is evidence of that. The Holy Spirit also works through natural processes, however, and the better we understand those, the better we can cooperate with him.

Limited Audience

Despite the huge claims as to the size of the audience, investigations show that religious television does have a limited viewership, particularly in the light of the fact that it must compete against the major entertainment networks.

Now, however, the research of Jeffrey Hadden and Charles Swann has shown a shocking difference in the actual size of viewing audiences and those claimed by the telecasters. They found that, according to Arbitron, the total number of viewers of sixty-six syndicated religious programs in an average week in 1980 was 20,500,000. This was less than one major figure claimed for his program alone (Hadden and Swann 1981, 50).

These figures, however, must be qualified by another consideration. If a viewer watched five programs in a row on a given Sunday morning, he or she would be counted five times. Thus the 20,500,000 total does not mean there were actually that many different viewers. The actual total could be considerably less. On the other hand, they also point out that the 4,200 cable systems operating at the time with 15 million subscribers were not taken into account. This would no doubt add to the total number of viewers. Hadden and Swann concluded that, when all the factors were weighed, Arbitron was, in all likelihood, fairly accurate as to the number in the viewing audience (ibid., 53-54).

These same researchers found that most of these programs draw a disproportionate share of their viewers from the South, and that "virtually all the syndicated programs have audiences of which two-thirds to three-quarters are fifty years of age and over." About two thirds of these are female (ibid., 61-62). This simply confirms the fact that there are large segments of the population that are not being reached by religious telecasts to any significant degree.

One-Way Impersonal Communication

Electronic broadcasting faces yet another limiting factor. Despite all that can be done, it is largely a one-way communication. It is, therefore, by its very nature impersonal and nonrelational. The speaker is not known by his listeners, nor does he know them.

Hadden and Swann perceptively point out, however, that a combination of casuality, intimacy with supporting cast, live audience, and computer mailings using the name of the addressee in the letter enables susceptible and willing people to imagine a face-to-face relationship with the performer (ibid., 65-66). At best, however, it is an illusion. It is strictly one-way communication although, apparently, many are content to have it that way. Social scientists and public opinion experts agree that face-to-face discourse is a far more effective instrument of pedagogy and persuasion.

Nonvulnerable Messengers

Closely related to the matter of impersonal communication is the fact of nonvulnerability. Jesus was vulnerable. It is often stated that Jesus may have spoken to a total of twenty or thirty thousand in his lifetime while, via television, one might do far better in one presentation. Yet Jesus' contact was of a far different nature. He walked among his audience. His life was open to them. He touched them and they him. He was subject to criticism, abuse, and finally death at their hands. Such was his vulnerability. Thus does the world know and revere him as no other.

He would have been quite safe on television. His was a far cry from the picture on a large, sterile cathode tube that, despite every device, remains removed in space, impersonal, and nonrelational after all.

Entertainment Medium

A further drawback of television is the fact that, by its very nature, it is an entertainment medium. Marshall McLuhan's "the medium is the message" has been echoed repeatedly. He means, of course, that the medium is a message itself, and consciously or unconsciously people think of television in a certain way. The vast majority of viewers turn on their set for entertainment, and this may explain why programs with a large dose of that element often do best in attracting an audience (compare Spring 1982, 36-37).

Opinion Leaders

The most significant weakness of all has to do with opinion formation and the decision-making process. Authorities have already been quoted who do not believe the electronic media are the best means to bring about major decisions. This is shown to be true, in part, by research that reveals the power and importance of opinion leaders or influentials in any group. Most people are not as influenced by the media message as they are by attitudes of peer leaders toward the information.

Also, many people look to influentials because they perceive too great a distance between the conveyor of information and themselves. They are not enough like that person, for example, the television preacher, to see him as credible and thus accept his information. He is, after all, unknown to them. Thus, they turn to an opinion leader in their peer group as interpreter. They check out the experience of one or more persons like themselves.

The opinion leader is ordinarily a high status person who has wide exposure to the media, significant social participation, innovative ability, and who is a modern-thinking person. What the opinion leader knows and whom he or she knows outside the peer group who can provide information are important factors in opinion leader status (Rogers and Shoemaker 1971, 217-22; Severin and Tankard 1979, 203-205).

This is why people consult them. They are assumed to be credible, possess superior knowledge of experience, and, unlike the media persuader, have nothing to gain. The more important a given decision is, the more likely the opinion leader is to be consulted (Engel 1979, 162).

This application of this to lay personal evangelism cannot be passed without comment. This is why the trained lay witness must be ready on the front line. The mass media may indeed raise questions, but the trained Christian who has become influential in Christian things by virtue of experience, knowledge, acquaintance with important Christian people, and credibility must be there to speak the appropriate word for Christ.

Opinion leaders and nonopinion leaders alike are open to influence by the mass media that can lead to a decision. When major matters are at issue, however, it is more often than not the opinion leaders that provide the decisive influence (Emmert and Donaghy 1981, 364).

An interesting article in *The Wall Street Journal* unintentionally gives an illustration of the role of influentials:

> Judy Christianson, a visiting nurse in Cleveland, first became aware of the Church of the Covenant last spring when she heard one of its radio ads. That

didn't draw her into the church, but she was intrigued and started asking her friends about it.

"I found people I knew and respect who were members," she says, so she began attending. This fall she became a member. "Radio ads don't do it by themselves —you have to ask around to validate what they say," she says (Yao 1979, 7).

This is what communications experts see as one of the essential functions of mass media. It raises questions and plants ideas, but to hope for great numbers of conversions from its influence alone may well be to expect from those media what they cannot do. And if this is true of the decision itself, it may be even more true in regard to helping the convert into vital church membership.

Mass Versus Interpersonal Witness

One of the most widely quoted books in this area is *Communication of Innovations* by Rogers and Shoemaker, 1971. This source summarizes the relative strength of mass media as opposed to interpersonal channels in a most helpful way.

Mass media can:

1. Reach a large audience rapidly.
2. Create knowledge and spread information.
3. Lead to changes in weakly held attitudes.

Interpersonal channels . . . :

1. Allow two-way exchange of ideas. The receiver may secure clarification or additional information about the innovation from the source individual. This characteristic of interpersonal channels sometimes allows them to overcome the social and psychological barriers of selective exposure, perception, and retention.
2. Persuade receiving individuals to form or change strongly held attitudes. (Rogers and Shoemaker 1971, 252-53).

What is said about interpersonal channels here is of the utmost importance for personal evangelism and reveals the indispensable nature of interpersonal witness.

Concerns

Noninvolvement

There are some pressing concerns being expressed about the electronic church. Even though some programs do stress involvement in a local church, and while there is evidence that some people have been encouraged to deeper participation (P.R.R.C. and Gallup 1981), it is strongly suspected that many viewers are glad to settle for less. I have spoken face-to-face with some who have apparently decided to give their allegiance to the television church, and not a few pastors report similar experiences. While this may be better than nothing at all, such an arrangement leaves people largely uninvolved beyond the sending of offerings. They will probably bear no responsibility for the spiritual training of children or others in their community. Their spiritual gifts may go totally undiscovered and remain unused, except for the gift of giving. They will never experience the joys of Christian fellowship within a local body or the growth pains of learning and struggling to do spiritual work with imperfect fellow believers. The call to real community and the participation in body life will have passed them by. They have chosen an easy road that lacks fulfillment, and one, incidentally, that is unknown to the New Testament.

Nonprophetic

Since television viewers will not generally receive messages that are too different from positions they already hold, a rather limited, narrowly focused message becomes a necessity. Viewers may not be discomfited too radically or too often, or they will hunt something that produces less dissonance. Matters of social evil, injustice, poverty, and oppression are seldom to be heard in contexts that reveal the listener's guilt and need to change. Thus, opportunities for growth in these crucial areas go begging.

Easy answers to very complex problems are commonplace, and the possibility of quick miracles for any problem are emphasized. Promises of prayer, sometimes with a hint of sacerdotalism, are extended. However, the thinking viewer must know that amid thousands of letters, real personal concern is hardly possible.

Accountability

Not least are concerns about the large amounts of money collected. While some do publish statements concerning the use of funds, others leave large questions unanswered by their apparent unwillingness to offer public accountability.

Another concern is the amount of money that has to be expended in order to raise money. Responsible stewards must seriously question the extent to which this is a wise investment of funds (compare Fore 1981, 939).

Primacy of Personal Local Church Evangelism

It is precisely in areas where these media are weak that personal evangelism, launched and centered in the local church, can be strong. The audience is still sovereign, but the personal witness who makes a trip to the home or who is buying lunch for some unsaved person is far more likely to get a serious hearing. It is not so easy to turn off the caring person who speaks with genuine concern and who has gone out of the way for an opportunity to share.

This is personal, face-to-face communication. Properly done it has no "hit-and-run" characteristics. Needs that surface can be met. Dialogue can take place. The message can be aimed and made relevant to the context.

Personal witnesses are vulnerable. They are open to abuse, ridicule, rejection, or intimidation. They can be shown out or thrown out. Such a thing rarely occurs if the spirit and approach of the witnesses are at all appropriate. More often they are accepted or at least tolerated, and they have opportunity to share their message and show their concern.

Persons won by this means can usually be led into the local church and into groups conducive to growth and development. They can experience Christian community, spiritual fellowship, gift discovery, Christian service, meaningful existence, and a deeper understanding of their responsibility in the world.

Local churches can offer responsible discipleship in which complex issues are explained. Prayer groups can offer support and assistance that is deeply personal and genuinely concerned. Contributors can see where the offering goes and may have a voice in determining its use. In short, the local church can offer evangelism and follow-up discipleship on an extremely personal and superior level.

Expectations

A number of factors suggest that there may be improvement in the future evangelistic thrust of the electronic church. For one thing, there seems to be a new awareness that those who use mass media should have some understanding of the field of communications. As that understanding grows and as more trained personnel assume responsibility, there should be corresponding shifts toward using television to do what it does best. In fact, it is already taking place. One Christian network is already offering a wide range of programs including newscasts by a former Miss America, entertainment for children, Wall Street analyses, and a Christian soap opera (Spring 1982, 36-37). Since drama is well suited to television, the soap opera and other dramatic productions should be a very effective low-key way to present the message. The variety of offerings should help attract a more diversified audience as well.

The entry of mainline denominations in a far greater way should help in relating to the local churches and greatly increase evangelism potential. Follow-up and feedback may be greatly facilitated.

The expansion of cable television will open the way for many local churches to participate. Local church telecasts have demonstrated their potential in church growth and evangelism as interpersonal relationships with responsive viewers becomes a real possibility (compare Nicholas 1983, 35).

On the negative side, increasing competition for viewers and dollars may also be a pressing reality as new young preachers make their way into the field (see Buursma 1983, 4). Some feel that the viewing audience peaked in size in 1977-78 and that a saturation point has already been reached (Horsfield 1982, 87). The viewing constituency has not been at the 1977-78 level since that time, but the diversified formats may succeed in attracting new viewers.

Dollars are another story. As competition increases, there could be some radical retrenchments. Passing time may see the waning of the appeal of the electronic church and less willingness on the part of constituents to respond to request for gifts.

One thing is certain: we will soon know more about the actual effect of the electronic church. Much research is going on, and future chapters like this one will have fewer qualifiers like "perhaps," "it seems," and "possibly."

Whatever the case, the fact that the electronic media are not nearly as effective in evangelism as many suppose and the vastly superior nature of face-to-face contact over the impersonal emphasizes once again the tremendous importance of the local church. It is on the local field that life-transforming evangelism can take place in the New Testament spirit and in direct vulnerable relationship with pagan society. There secular persons can be met on their own ground. No substitute for the local church has yet been found, and especially is this true in evangelism.

Not infrequently people have said, "Oh, if television had only been available to Jesus. Just think of the multitudes he could have reached."

People who have earnestly thought about it may more nearly agree with James Taylor who said, "I take the opposite view. I think that if Jesus had had TV, if Paul had had a printing press, Christianity might not have survived. The early Christians would have been tempted to leave the job of evangelism to the communication experts. "More people would have known about Christianity. But far fewer would have been converted" (Taylor 1979, 614).

Fortunately, however, the early church had no choice. It confronted the world in powerful face-to-face, interpersonal, vulnerable encounter despite the risks involved. Multitudes were converted by that means. Christians today are the descendants of that success.

We can be thankful for the potent things electronic media can do. Hopefully, we will learn much about how this can be used more effectively in evangelism, but the essentials of the task of evangelism must still be done largely by personal witnesses through the local church.

9
Commonsense Principles
of Personal Evangelism

There are a number of principles that seem to fit best into a chapter by themselves. They must be a part of any thorough course in personal evangelism. Often knowing what not to do is as important as knowing the appropriate positive actions. Some, therefore, are best expressed negatively, others positively. Mostly they represent good common sense. The observance of them will go a long way to facilitate communication.

Learning to Listen

Importance of Listening

It is strange that so many books on witnessing have so little to say about listening. Experts on the subject now tell us that good listening may have more to do with our success in whatever enterprise than almost anything else we do. The importance of this art is being widely recognized.

A recent investigation has shown that managers now consider the development of listening competency as the most critical ingredient in their success (*U.S. News* May 26, 1980, 66). Its importance in the area of psychology and pastoral care is well known. Yet many books on personal evangelism seem most concerned with getting the message across and contain little on listening. This, I believe is a large oversight.

There are excuses and dodges that should not be allowed to sidetrack us. Decisions are certainly important, but there is still an indispensable role of listening that must not be ignored. It will usually be the case that we first have to listen carefully in order to be heard.

The Bible is not silent concerning this important activity. We find Job imploring his friends to listen to him.

> Oh that you would keep silent,
>   and it would be your wisdom!
> Hear now my reasoning,
>   and listen to the pleadings of my lips (Job 13:5-6).

Like many today, Job's friends were far better at speaking than listening. James exhorts, "Let every man be quick to hear, slow to speak, slow to anger" (Jas. 1:19). Most people do just the opposite. They are slow to hear, but quick to speak and show anger.

Hearing Versus Listening

There is a vast difference between hearing and listening. Hearing is simply receiving "stimuli over auditory pathways" (compare Khang 1972, 23). It occurs automatically. Listening is far more complicated. It has to be taught or studied. "It is more than merely *hearing* what someone else is saying." It also includes "interpretation of what is said . . . evaluation, which involves weighing the information . . . and responding" to what was heard and evaluated (*U.S. News* May 26, 1980, 65). The shocking thing is that people do this at an average efficiency rate of "only 25 percent" (ibid.)

The reasons for this inefficiency are not hard to find. For one thing, most people receive little or no training in listening. Though it is beginning to receive attention in the schools, most emphasis is still upon reading and writing skills. Second, people like to be the center of attention and hear their own voice speaking. They have a built-in need to be heard and easily overlook the needs of others in the urgency of meeting their own. Third, we all think much faster than we speak. People speak between 120 to 180 words a minute but think four or five times that fast (Lane 1980, 183). We think of other things while trying to listen. The mind wanders and misses much of what is said. Fourth, people hear selectively. There is so much noise about us in many situations, we unconsciously exclude some sounds and concentrate on others. For example, when talking on the telephone with the television on, we exclude the television and concentrate on the caller's words. We can, however, easily let other sounds be a distraction. Finally, we are programmed not to listen carefully. We have learned that most things will be repeated. A surprising number of people almost always say "what?" or "huh?" the first time they hear anything. Teachers make the same announcements many times. The same is true at church and at work. The result is that listening efficiency is low.

Listening and Communication

When there is a failure in listening, two fundamental principles of interpersonal communication are ignored (Borg 1981, 31). One is that real "communication is a two-way street." For interpersonal communication to take place, there has to be the initiation of a line of thought and a response to it. Some authorities go a bit further and require an initiation, a response, and a response to the response (Brown and Keller 1979, 4). Moreover, the responses have to be related one to the other. In other words, when there is no listening, no significant communication between persons has taken place. Second, "a level of trust and understanding" is necessary for the efficient communication of new ideas. Careful listening recognizes the importance of both principles.

Most people simply cannot accept a message from a stranger. Children are taught from earliest days to distrust unknown persons. Strangers can be criminal, dishonest, or potentially hurtful in other ways. We have the most confidence in those we know and believe to be honest and trustworthy. Listening is the best possible way to build that relationship.

When we listen carefully to others, it is a silent compliment. Listening says, "You are worth my time and interest." It is an unselfish exercise in sharing that demonstrates care and concern. At the same time it is meeting a basic need common to all: the need to be heard. It is a form of Christian love. "Of all the actions that can make another human being feel significant and worthwhile, there is none more vital than skilled listening. Still, it is the most overlooked" (Conklin, 1979, 80).

It provides the key to knowing our prospect and where to begin in witness. We have to begin where people are, and the only way to understand them in their situation is to ask questions and listen to their responses. It is in this kind of listening that we discover the most natural and relevant ways of sharing Christ.

Our listening helps people understand and communicate with themselves. Drakeford points out that people can best understand their own thoughts by expressing them to someone else (Drakeford 1976, cassette). It is by getting them out into the open that they can be examined and corrected.

When people express their beliefs, arguments, and objections, the witness has the opportunity for affirmations, truth sharing, and providing answers. The non-Christian may be testing his views for the first time, and it is an altogether important thing to do.

Listening also determines the quality of the speaker's response. Skilled listening draws out the best in the speaker. Black churches have a unique way of doing this for their preachers. The same dynamic needs to occur in person-to-person intercourse.

Improving Listening Skills

Fortunately, listening is a skill that can be developed and improved. Because listening is so crucial to a proper relationship for witness, the following suggestions for listening improvement should be considered carefully.

First, concentrate intensely on what is being said. Purposely show that you are following the speaker's words by using occasional nods, gestures, facial expressions, eye contact, or postures. One must not overdo it, but the appropriate use of these responses will help draw the best from the speaker and aid the listener in concentrating on what is being said.

Second, help shut out distractions by using brief questions or comments that draw the other person out. Expressions like "I see!" "Really!" or "Is that right?" in a sympathetic tone can assist both sides of the communication.

Third, the listener should try to think where the speaker is heading. He or she can anticipate what the outcome may be while evaluating and reviewing what has already been said.

Fourth, plan to recall and make notes on the conversation, much as a professional counselor does, immediately following the encounter. The assumption of that responsibility can sharpen all the listening skills.

Fifth, listening between the lines can be a helpful practice. What is not being said may be very important along with the manner and tone of what is being expressed.

Sixth, note the body language. It may or may not reinforce the verbal message. Attention to the nonverbal communication can be even more important than to the verbal. What is being done with the hands? What does the posture and facial expression say? Note the eyes especially, along with the gestures, vocal tones, and inflections.

Seventh, keep giving the speaker the opportunity to talk. Ask a new question, or ask for more information about something already said. Resist the temptation to begin telling your own story until you have given your prospect a full opportunity. The one who can do this is always considered an excellent conversationalist.

Learning to listen does more than make productive witnesses. It will bring blessing to every area of a person's life.

Avoiding Arguments

The witness must studiously avoid arguing. Well-trained Christians can often win an argument, but they seldom win the person with whom they argue. Even more important, the task of convincing belongs to the Holy Spirit (John 16:8-11). He is the only one who can win both arguments and the person.

Such restraint is far more difficult than it sounds. Imagine an excited young man enthusiastic and happy in a new-found faith. He goes to share what he has discovered with an old acquaintance only to find him hostile to Christianity and full of excuses for his attitude. It is not easy for one so recently delivered from such a stance to resist arguing against what he knows now to be so futile and false. Neither is it always easy for the well-trained pastor to refrain. He is a man with college and seminary degrees, usually seven years of higher education or more. He has long experience as a pastor and interpreter of the Bible. He encounters a man with no training at all who has only the most minimal exposure to any church, yet he claims to have worked out his own religion and debunks everything Christian. There may even be a wife and children suffering from his godless ways, and he is completely blind to his problem which is so obvious to everyone else. It is only the love of Christ that constrains the pastor to try and share his good news with kindly spirit and avoid any hint of argument. The temptation to speak plainly and "set such a person straight" is strong indeed. Nevertheless, such restraint is not optional if lost persons are to be won.

In such cases it is usually best to listen for something with which one can honestly agree, at least in part, and begin there. It is an established fact that no one likes to be contradicted or bested in argument. When that occurs, it usually serves to increase defensiveness and harden the person in his or her stated position. Meantime, the argument has ruled out the possibility of establishing the relationship of trust usually necessary to effective communication. Such wisdom must be developed and practiced. As Jesus said, "Behold, I send you out as sheep in the midst of wolves; so be wise as serpents and innocent as doves" (Matt. 10:16).

Eliminating Judgmental Attitudes

A third principle is that judgmental attitudes must be studiously avoided. We do not win people by registering shock at their conduct or by condemning their behavior.

In a day when narcotic use and addictions are so common, sexual expression and obscenity so open, and violence and inhumanity so blatant, Christians can indeed encounter shocking situations. One must remember that it was just such persons that Christ came to change. There are plenty of shocking situations in the Scriptures. Two women had eaten a child and were arguing over the eating of another (2 Kings 6:28-29). Parents had sacrificed their children to pagan idols (2 Kings 16:3; Isa. 57:5). A woman was discovered in the very act of adultery (John 8:1-11). Men were using a deranged slave girl for personal profit (Acts 16:16), and a man was living with his stepmother (1 Cor. 5:1) to mention a few.

Jesus was not shocked at the unjust extortions of Levi, the Samaritan woman's five husbands, the rebellious activities of Simon the Zealot, or the ill-gotten wealth of Zacchaeus. He simply called these persons unto himself. In fact, he warned about harsh censorious judgment of people (Matt. 7:1). While Paul did have something to say about Christian responsibility in judging the conduct of erring fellow Christians, he was explicit in warning against judging those on the outside (1 Cor. 5:9-12). Witnesses simply cannot be shocked at how low people can sink or cease to be amazed at the heights to which Christ can lift the fallen.

Though some strides in Christian understanding have been made in recent years, there are still many Christians who are hindered by a crippling legalism. It not only hinders them in their openness to people; it robs them of enriching relationships with many Christians. The Bible does speak about certain things being clearly wrong. For example, fornication, stealing, murder, selfishness, covetousness, ignoring needs of the hungry and suffering, and injustice can never be right. On the other hand, there are matters not clearly set out in Scripture and about which Christians do not agree. Here room must be allowed for differences of interpretation. There are areas where everyone must be "fully convinced in his own mind" (Rom. 14:5) and where the Christian's concern is to "no more pass judgment on one another" but to never "put a stumbling block or hindrance in the way of a brother" (Rom. 14:13).

In the case of the unsaved, for narrowly legalistic Christians to try and change their conduct before their attitude and relationship toward Christ has been transformed is "cart-before-the-horse" futility. It can so alienate the lost person that future contact becomes extremely difficult or even impossible.

Paul Little has pointed out how easy it is to condemn others without intending to. Suppose a non-Christian asks you to join him in an alcoholic drink or in some other activity that you have ruled out in your desire to please Christ. If you reply, "No, I don't drink" or "That's something I don't do as a Christian," you have really condemned his intention and perhaps made him think that your "don'ts" are an inherent part of the gospel message. Little wisely suggests rather than say "no" in the above spirit, that you recognize the kindness and generosity of the invitation they have given, and suggest an alternative. For example, "Thank you. I don't care for a drink but I would enjoy a coke" or "I don't believe I'd enjoy the pornographic movie, but I would be delighted if you will call me when you are going to a concert" (Little 1966, 41-43). These are valuable suggestions for witnesses who are trying to build a relationship of trust and avoid any hint of condemnation.

Observing Common Courtesies

Christian courtesy is always appropriate. Though these are simple matters, they can be the determining factors in acceptance or nonacceptance on the part of the prospect.

Begin by getting the person's name correctly and remembering it. People like the sound of their own name when pronounced properly. It is simple courtesy as well as good psychology.

It is a good idea to ask permission to ask personal questions, though perhaps not always, as some suggest. "May I ask you a rather personal question?" can often take the edge off tension that might otherwise arise. It is also the polite thing to do.

One should be careful to observe another's private space. Most of us have had the uncomfortable experience of conversing with someone who stood too close. Stepping backward does little good if they continue to move right in. Such discourtesy, though unconscious, usually cuts off effective communication.

Visitors in homes must be especially kind and attentive to children for obvious reasons. When children create a situation where it is difficult to be heard, one visitor should take the responsibility to entertain them so that the other can talk.

Visitors should always be sure they are not intruding on previous plans of the prospects. If so, make a later visit. Even if there are no previous plans, visitors should not stay overly long unless requested to do so by the prospects.

Simple courtesies like being careful not to interrupt others when they are talking, being sure one's shoes are clean before entering someone's home, and expressing gratitude for the visit can go a long way in facilitating communication.

Television is an incessant problem encountered by home visitors. If the prospects are watching a favorite program or a special presentation in which they are obviously interested, it may be wise to come back later or another time. If they extend an invitation, watch it with them and speak when it is over. Few avid football fans are won while an important game is being telecast, but a lot of them could be further alienated from the church by unwise visitors.

Avoiding Manipulation

Manipulation occurs whenever a person's free choice is compromised (Griffin 1976, 28). Everett L. Shotstrom defines a manipulator as "a person who exploits, uses, and/or controls himself and others as things in certain self-defeating ways" (1967, xii). He adds that all persons to some degree manipulate others. Since it is so common, the witness must be aware of its nature and alert to its possibility.

There are a number of ways that a personal evangelist might be manipulative of others. If the primary concern becomes that of adding another statistic to the total, something about which the witness can boast, then the whole motivation has become manipulative. If only a part of the gospel is shared, that is, the easy part that sounds rosiest to the prospect or if the truth is compromised or embellished in any way lest the person turn away or if the potential convert is spellbound by the messenger (for example, an outstanding celebrity such as Miss America) rather than the message, then manipulation is a possibility. Manipulation can occur in mass evangelism efforts, in other ways, and even within the church. Hyperemotionalism may sometimes take people beyond the place where the Holy Spirit would lead them. People must always remain free to say no.

On the other hand, it has been pointed out that it is not as easy to manipulate others as some suppose. James Engel champions the view that everyone is equipped with God-given filters which protect the individual against unwanted influence and enable persons to resist changes in belief that are not perceived as meeting felt needs (Engel 1975, 27,40-42). Nevertheless, in the sense described above, manipulation is always a possibility.

Paul stated his working principles in succinct form in 2 Corinthians 4:2-3. It is the kind of passage that a sincere witness would do well to memorize. "We have renounced disgraceful, underhanded ways; we refuse to practice cunning or to tamper with God's word, but by open statement of the truth we would commend ourselves to every man's conscience in the sight of God."

Using the Bible Wisely

The Bible is the sword of the Spirit, and it is invaluable in the task of sharing the faith. On the other hand, people do not always use it wisely.

A large Bible can easily put a prospect on the defensive. A small Testament for pocket or purse makes much more sense. Leave the heavy artillery in the car. If need for it arises, the witness can get it later.

Use a modern version like the *Good News Bible* or the *New American Standard Version.* The King James Version is beautiful and well loved by many, but the need is for clarity rather than beauty. The Bible is not an easy book to read, and one steeped in archaic language adds unnecessarily to the problem.

Secular people often understand short passages only after careful explanation. Long passages are usually totally nonproductive. The prospect's mind wanders, and the thrust of the conversation is easily lost. It is better to quote or read short, clear, passages without the references.

One cannot assume that people know much about the contents of the Bible. Surveys show otherwise. Even simple statements about the Bible may require some background information. Phrases like "I'm sure you know" or "I know you understand" are best left out. On the other hand, a witness must not talk down to a prospect or show any pride in what he or she may understand.

It is almost always a good idea to leave a prospect something to read. Marked New Testaments in modern English with some questions and instructions for locating the answers have demonstrated their usefulness. These can be purchased inexpensively, and most churches can afford to keep some available. Persons do not always reveal how they feel. The most aloof can be crying inside. Pride can be an insurmountable barrier. Leaving a Bible behind with instructions and usable helps can greatly enhance the efforts of the witness.

Refraining from Petty Criticism and Talebearing

A further principle is that some care must be exercised in selecting subjects of conversation. It should be a hard-and-fast rule never to speak critically of another church, person, or pastor. Paul's admonition to Titus to "speak evil of no one" (Titus 3:2) is a good one. To transgress this principle is always counterproductive.

It is also a good idea not to speak too glowingly of church members whose names come up in conversation. While you may be able to commend them quite sincerely, you never know what your prospect's relationship with them has been. To praise someone about whom your prospect has negative feelings is to reinforce their suspicions of hypocrisy in regard to the church and churchgoers. The same caution applies to the church. Any word about it should be positive, but churches have long histories, and it is never possible to know what understandings or misunderstandings are abroad.

Needless to say, witnesses should never carry tales from previous visits. What has taken place in previous encounters with other people is not to be shared.

Avoiding Discomfiting and Embarrassing the Prospect

Home visitors should avoid creating negative impressions before the contact begins. Praying in the car in front of the prospect's house in clear sight of occupants and neighbors can have a very adverse effect upon the visit. Pray, of course, but do it before you leave the church (compare Kennedy 1977, 112).

Callers should clearly identify themselves and their church at the door. An easily read badge with the church name and that of the caller alleviates suspicion. Briefcases or a handful of tracts or magazines may tend to give a cult image.

No prospect should ever suffer embarrassment unnecessarily. If we are to win people, we must be very sensitive to their feelings. Discussing spiritual matters makes many people very uncomfortable. Unfortunately, this is true even of many Christians. Therefore, it is very important to deal with most prospects privately.

For many people, to show spiritual interest or need is a sign of weakness. It speaks of a kind of inadequacy, a denial of the "all-sufficient person" image, an ideal created largely by novelists and filmmakers. Spiritual concerns are conversationally taboo within the peer groups of some people, and a nonprivate broach of the subject can result in real anger and hostility.

For those reasons, the witness must be very sensitive to each situation. He or she must be willing to come back at a more opportune time or wait for an appropriate moment. These cautions may be especially important in the case of an unsaved husband who has a Christian wife. Often the wife's Christianity has been a source of tension in the home. The church has become "the enemy," and the wife's Christian friends are a part of the army that is "out to get him" and take him captive to the altar. If the witnesses try to win him in the wife's hearing, they may be regarded as more of his wife's allies arrayed against him.

Of course, there are exceptions, and privacy is not always necessary. One might witness to a man and wife together, both of whom are unsaved, or even to a whole non-Christian family. It is often wise to deal with children in the presence of one or both parents. It may be a natural way of sharing Christ with the parents also. In any case, parents should always be made aware of the decisions of children.

Situations vary so much that common sense, good judgment, and sensitivity to the Holy Spirit alone will dictate the path of wisdom. In every case it will remain a principle, however, that embarrassment must be avoided wherever possible.

Genuine warmth and friendliness supported by a smiling face are always in order, and humor wisely used is a great asset. If your prospect can smile and laugh with you, you have already made great strides toward a communicative relationship.

Maintaining Goodwill

Enthusiastic witnesses must be cautioned against going ahead of the Holy Spirit. We have already seen that decisions often require time. The good leaven has to do its work. We must never presume to do the Spirit's work for him and go too far with an unready prospect.

Goodwill must remain for whomever makes the next visit. It could be you. This calls for a prayerful, loving approach and a constant sensitivity to the responses and feelings of the prospect.

Importance of Good Grooming

Another important principle is that good grooming is worth the effort. It is no longer a question whether a person's grooming affects the impressions they make. A large amount of research has shown that it does. In personal witnessing, first impressions can be extremely significant. That alone could make the difference in whether one gets a hearing or not. It can also make a difference in the degree of acceptance accorded the witness on the part of the prospect.

John T. Molloy, author of *Dress for Success,* is paid large fees by corporations just to tell their executives how to dress properly. Molloy's research showed that one reason many executives bought IBM equipment was the moral quality of the company seemingly conveyed by the dress code for the salesmen. The white shirt played a large role in creating that impression (1975, 32-35). His famous experiment with the beige and black raincoats showed that one's appearance has a great deal to do with the reception experienced and work achieved (ibid., 24-26). Other experiments showed that well-dressed people have a much better chance of getting their checks cashed and properly attired persons a much greater chance of getting a job (ibid., 30). Preachers are no exception.

Molloy's investigation also revealed that ministers who dress in accordance with their role are accorded greater authority than those who do not. While different groups are variously affected by certain styles of dress, some things like bow ties, red, pink, or lavender shirts, and short sleeves are taboo from a business point of view. Careful tie selection, shined shoes, and combed hair seem to be extremely important (Jemison 1980, 6). Since such things are proven to influence how people feel about others, should the Christian servant be any less concerned about his or her appearance than the businessman?

Of course, dress will vary with the occasion. Attire suitable for home visits would surely be different from that appropriate for beach ministry. In some situations common sense must rule, but the serious witness will make a study of the matter and eliminate anything that has a likelihood of making bad impressions or creating barriers.

Sometimes sincere Christians are careless about other matters of grooming. Untrimmed hair protruding from the nose can be particularly repulsive. Some Christians, otherwise clean and neat, wear glasses that are grimy and greasy. Spots and stains on ties, shirts, or blouses along with missing buttons are not calculated to inspire confidence. Bad breath and body odor are always inexcusable in this day of soaps, pastes, and sprays. Non-Christians who are exposed to this kind of witness may tend to associate Christianity with this style or lack of style in dress or grooming. Such associations once made are not easily overcome.

As a small boy in depression days, the church I attended had extremely poor facilities. The auditorium was ugly, old, makeshift, and uncomfortable. By contrast, the school I attended across the street had a fine auditorium. In my boyish mind, the school was much more important than the church because the auditorium was so much better. It was a long time before I ceased to associate Christianity with drab buildings, creaky aisles, and drafty rooms. It is entirely possible for nonbelievers to associate Christianity with the careless grooming and dress habits of some of its adherents.

It is never possible to cover every contingency that may arise, but this chapter contains many practical suggestions about real situations. Our task is to serve the prospect at whatever inconvenience to ourselves. The sincere witness will remain alert to any possible action, practice, or habit that might hinder his or her witness. Servants of the King of kings should always endeavor to be at their best in every kind of situation.

10
Facing Common Excuses

Excuse making began in the Garden of Eden. After Adam had eaten of the forbidden tree, God asked, "Have you eaten of the tree of which I commanded you not to eat?" Adam's guilty response was, "The woman whom thou gavest to be with me, she gave me fruit of the tree, and I ate." God then questioned Eve, "What is this that you have done?" She replied, "The serpent beguiled me, and I ate" (Gen. 3:11-13). Adam's excuse was the actions of his wife, and Eve's, the beguiling nature of Satan.

Moses had no trouble finding excuses for not going down to Egypt as God commanded (Ex. 4:1-13). Aaron had a ready excuse when Moses came from the mountain and found the people in open immorality (Ex. 32:24).

When God ordered Gideon to lead Israel out of the hands of the Midianites, he quickly offered an excuse having to do with the weakness of his clan and his own insignificance in his family (Judg. 6:15). For Jeremiah his youth seemed like a sufficient reason for declining God's call (Jer. 1:5-6).

Jesus encountered excuses (Matt. 8:21; Luke 9:59-62; John 4:20) and spoke a parable which revealed to the ready inclination of people to devise them (Luke 14:15-24). Paul's experience was similar (Acts 24:25), and such has been the lot of Christians since those days. Therefore, we should not be surprised to encounter them in most non-Christians, or when we suddenly discover them in ourselves as we struggle to carry out the full will of God. The fact is that, following conversion, there is a shift from creating excuses for not believing to rationalizations for not obeying.

The Nature of Excuses

Rationalizations for Unbelief

The excuses of non-Christians may be of several kinds.[1] First, there are those that serve as rationalizations for unbelief. They are bricks in the walls people build between themselves and God to justify their paganism and enjoy their sin. "I know a man who claims to be a Christian, and, if he is, I certainly don't want to be one"; or, "The church my parents belonged to when I was a child had one fight after another." These are examples of excuses that serve that purpose for many people.

Intentional Diversions

Excuses may serve as an intentional diversion on the part of a somewhat hostile prospect, a deliberate effort to stump or confuse the speaker. The prospect may feel that a certain objection is unsolvable; and, since the witness won't be able to give a reasonable answer, he or she has no obligation to continue listening. "No one knows where Cain got his wife," or "You can't really prove that God exists" might be examples of that sort.

A Plea for Breathing Space

The excuse can be a plea for room. Possibly the evangelist is too agressive or is coming on too fast. The excuse is thrown up as an attempt, conscious or otherwise, to lessen the pressure. For example, "I think I should take a course in religion at the local college before I make my decision," or "I might become a Christian someday, but it is out of the question now."

An Expression of Doubt

It can be an expression of honest doubt, something that really does constitute a stumbling block for a thinking person. For example, "I don't think I could live a Christian life," or "I don't see how one man's death can serve to atone for the sin of all men."

A Cry for Help

The excuse may also be a cry for help. It may be someone who really wants to believe but has a personal problem causing real concern. In that case, it is really a question as much as an excuse. "I've been divorced and remarried, and I don't believe God will accept me"; or "If I became a Christian, I might have to quit my job."

It may sometimes be more accurate to name these hindrances or obstacles rather than excuses. Whatever they are, they are problems for the witness and must be handled as skillfully as possible.

General Principles of Response

Serious Consideration

The typical book on "soul-winning" advises the witness to acknowledge the excuse, respond as briefly as possible, and get right back to the main issue. Many point out that that is what Jesus did with the woman at the well (John 4:5-42). Doubtless there are cases where that is what ought to be done. The woman of Sychar, however, did have a good background of religious exposure quite similar to that of the Jews, and her excuse (4:20) may well have been a part of her attempt to avoid God. Where that is the case today, getting back to the issue could well be the appropriate thing to do. On the other hand, many people today have no such background of preparation. Some have literally no knowledge at all, and our response to the excuse or obstacle should be quite different.

Whatever the excuse, it should never be treated as unimportant. Though it might seem superfluous to the witness, the prospect may be quite serious, and it may serve as an effective hindrance to decision.

Sometimes a witness may ask to postpone giving an answer until finishing a certain line of thought. There may also be times when an answer will have to be searched out and a return trip made as Kennedy suggests (1977, 79-80).

A Basis for Proclamation of the Gospel

Not only do many know little or nothing about Christianity but also what they do know may be largely distorted. Most advice on handling problems is built on the old assumption that people know enough to make a decision and only need persuasion. This we have seen to be entirely unfounded. Many people have only the barest understanding of the existence of God, and that may be clouded. For this reason when excuses arise, rather than answering quickly and then passing by the issue, it may be much wiser to use these times as opportunities to proclaim and explain the gospel. This we can do by answering the excuses as relevantly as possible from the Scriptures and relating them to further proclamation and explanation. In other words, in the light of the decision-making process, what is called for in many cases is a radically different approach. Many excuse makers need a deeper understanding of the gospel and its claims on their lives.

After all, this is one of the distinct advantages of personal encounter. Questions and problems may be dealt with decisively and thoroughly on a face-to-face basis, something impossible for other types of evangelism. This indispensable advantage is often lost because of ill-advised and hasty methods of dealing with excuses.

Agree and Expand

To contradict the excuse is rarely productive. It is far better to find something from the prospect's statement with which to agree or to commend, at least in part. Of course, this must be honest; and agreeing, even in part, is not always possible. Even when a witness must disagree, however, it can be done obliquely. For example, "Have you ever thought about this?" Or, "I like what Paul said about that" and then give Paul's word. It should never be, "I just can't agree with that," or "The Bible says that is dead wrong."

When one finds even a small point with which to agree, he or she can expand on that truth from the Scriptures. Thus, in an indirect way, the gospel can be presented, and the excuse maker may be able to sense that the gospel contradicts the objection without our help.

Symptoms and the Disease

Often an excuse is a reflection of a non-Christian presupposition or belief. "I'd have to give up too much to become a Christian" is an excuse reflecting a belief that real enjoyment and satisfaction is found in the non-Christian life-style, and that little satisfaction is to be found in the Christian realm. "The church only wants money" may reflect the belief that happiness is the possession of material wealth; and the church tries to rob people of that, although nonbelievers might not state it quite that way. The witness' response will depend on what the excuse reveals.

Physicians treat both symptoms and diseases although it is usually more important to treat the disease. Sometimes only symptoms can be treated as in the case of the common cold. In other cases such as athlete's foot, the symptoms and the disease are dealt with simultaneously. At least, it appears that way from a layperson's point of view. Sometimes the symptoms are relatively unimportant as in the case of the yellow color that goes with jaundice, but treating the disease is all-important. I believe that such is the case with excuses. Common sense will often dictate the proper course. Sometimes the witness will deal with the symptoms, sometimes both symptoms and the disease, and occasionally speak only to the disease itself.

Frequently Encountered Excuses

"There Are Too Many Hypocrites in the Church"

This may well be the most frequently encountered of all. It can be expressed in different ways. A person might say, "I was badly treated or cheated by some church members," or "I know some Christians where I work, and I don't want to be like them," or they may point to some prominent "Christian" who has been exposed in connection with a scandal of some sort.

An example of a productive approach might be as follows: "You are right, of course. There are hypocrites in the church. That was something about which Jesus himself was deeply concerned." Follow such a statement by showing that the Lord is quite capable of taking care of hypocrites.

In Matthew, Jesus said, "Not every one who says to me, 'Lord, Lord,' shall enter the kingdom of heaven, but he who does the will of my father who is in heaven. On that day many will say to me, 'Lord, Lord, did we not prophesy in your name, and cast out demons in your name, and do many mighty works in your name?' And then I will declare to them, 'I never knew you; depart from me, you evildoers' " (Matt. 7:21-23).

Almost the whole of Matthew 23 is addressed to the scribes and Pharisees whom Jesus calls "hypocrites" (23:13), "blind guides" (23:16), "blind fools" (23:17). He addressed them as "You serpents, you brood of vipers" and asked them, "How are you to escape being sentenced to hell?" (23:33). Here is some of the most scathing language in the New Testament addressed toward those who pretend to be what they are not, and it comes from Jesus himself.

The Book of Acts (5:1-11) records a case of early church hypocrisy. Ananias and his wife, Sapphira, sold a piece of land. They gave what they represented to be the whole amount to share with the poor, but they kept back part of it for themselves. The extreme displeasure of God with such conduct was evidenced by the fact that both died as a consequence of their dishonesty. While God does not always deal so harshly with people today, his attitude toward such deception is nevertheless clear. Since the Lord is the one "who will bring to light the things now hidden in darkness and will disclose the purposes of the heart" (1 Cor. 4:5), we can be sure that such hypocrisy is no secret to him, and he will deal with it in justice and righteousness. All such inconsistency can be safely left in his hands.

At the same time, the Bible declares, "Each of us shall give account of himself to God" (Rom. 14:12). As disturbing as hypocrisy in others may be, we cannot let it hinder us from looking after our own spiritual welfare. Although there is a degree of hypocrisy in everyone, blatant hypocrisy must simply help us see that once we become believers we must aim for the life of complete commitment. We must avoid at all costs becoming what has been so unattractive to us in others.

There is something else that can be said to persons offering this excuse. The fact that they pointed out the problem indicates that they realize that confessing Christ means living a transformed life. Their concern about hypocrisy shows that they recognize the inconsistency of professing belief but living like a nonbeliever. Commend their insight and understanding and point out that the Bible says, "If any one is in Christ, he is a new creation; the old has passed away, behold, the new has come" (2 Cor. 5:17). We do not make this change in our own strength, however, but by the power of God who lives within us.

Note again what I have suggested. Avoid condemning or contradicting the statement of the prospect. Agree, if possible, with something the prospect says. Commend his or her insight in seeing the inconsistency of hypocrisy and the understanding that real Christianity demands far more. Use Scripture to show that God knows everything about us, that he will justly deal with such sin in others or in us, that each one must give an account of himself, and that the Christian life is indeed a new kind of existence. In this way a witness can avoid argument, further proclamation can take place, and the relationship necessary to communication can be enhanced. While this method takes more time, it is more thorough and productive in terms of lasting results. Excuses provide opportunities to answer questions and to explain spiritual truth that can build the necessary understanding for a faith commitment to God.

"The Church Is Just Interested in Money"

Once again we can agree cautiously and in part. While it would not be wise to discuss details with the prospect in that criticism of others would be involved, there are grounds for such charges today. Some television personalities use an inordinate portion of their time asking for money. Others put on considerable pressure by means of computerized mail, irrespective of recipients (Hadden and Swann 1981, 103-124). Some Christian organizations have solicited from non-Christian businessmen and unsaved parents of Sunday School children. This is not to say that money must not be raised or that Christians should not be encouraged to give. It is to say that unwise and inappropriate action by a few has caused widespread misunderstanding on the part of many.

One possible approach to this problem might be as follows: "Mr. __, I believe there is truth in what you are saying. It is unfortunate that occasionally some Christian leaders have used unwise methods to raise funds for their work. But let me speak for myself and, I sincerely believe, for my church. We are far more interested and concerned for you as a person than for any money you may or may not have.

"Certainly persons were at the very center of Jesus' concern. While he was concerned about the relationship of people to material wealth, his basic concern can be summed up by one of his best-known sayings: 'Seek first his kingdom and his righteousness, and all these things shall be yours as well' (Matt. 6:33). People, more often than not, reverse the order. They seek 'things,' that is, material wealth, and leave the kingdom till last or seek it not at all. For Jesus, the kingdom was always first and foremost in importance. He also warned us that 'A man's life does not consist in the abundance of his possessions' (Luke 12:15), although the majority think it does. On another occasion when he was hungry, he said, 'Man shall not live by bread alone, but by every word that proceeds from the mouth of God' (Matt. 4:4). Even in a state of physical hunger, he spoke of the indispensable nature of God's truth. You are surely right when you imply that there are other things which should be emphasized first.

"On the other hand, Jesus was concerned that people neither misuse material things nor be used by them. It is awfully easy to be controlled by money rather than to control it. There are a number of warnings about this in Scripture. 'No one can serve two masters; for either he will hate the one and love the other, or he will be devoted to the one and despise the other. You cannot serve God and mammon' (Matt. 6:24). Paul warned, 'The love of money is the root of all evils; it is through this craving that some have wandered away from the faith and pierced their hearts with many pangs' (1 Tim. 6:10). Thus you can see something of the teaching of the New Testament in regard to material things. There is much that the Bible would teach us about the use and misuse of 'things.'

"There is one other Scripture that your statement calls to mind, and it is a significant one. In speaking about personal giving, Paul laid down an important principle; 'Each one must do as he has made up his mind, not reluctantly or under compulsion, for God loves a cheerful giver' (2 Cor. 9:7). A person must give what he can give cheerfully. There is to be no compulsion or reluctance, and each one makes his or her own decision. While our church will try to teach faithfully all the Bible says about giving, we do recognize this important principle, and I trust that any undue pressure or insistence is ruled out. The first thing always is to help people establish a saving relationship with Christ."

Once again I have suggested more material than one would usually use, but it demonstrates an approach. The witness can agree to some extent, throw light on the matter from the Bible, and, on the basis of the Scriptures, get back to the importance of a relationship with Christ.

Depending on the situation, another approach might be used to show that while the churches do ask for money, they are strictly nonprofit enterprises. While there have been misguided exceptions, churches are designed to be the most unselfish "organizations" on the earth. The church is mission. Its very health is measured by its concern for others. Throughout the world the churches have built hospitals, schools, orphanages, leprosariums, and other eleemosynary institutions. They have changed countless inhuman situations, cruel laws, pagan superstitions, and unjust structures. They have taught millions to read and write their own language, introduced hygiene, dug wells, taught agriculture, raised hopes and expectations, and, best of all, led thousands to a knowledge of Jesus as Lord and Savior. They have indeed asked for money, and will continue to do so, but in order to lift and bless humanity as no other entity on earth. None of us are sorry about the money raised and used in those ways.

"I Think I Would Have to Give up Too Much"

This too is a large obstacle for many. In fact, most of the people to whom we witness are, to some degree, in love with the present world. That is the real problem. It is their presupposition that real satisfaction is to be found in pursuing the typical goals of persons in the secular world. Persons who are sincere in this response usually need some time for the gospel to do its work. Once again let us follow the pattern as before: agreement or compliment, use of Scripture to explain and proclaim, and then proceed with the gospel presentation.

"I think it is good that you realize that the Christian life is costly, and that it would eventuate in change. That is an important understanding, and it shows you have done some solid thinking about the gospel.

"Jesus did make some revolutionary demands. He warned that love and loyalty for him must take precedence even over family relationships (Luke 14:26). His followers are those who deny themselves and take up their cross daily (Luke 9:23). Loyalty to Christ must be more important than 'things' for he said, 'Whoever of you does not renounce all that he has cannot be my disciple' (Luke 14:33). So the demanding nature of the gospel is crystal clear. It is not strange that you are thinking about this, because sincere people cannot do otherwise.

"On the other hand, have you considered what you would gain? Jesus provides some priceless things the world cannot give. He promised peace of a sort that only he could provide (John 14:27). The Bible promises forgiveness and a good conscience (Acts 10:43; 1 Pet. 3:21) as well as a new and all-encompassing purpose in life (2 Cor. 5:15). Jesus said he came to make possible a more abundant life now (John 10:10) and eternal life beyond (John 3:16). Paul said that life's real fulfillment is to be found only in Christ (Col. 2:9).

"When Paul compared his former life to what he had found in Christ, he said, 'Whatever gain I had, I counted . . . as loss because of the surpassing worth of knowing Christ Jesus my Lord. For his sake I have suffered the loss of all things, and count them as refuse, in order that I may gain Christ' (Phil. 3:7-8). Paul hadn't lost or given up anything that hadn't been replaced many times over with something better. God is not a cosmic killjoy contrary to a widespread misconception. Genuine joy is one of the things the gospel brings, joy without remorse, guilt, or regret; and it is something that lasts forever. You will find that what was true for Paul will be true for you.

"When I lived in the Midwest, there was a pin oak tree on our church property. The unique thing about a pin oak is that although its leaves turn brown in the fall, they do not fall until spring when new growth comes and pushes them off. The Christian life is like that. The new things which Christ brings displace the old. There is simply no longer any room for those things. It is not so much what you give up. It is that you have so many better things from which to choose."

"I Don't Feel As I Think I Should"

This statement is usually encountered when a person is invited to accept Christ. It can mean at least two things. First, it may be an expression of concern from persons who are near to making a decision for which they lack sufficient preparation. They sense this and express it in terms of an absence of feeling. Perhaps the sense of conviction is not deep enough in which case further proclamation is necessary, possibly with added emphasis on sin and its consequences. Second, it may be a reflection of background. If a person has been exposed only to highly emotional-type churches or if a Christian friend has shared a deeply moving conversion, the prospect may feel that that is the sort of experience he or she must have.

It is often helpful to explain that such experiences can be influenced by factors such as age, previous experience, and personality makeup. Use the material in chapter 3 on the nature of conversion and show the prospect that no two experiences are exactly alike.

The Bible has little to say on the feelings of a person prior to conversion other than that there must be a conviction for sin (Acts 2:37; 16:30). On the other hand, it does have something to say about feelings after conversion. Of the people of Samaria who heeded the preaching of Philip and witnessed the signs which he did, it is written, "There was much joy in that city" (Acts 8:8); and the Ethiopian eunuch won by the same man, "went on his way rejoicing" (Acts 8:39). From a biblical viewpoint, prior to conversion there *must* be conviction of sin and a sense of need. After conversion there *may* be a sense of release, gratitude, and joy. Whatever else a person senses may largely be due to factors peculiar to that individual.

"I Was Made to Go to Church as a Child"

It is surprising how many people present this both as a reason for never attending and as an excuse for their resistance to hearing the good news. Such a response reeks of immaturity. In most cases, it would be quite laughable were it not for the fact that it is usually spoken in utter seriousness and with some hostility directed as much toward the absent parents as to the concerned witness.

A person calling in the homes of Sunday School or bus children sometimes encounters another aspect of this excuse. "I had religion poked down my throat as a child. I'll not influence my children one way or the other. They can make up their own minds when they are old enough."

It is not unusual for people to feel that they have been mistreated by their parents. All parents make mistakes, and some actually mistreat their children so as to inflict permanent injury of one kind or another. Few, however, have injured their children by insisting that they attend church. In many cases a big smile and a touch of humor will serve as a good response to this excuse. "I believe I know what you mean. Parents do make children do things they do not like to do. My parents made me take medicine, clean up my room, cut grass, wash dishes, and take baths. Sometimes they had to make me go to school and, occasionally, even eat. When you stop to think about it, we now do all these things on our own. It's odd, isn't it, that all our hostility seems to settle on the issue of church when we realize, consciously or unconsciously, that, with few exceptions, all those things were done for our good?" (Don't forget the big smile.)

In one of Paul's letters he speaks of "forgetting what lies behind and straining forward to what is ahead." He said, "I press on toward the goal for the prize of the upward call of God in Christ Jesus. Let those of us who are mature be thus minded" (Phil. 3:13-14). One of George Truett's best-known sermons is based on this text. In it he lists some things that should be forgotten. Life's injuries are prominent in the list (Truett 1917, 48). Anything that hinders or cripples us in any way should be forgotten, as nearly as it is possible to do so.

The witness may also say, "I believe that despite your feelings about those early years, your attending those classes and worship services is of real value to you. Studies have been done which show that persons who attended Sunday or church school as children are far more likely to become active Christians as adults than those who did not (Bibby 1978, 131-32). You learned things nonattenders do not know. You were exposed to the great truths of Christianity both in spoken word and song. In all likelihood you memorized a few Scriptures. These have given you some knowledge of the great facts of the gospel: for example, that Jesus is the Son of God, the Savior of the world; that man has a serious problem that we call sin; and that there is a way of forgiveness and of entering into a new kind of life that is satisfying and fulfilling. I believe that background is going to stand you in good stead as you think seriously about spiritual things."

The last few sentences of this example can be expanded as the situation may dictate, and the witness may be able to move on in presenting the gospel.

As for parents who feel it virtuous not to influence their children in spiritual matters, we must help them see that there are all kinds of forces seeking to sway young people in nonspiritual directions. Drugs, alcohol, sexual experimentation, and crime involve young people at a very early age. The peer group, television, movies, novels, and actions of their models are all aspects of influence that may urge them to try one or more of these things. If a child is left to those influences alone, there is great probability that some involvement and experimentation will come. Many parents recognize that children need help in these areas and welcome whatever the church can do. Others can see that children ought, at least, to be exposed to another view.

"I Don't Need the Church. I Can Be a Christian Without It"

If this is a simple diversion, then the traditional suggestion of dealing with it as briefly as possible and moving on is probably best. This is rarely a problem once a person is truly converted. One might suggest, "Don't decide about the church until you decide about Christ. Let's just talk about him for now." Then, proceed with presenting Christ as Savior and Lord.

If a witness feels the excuse represents a misunderstanding about the church membership, then an explanation of the early church pattern in Acts may well clear the fog as well as furnish additional proclamation. We can agree with them in a technical sense, yet the idea of being a Christian and remaining aloof from the church is foreign to the New Testament. The Acts pattern is repentance, baptism, and becoming a part of the fellowship (Acts 2:37-47). Although the word *church* is not used in verse 47 as in the King James Version, it seems abundantly clear that that is Luke's intent.

The prospect should be made to understand that the church will always be imperfect, but nevertheless usable and valuable to God, as well as necessary for us. God can use imperfect things just as we do. My car is far from perfect. It always has something that could be repaired, yet it provides useful transportation. My house is not a perfect house. Something always needs attention, yet it provides shelter. God's church needs improvement at many obvious points, but it is usable to him as the body of Christ.

"Christ loved the church and gave himself up for her" (Eph. 5:25). One cannot wisely reject what was so important and precious to the Lord. The church is the bearer of the gospel. To it was given the commission to carry the good news to every person on earth. It is through the church, the body of Christ, that Jesus continues his ministry. Every believer is a member of that body to worship, learn, and serve in the world.

Not only is the church God's design to meet needs of the world, but it is also to minister to the needs of those within it. We are social beings with social needs. The church is God's new people with whom we can experience satisfying community. This fellowship is designed to meet some of our deepest longings. It is essential to our spiritual health and growth. It is impossible to serve and know Christ as Lord without being part and parcel of his church.

It may be that a person offering this excuse has had an unfortunate experience with a church. Simple things like being embarrassed by a Sunday School teacher, being left out of a Sunday School picnic or the free treat at a Christmas program, or a bad experience of a relative or friend can become an excuse behind which people hide for years. A simple invitation to talk about it can help. For example, "You sound as though you might have had a very unhappy experience with the church. Would you mind telling me about it?" Such may be sufficient to help the individual ventilate the hostility and create a more receptive spirit.

"I Am a Very Busy Person"

This excuse takes many forms. "I travel a lot." "I work long hours." "Even if I became a Christian I wouldn't have time to do anything about the church." "Sunday is the only day I have for recreation." These statements are all expressions of the person who thinks he or she has insufficient time for spiritual things.

All of us can sympathize with the pressures of time. Such is the nature of urban life. Many people who offer this excuse do work hard. They are ambitious to get ahead and to provide well for loved ones. Many causes and organizations compete for their spare hours. This is certainly not all bad, and we can genuinely compliment them for filial concern, their desire to make something of themselves, and their involvement in community and social organizations.

On the other hand, loved ones need much besides material things. In fact, Jesus' word about the great priority, "Seek first his kingdom and his righteousness," is useful here as well as for other excuses (Matt. 6:33). It is always a matter of priorities. There are things that each one of us do not have time to do; we choose the things that seem most important and use our time for those. It is also true that our priorities change, and we can express the earnest hope that the priorities of our prospect may change in reference to spiritual things.

There are many Bible passages that emphasize the priority of the spiritual. In the Old Testament we find the psalmist saying,

> The fear of the Lord is the beginning of wisdom;
> a good understanding have all those who practice it (Ps. 111:10).

Then we find the Proverb writer saying,

> Wisdom is supreme; therefore we get wisdom.
> Though it cost all you have, get understanding (Prov. 4:7, NIV).

These have their roots in right relationship with God.

Paul urged Timothy, "Take time and trouble to keep yourself spiritually fit" (1 Tim. 4:7, Phillips) but the admonition was for all, for Timothy was to "Command and teach these things" (4:11). The Colossian letter is addressed specifically to Christians when Paul tells them to make "the most of the time" (4:5), but once again it is an applicable principle for every person. Paul means that our opportunities have limits. If we do not seize them, we lose them. We must be good stewards of the times and opportunities that are ours. Many people are losing their spiritual opportunities by giving them too low a priority.

The Living Bible has an arresting paraphrase of Ecclesiastes 7:2: "It is better to spend your time at funerals than at festivals. For you are going to die and it is a good thing to think about it while there is still time." The fact is that every person has time for spiritual things and should take time for them now. It is only a question of priority.

"There Are So Many Denominations"

The witness may begin his answer by expressing appreciation for the question. It is, once again, a natural question for a thinking person, and it reveals that the person has some awareness that a vital relationship with Christ ought

to contribute to oneness rather than diversity. We can certainly agree about
the desirability of unity.

We can readily admit that denominationalism is not ideal. It is a part of
human imperfection with which we have to live until the time when God
delivers us from the presence of evil. God did not cause the fragmentation. On
the other hand, it is a far better arrangement than in former times when people
were forced by political considerations to support and belong to churches with
which they conscientiously disagreed.

It is important to show, also, that there is more unity among churches than
most people see. There are large areas of agreement among major denominations. For example, many would agree about the central truth of John 3:16,
Romans 3:23, Romans 5:8, and 2 Corinthians 5:19. By explaining the thrust
of each of these, the witness can further proclaim and explain the gospel while
answering the prospect's objection. These areas of major agreement also explain why so many churches can cooperate on important matters such as
city-wide evangelistic campaigns or questions of moral concern.

It is also true that every sincere Christian past, present, or future is a part
of the body of Christ: the universal church. In spite of earthly divisions, all
genuine believers will spend eternity together in the kingdom of heaven.

Such diversity is the result of our freedom of choice. All persons can choose
the church that most nearly helps them express their beliefs and worship
according to conscience. While such diversity may not be best from many
standpoints, and while unity is an ideal for which to strive, few persons would
surrender it in exchange for any arrangement robbing them of freedom. It is
in reality a magnificient privilege for which people have been willing to die.

"I Believe That Jesus Was a Good Man and a Good Example but Not the Son of God"

This often repeated cliché and widespread misunderstanding is really one of
the easiest excuses to answer. It is plainly self-contradictory. The witness can
begin by agreeing that Jesus was indeed a good person and a good example
and by expressing appreciation for the fact that the prospect has recognized
this.

The prospect may then be led to see some of the claims Jesus made for
himself. When the woman of Samaria said, "I know that Messiah is coming
(he who is called Christ); when he comes, he will show us all things." Jesus
replied, "I who speak to you am he" (John 4:25-26). To the Jews who sought
to persecute Jesus because he healed on the sabbath he said, "My Father is
working still, and I am working" (John 5:17). John then adds, "This was why
the Jews sought all the more to kill him, because he not only broke the sabbath
but also called God his own Father, making himself equal with God" (John
5:18). To Philip he said, "He who has seen me has seen the Father" (John
14:9). To the Jews he said, "I and the Father are one" (John 10:30). There are

many other sayings very similar to these where Jesus obviously claimed to be more than just a man or even a good man.

What the prospect must see is that Jesus was either all he claimed to be, or he was not a good man or a moral example. If he was not the Christ as Peter declared (Matt. 16:16), then he was the foremost imposter of all time. If he was not God incarnate, as Paul said (2 Cor. 5:19), then he misled more people to false hope and security than anyone who ever lived. He cannot be a good man and not be all he claimed at the same time.

Since the Gospel of John was written so that people "may believe that Jesus is the Christ, the Son of God, and . . . believing . . . have life in his name" (20:31), it would be well to encourage such prospects to read and ponder this Gospel carefully. If they can do so with a reasonably open mind, there is every likelihood they will come to solid belief in Jesus as Savior and Lord.

"I Intend to Be a Christian Someday but Not Now"

People who give this excuse are often favorably disposed toward Christianity. They may have Christian relatives or friends and attend church or Sunday School occasionally. Many of them really do plan to confess Christ, but they are not ready to give up the sinful activity they enjoy and know to be in the way.

We can begin by commending their intentions and trying to show them the wisdom of making "someday" today. While we must not exert undue pressure, we are obligated to share pertinent passages of the Bible that deal with this sort of attitude. Such people are gambling with their future. They are "betting" that they can go on doing as they please and enjoying sin, and that God won't permit any untoward thing to happen to them. Indeed God is patient and wonderfully merciful. On the other hand, when Paul reviewed Israel's history (1 Cor. 10), he referred to rebellious times when, despite their previous knowledge and experience with God, they persisted in desiring evil, and misfortune came to them. Paul wrote, "Now these things are warnings for us, not to desire evil as they did" (1 Cor. 10:6). These were people who knew what God expected but refused to do it. It is never wise to go on living in such negative relationship with God (compare Ps. 95:7b-11).

Persons like this compound their problem with each passing day. They increase their sin, in that they fail to do what they know is right (Jas. 4:17). To hear the truth adds to the responsibility for doing it. To hear the truth and to refuse to do it adds to the weight of judgment (Luke 12:47-48).

Some are thinking, *Tomorrow I will do it,* but the Scriptures warn, "Do not boast about tomorrow, for you do not know what a day may bring forth" (Prov. 27:1). James also warns those who arrogantly plan the future without taking God fully into account: "Come now, you who say, 'Today or tomorrow we will go into such and such a town and spend a year there and trade and get gain'; whereas you do not know about tomorrow" (4:13-14). Life is transitory. No person really has assurance of tomorrow. "What is your life? For you are a mist that appears for a little time and then vanishes" (4:14). Life's opportunities are brief and pass quickly. One who procrastinates is in great danger of missing them entirely.

It is not only the brevity of life about which the Bible warns. There is also the matter of the return of the Lord. Because that is always a possibility Matthew admonishes, "Watch therefore, for you do not know on what day your Lord is coming. . . . Therefore you also must be ready; for the Son of man is coming at an hour you do not expect" (Matt. 25:42,44).

The tragic thing is that such procrastinators do not see that they are really robbing and hurting themselves. Sin leaves scars. Every day of self-will and disobedience multiplies and enlarges the scars. Each day of rebellion cheats them out of being all they could be in the will of God. They are losers, and the suffering world that needs their witness and service is also deprived.

Sin's blindness allows persons to think that they can plan their lives better than God. That is never the case. It is in the center of God's will that people are fulfilled and nowhere else (Col. 2:9).

There are many other excuses, of course. These serve merely as examples of the more common ones and suggest ways of dealing with them. It is a good idea for a serious witness to keep a notebook. Each new excuse encountered should be recorded, and appropriate Scripture and illustrations searched out for future use. In this way, the witness can become adept at answering helpfully and constructively and will soon be able to instruct others as well.

---

[1] The ideas for the outline under the Nature of Excuses came largely out of a Doctor of Ministry Seminar at Fuller Theological Seminary, January, 1983.

11
The Harder Questions

Some obstacles that arise go beyond mere excuses. They are the more difficult questions. Some involve real theological problems. Most of them come up repeatedly. In some cases, there are no complete answers. For example, through the centuries the greatest minds have wrestled with the problem of suffering with incomplete results.

Sometimes it is helpful to point out that Paul, speaking of God, said, "How unsearchable are his judgments and how inscrutable his ways!" (Rom. 11:33). Indeed his ways and his thoughts are higher than our thoughts (Isa. 55:8-9). Our efforts often represent the finite struggling to fathom the infinite. It is not strange that we are unable to comprehend everything fully. Yet, we can usually give answers that are sufficiently helpful to surmount the obstacle and open the way to further witness.

Our answer should correspond to the intensity and concern that accompanies the question. In most cases, the reader will find in these suggested answers far more material than can be used. Selectivity will be necessary.

Those Who Have Never Heard

"What about those who have never had an opportunity to hear about Christ?" Anyone who has witnessed consistently in recent years probably has encountered this question. It is an important one for thinking people. The current atmosphere of concern for justice, fairness, and human rights has accented the urgency of inquiry. The possibility that God has been unfair in offering the gospel to some and not to others can be a real obstacle in serious consideration of the Savior. Christians, too, including some leaders and pastors, have uneasy thoughts and are not sure how to answer this question. Persons considering missionary service in distant lands almost always wrestle with this issue.

Many non-Christians who ask this question will be aware that Christianity makes exclusive claims. Evangelistic campaign themes like "Christ, the Only Hope" or "One Way" have publicized Jesus' assertion in John: "I am the way, and the truth, and the life; no one comes to the Father, but by me" (14:6). This has been the traditional position of the church, and, with some explanation, it is an important one to maintain. Giving an answer affords excellent opportunities for further proclamation and for explaining something of a Christian's mission responsibility. At the same time, it can contribute to the warning against "cheap grace."

The Fairness of God

The first thing to affirm is that God is absolutely just. This is part of his holy nature. "The Lord of Hosts is exalted in justice, and the Holy God shows himself holy in righteousness" (Isa. 5:16). God is also perfect love, "For love is of God, . . . for God is love" (1 John 4:7-8). Perfect holiness and love always act fairly. When Abraham was interceding for the righteous of Sodom, he asked, "Shall not the Judge of all the earth do right?" (Gen. 18:25). He was not disappointed. He found God both righteous and merciful. Job's friend, Elihu, spoke wisdom when he said, "Of a truth, God will not do wickedly, and the Almighty will not pervert justice" (Job. 34:12).

God's Earnest Desire

Moreover, it is not God's will that any person should be lost. "The Lord is not slow about his promise as some count slowness, but is forbearing toward you, not wishing that any should perish, but that all should reach repentance" (2 Pet. 3:9). When Paul wrote to Timothy, he spoke of "God our Savior, who desires all men to be saved and to come to a knowledge of the truth" (1 Tim. 2:4). God instructed Ezekiel to tell Israel, "I have no pleasure in the death of the wicked, but that the wicked turn from his way and live" (Ezek. 33:11).

For many, this answer will be sufficient. The Holy Spirit may have brought them to a point where the assurance that God is fair and desires the salvation of all is all they need to move on toward Christ. Others will inquire further and desire a more complete explanation.

Unfortunately, the Bible does not deal in a specific way with the fate of those who have no opportunity to hear. We must admit there is much we do not know. Even the most conservative commentators oppose dogmatism on this matter (Sanders 1966, 9).

Responsibility of Those Who Have Not Heard

For those who desire to dig more deeply, there are a number of suggestions. It is often pointed out that people who have no opportunity to hear of Christ will not suffer condemnation for failure to believe in him. They will not be responsible for what they could not know. Their condemnation will be the consequence of failure to live up to the light which they have had.

Paul explained in Romans 2:12-15 that something of God's moral requirements are written within the human heart. Consequently, everyone has a moral standard of some sort, and the activity of the conscience is evidence of it. For non-Jews, the revelation of conscience is the light for which they are responsible. The violation of that standard is the reason for their condemnation. Jews, on the other hand, had the written law and were responsible to live up to that light. If a person could live up to whatever light he or she has, justification would be the result. However, since all commit sin and fail to live up to whatever light they have, this tells us that people are lost.

Furthermore, the Bible speaks of degrees of punishment based on what a person understands of the Master's will (Luke 12:42-48). The more an individual knows and understands of God's will, the greater his responsibility. The principle is stated as follows: "Every one to whom much is given, of him will much be required; and of him to whom men commit much they will demand the more" (Luke 12:48).

In Romans 1, Paul was talking about the Gentile world. He made it clear that God has given a revelation of himself in nature. The created universe reveals his power and Deity to such degree that no person can have an excuse for not knowing. Psalm 19 confirms the same truth.

One writer suggests that in the light of this and based on Matthew 7:7-11 and Jeremiah 29:13, "that if a man responds to the light he has and seeks God, God will give him a chance to hear the truth about Jesus Christ" (Little 1966, 69). Before you adopt this view, however, you should do so with the awareness that the Matthew passage is in a context where Jesus is encouraging his followers to pray. This is especially clear from Luke where these verses fall immediately after the Lord's Prayer and the exhortation to importunity and just before Jesus' illustration of how even earthly fathers delight to answer requests of their children. Whether "seeking" in this context can have the broader meaning that Jesus did not give it is open to question.

The same is true for the Jeremiah passage. It is addressed to the exiles in Babylon. They are a sadly backslidden lot, God's covenant people, suffering under severe judgment. Yet by God's grace they are a people with a future, and there will come a time when they will pray, and God will hear them. They will seek him and find him when they search for him with all their hearts. This is God's promise to his estranged covenant people who have had priests, judges, prophets, and a long history of spiritual experience. It is not a promise directed to the world at large in this context. Whether it can so easily be given the broader meaning is open to question, although it does coincide with the loving and gracious nature of God.

There are more general passages about seekers, however, that might be given a broader meaning more easily. For example, "Without faith it is impossible to please him. For whoever would draw near to God must believe that he exists and that he rewards those that seek him" (Heb. 11:6).

Further Suggestions

Another writer refers to the eunuch of Acts 8 to whom God sent Philip and says, "Here is a great biblical principle: No one has ever remained lost without Christ who really wanted to be found. . . . God will bring a Philip into every seeker's life" (Wood 1977, 109).

Indeed God did send a bearer of truth to the eunuch. He did this for Cornelius as well (Acts 10). The question is, can this be assumed as a principle applicable to all based on the fact that God did this for two men in the founding days of the church?

Another suggestion has to do with the interpretation of 1 Peter 4:6. Dale Moody sees the preaching in this disputed passage as directed to the "dead who had no chance to hear the Gospel before they departed this life" (1981, 496). He points out that this would not be a second chance in that they had had no first chance. In this way they could be judged on the same basis as those who heard the gospel during their lifetime (ibid.). If this is the proper interpretation of this controversial passage, it would be of incalculable benefit to those who died prior to the time of Christ's resurrection.

Another possibility is one found in varying forms concerning Abraham's salvation. In the light of Romans 4:3, it should be a problem to no one to speak of Abraham as saved. The same would be true for Moses, David, and others. But how were they saved? The answer is that they were saved through Christ who was to come. Indeed, they partly discerned his coming and bore testimony to it, though they did not know his name or how he would come. Other faithful Old Testament saints understood even less. Yet when they realized they were sinners and exercised faith in God, they were accepted and forgiven. It is true that they also brought a sin offering, but the offering was only a symbol and a foreshadowing of what was to come. It was repentance and faith that brought forgiveness (Ps. 51). That Christ was active though unknown in Old Testament times is clear from several passages in the New Testament (1 Cor. 10:4; 1 Pet. 1:11; John 8:56).

If the Old Testament saints were saved by repentance and faith, though they often understood little or nothing of the Christ who was to come, could it not be true of anyone else in whose heart the Spirit of God worked? By virtue of God's revelation of himself in nature (Rom. 1:19-20) and of his moral requirements within the heart (Rom. 2:12-15), could not such a person sincerely repent of sin and cast himself upon the mercy of this God and be saved? This salvation would be through Christ alone, although those who responded would not know his name. It would not be a salvation of works, for the Scriptures everywhere deny such a possibility.

This idea is supported by the fact that even before God gave his promise to Abraham, he made himself known to certain other persons. As far as we know, he did this without a messenger or Scriptures. There was Melchizedek and Balaam, for example. In the case of Melchizedek, Moody remarks, "If his relation to God was not genuine, it is strange indeed that both the Old Testament and the New make him a good model of the Messiah" (Ps. 110; Heb. 7:1-17) (1981, 57).

Jesus had said, "Before Abraham was, I am" (John 8:58). Just as the preexistent one made himself known to some before Abraham's time and after, though not by name, it is reasonable to think that the postexistent Jesus can do the same thing in the present time (ibid., 61). Such a belief was held by some of the early church fathers, Justin Martyr being among the first.

It is also pointed out that, on occasion, missionaries have reported the immediate response of some who have already met the God they preach and who respond immediately to the demands and privileges of the gospel (Rutenber 1960, 180; Anderson 1971, 105). The extent of this activity cannot be known, but Rutenber suggests that it is a rare phenomenon (1960, 180).

If such a proposal is valid as a number of scholars think, it would in no way negate the missionary imperative. If there were some who repented of sin and cast themselves upon the mercy of God, they would still be in desperate need of assurance, teaching, growth, and a message to share. The vast unrepentant multitudes would need the whole missionary message.

Unfortunately, there are no direct passages to give clear support to these suggestions, appealing though they are. While they seem appropriate to a merciful God, we cannot be absolutely certain about any of them. The hope they offer seems small in the light of the lost billions. At least, it does not appear that any great numbers are being saved apart from the proclamation. They are, I think, debatable possibilities. The final answers lie with God.

Certainty

What is certain is that the church has a gospel that must be shared with the whole world. The proclamation of the gospel is God's plan for rescuing persons today, and this is the only sure means by which the lost may be saved. Those certain to be lost are those who have the gracious opportunity to hear but will not. The very hearing of the gospel increases the spiritual responsibility of the recipient to respond. For "Every one to whom much is given, of him will much be required" (Luke 12:48). "He who has ears to hear, let him hear" (Mark 4:9).

The Bad Things that Happen

This, of course, is the old problem of evil, and the question takes many forms. It is perhaps the major obstacle to belief in the lives of many today. Though this problem is no more intense than it has always been, it may seem so because instant communication and modern media expose the calamities of the world for all to see.

A Perplexing Problem

The witness might begin by pointing out that this is a question thinking people might ask. One can agree about the perplexing nature of the problem and suggest that their interest in the matter indicates a worthy sensitivity to what seems unfair and unjust in the world.

We have to admit that we have no complete answer. Great minds have wrestled with the problem from earliest times. God has not revealed all we would like to know. On the other hand, we have some understanding, and we can express our deep conviction that Christian answers make sense and have been helpful to multitudes through the years.

The old argument used to fault God is stated as follows: evil in the world indicates that God is not all good, or he isn't all powerful. If he is all good, he must lack power to prevent evil; or if he is all powerful, he is not good enough to prevent it. Many have happily appropriated this objection and excused themselves from seriously considering biblical claims.

To state it simply, God is both all good and all powerful, but evil is the price of freedom (Manson 1951, 157-58). God created persons with the power of choice. He was not compelled to do so. He could have created persons as automatons without the power of choice who invariably acted in God's will. Such persons, however, would not be moral beings. As Gordon Lewis puts it: "Not even omnipotence itself could create a moral being without the possibility of disobedience as well as obedience. Omnipotence can do everything it chooses in the way it chooses, but it cannot do contradictory nothings like creating a will which cannot will" (Lewis 1974, 40).

The Genesis account of the fall records the misuse of that freedom and the consequent sin that has corrupted human existence since that time. Both Genesis 3:14-19 and Romans 8:19-22 show that the cosmos also suffered serious disorder. The world is constituted in such a way that one person's evil affects many others who may have no part in that person's particular act or conduct. Natural calamities are the manifestations of the corrupted cosmos. The distorted nature of both persons and the cosmos are impartial realities.

A Caring God

Rather than blame God, it is important to see how much he cares about persons. Jesus came to show the world what God was like, and we find him totally concerned about the human predicament. He identified unmistakably with the sufferers, the poor, and the downtrodden. He manifested concern in the midst of pain and wept tears of genuine compassion. The irrefutable evidence of his love was the cross, and the guarantee of his continuing involvement, the resurrection. It is this that no person can safely ignore.

That is not all that is to be said about the problem of evil. It is important to understand that positive good can come from the most negative situations (Rom. 5:3-4; Jas. 1:2-5). Christ's own suffering and death is the primary example, but there are human ones. Bunyan's imprisonment produced *The Pilgrim's Progress.* Fanny Crosby's blindness produced a special kind of hymnic insight.

The Positive Side

Adverse circumstances often bring people to look to God. It is only when their own resources are exhausted that they are willing to try his. Experience is a great teacher. It is often out of suffering that people learn how to trust God and to minister to others (2 Cor. 1:3-4).

Sometimes God uses adverse circumstances as loving chastisement. Like a loving human father, he punishes his own for their benefit (Heb. 12:5-11). God often permitted unhappy circumstances to come to Israel that they might learn to follow him.

In the final analysis, the problem of evil should enhance the attractiveness of Christ. We cannot change the fact that evil is in the world. Christ, however, has provided a way of coping with it victoriously and, ultimately, of removing us from its presence. Those who are truly troubled by this question cannot lightly cast aside Christ's claims.

Doubt About the Credibility of the Bible

"I don't believe the Bible." People who say this usually fall into one of two categories. Some are just repeating what they have heard others say. Their view is not based on personal investigation but is rather a convenient reason for avoiding God. We have already seen that people often tend to reject messages that contradict their actions or beliefs. Many non-Christians earnestly hope the Bible is not true because they suspect it condemns their way of life and demands change. The other group consists of those who have had some Bible course at a secular college or university, possibly from a radically critical point of view. It may have involved comparative religion or the Bible as literature without any focus on the central concern of the Scriptures. Teachings on sin, forgiveness, and new life in Christ may have gotten little or no emphasis at all.

The Imperative of Sharing

In any case, if their views are to change, they need to hear the claims of Christ, for "faith comes from what is heard, and what is heard comes by the preaching of Christ" (Rom. 10:17). If we do not find a way to share the truth, they certainly are not apt to alter their opinions.

Many witnesses are almost defeated by encountering a person who says he or she does not believe the Bible. They tend to feel that it is no use to go telling something the prospect claims not to believe. Such is not the case at all, however, as Paul J. Foust illustrates so clearly in his book, *Born to Multiply*.

> It's the middle of the night and your bedroom window opens and a masked man steps through. You have a "45" in the drawer beside your bed. You open the drawer, pull it out, level it at him, and say, "Fellow, you just crawl back through the window!" Supposing he responds, "I don't believe in guns!" Do you suppose you might as well slide the gun back in the drawer? Not exactly, because there is a way of proving to this burglar that guns do work. You just squeeze, and he'll believe in guns! (Foust 1973, 53).[1]

The application is obvious. Witnesses must find a way to share the gospel in the power of the Holy Spirit so the nonbeliever may come to faith. They must go ahead and use their "weapon," for it does work.

As early witnesses began to move out into Gentile circles, Paul and others preached to those who had no faith in the Old Testament (the only Bible they had) or the gospel message. Not all who heard the message believed, but many did. Unbelief did not stop the witnesses: it was to unbelievers after all that their message was directed.

A Possible Procedure

If the prospect has had a university course or two, the witness might proceed by asking permission to share his or her own testimony. Following that, ask to share something from the Bible that in all likelihood got very little emphasis in the university. That, of course, is God's plan to redeem mankind. One must go no farther than the Spirit leads, but it is always the gospel that is "the power of God for salvation to every one who has faith" (Rom. 1:16), and it must, therefore, be shared as fully as possible.

The witness may proceed in a similar way with those mentioned earlier who use disbelief in the Bible as a convenient excuse for their spiritual illiteracy. One can, of course, express understanding for their unbelief and appreciation for their right to feel as they do. On the other hand, the witness should point out that no one really disbelieves all the Bible. There is much in it that everyone can accept. Ecclesiastes says: "The sun rises and the sun goes down" (Eccl. 1:5) (true in the popular sense); and "All streams run to the sea, but the sea is not full" (1:7). The psalmist says that the sea is "great and wide" and "teems with things innumerable . . . both small and great" (Ps. 104:25), and the Proverbs writer states that the "ant . . . prepares her food in the summer, and gathers her sustenance in harvest" (Prov. 6:6-8). The psalmist says that "birds . . . sing among the branches (Ps. 104:12), and "build their nests" in trees (104:17). The witness could then ask the prospect what particular part of the Bible he or she finds unbelievable, and then ask to show the central theme which has been accepted by so many over hundreds of years.

It is usually the case that people who offer this objection have actually read very little of the Bible. Point out that Bible truth permeates much of the great art and music of the world as well as much literature. William Barclay, among others, has said: "Whatever a man's religious beliefs be, and even if he has none, no man can claim to be fully educated unless he has read this monument to English prose" (Barclay 1979, 12). Such a challenge may be sufficient to get them to begin reading the Gospel of John.

People are helped by various things. The sincere witness must grow in sensitivity to the lost and be prepared for several approaches. Yet, in the final analysis, the Holy Spirit is the convictor. He alone brings about the decision.

The Good Moral Life as Sufficient

Common Misunderstandings

This position is an important one because there are so many who, consciously or unconsciously, embrace some form of it. This is usually the stance of the person who tells you, "I have a religion of my own." It is the "faith" of the person who says, "I live by the Ten Commandments," or "I live a lot better life than most people I know."

The witness can agree that a moral life is important. One can agree that doing one's best is good and observing the Ten Commandments has merit, though not in the sense the prospect may think. At some point, they will need to see that true Christian morality grows out of the new birth experience, and that it must be the result of salvation rather than a means to it.

It can be pointed out that this type of religion is good, provided one lives a perfect life. Only then can it suffice. In Galatians, Paul was addressing some people who had begun to depend upon keeping the Mosaic law for salvation. Circumcision was a declaration of that intention, and the beginning of an effort to keep all the Jewish law. To them Paul said a very startling thing: "I testify again to every man who receives circumcision that he is bound to keep the whole law" (Gal. 5:3). Law keeping was a method of salvation provided one could keep all the law. "For whoever keeps the whole law but fails in one point has become guilty of all of it" (Jas. 2:10). People who hold such views generally have no idea that perfection is required.

The Bible declares that such perfection is utterly impossible and warns that "by works of the law shall no one be justified" (Gal. 2:16). In modern terms, this means that no one can be saved by doing what is right or by living up to a certain standard set of rules. When people realize that we sin by ommission as well as commission and that sin has a large corporate dimension wherein we are all guilty, their exalted view of their own morality begins to pale.

Life in the Balance Scale

A tremendous number of people tend to think of their spiritual destiny in terms of a balance scale. They envision their good deeds on one side of the scale and their bad acts on the other. As long as they convince themselves that their good side is heavier than the bad, they feel reasonably secure. Or they may weigh their own morality against that of the majority of the people around them. As long as they feel more moral or righteous than most others, they comfort themselves with a sense of superiority and security.

The fallacy in their reasoning is that it is not their good acts or their neighbor's morality against which they must weigh themselves. The standard is nothing less than God's righteous demands, best seen in the person and life of Jesus. He is God's righteousness. When that comparison is made, Daniel's words to evil King Belshazzar take on meaning for us, "You have been weighed in the balances and found wanting" (Dan. 5:27).

Nicodemus is the classic case of this type of person. He was educated, respected, moral, and religious, but Jesus plainly indicated that these characteristics were not what saves. "Unless one is born anew, he cannot see the kingdom of God" (John 3:3). If human morality or personal good works could mean salvation, this man could have qualified; but as Paul said, it is "by grace you have been saved through faith; and this is not your own doing, it is a gift of God—not because of works, lest any man should boast" (Eph. 2:8-9).

Inadequacy of Human Righteousness

We have already seen how extensively Jesus used stories and illustrations to make his points. One of his parables speaks directly to this issue (Luke 18:1-14). Luke revealed the purpose of the story in verse 9. It was for those "who trusted in themselves that they were righteous and despised others." Here Jesus told of two men who stood in stark contrast one to the other. One was a Pharisee, a member of the strictest sect of the Jews; the other was a publican, a despised tax collector. The Pharisee's whole life revolved around the Mosaic law. He spent much time in religious observance. As he prayed, he thanked God that he was not like other men. He even mentioned their sins which he did not commit. Nearby was the publican, notoriously corrupt and, in personal morality, the direct opposite of the Pharisee. He was guilty of all the sins mentioned by the Pharisee and, what is more, lived by extortion and dishonesty. He had long since sold out to avarice and greed and was roundly hated by his own countrymen.

Quite in contrast to the self-righteous nature of the Pharisee's prayer was this sinful man's humble confession of sin and his plea for mercy. Irrespective of the vast difference in their morality from a human point of view, Jesus said the humble publican was the one who was justified.

The thing that must be realized is that whatever value people may place on human morality, God sees even the best of it as far too flawed for his kingdom. Only Christ's own righteousness imputed to the believer through faith will suffice.

Doubt About Life After Death

This obstacle is similar to the one about nonbelief in the Bible. We must find a way to share biblical truth if any change is to come about. Usually people who express such doubt know very little of Scripture teaching beyond the ideas of heaven and hell, which they have rejected. Neither are they acquainted with the evidence for the resurrection. Often their position is little more than a repetition of what someone else has said, and the possible awareness that such belief produces much less anxiety than that of giving account to a holy God.

The Nature of "Proof"

The witness can express appreciation for their frankness and their willingness to talk about their present beliefs. Then he can point out that many who do not believe have adopted this position because life after death is not subject to proof in the sense in which we usually use the word. Since it is such a central theme of Christianity, the witness should ask permission to share the evidence.

It may be wise to explain that while "test-tube" proof is not possible, there are many things that we believe on the strength of evidence. Sometimes the evidence is so strong and the degree of probability so high that it becomes unreasonable not to believe. The Christian believes the evidence for life after death to be of that nature.

Evidence from History

It is worth pointing out that back through the years of history the "belief in survival," though immensely varied, "is nearly universal. Tribal taboos and customs have often been dictated by it; great sophisticated civilizations, like that of ancient Egypt, have been built around it. The very universality of this belief has been held to offer some evidence for its truth" (Barry 1965, 173).

Modern Resuscitation

While it is not very important to Christians, we are now living in the era of resuscitation. Many people have now experienced clinical death and been revived. Hundreds of these have been interviewed, and while their experience was extremely brief and inconclusive as to any final destiny, these did seem to enjoy afterdeath experiences. This, of course, does not "prove" Christianity. It is evidence for life after death that may be of help to secular persons who are skeptical about this claim of Christianity.

Biblical Evidence

Christianity boldly claims to have an answer to this question. In fact, Christianity rises or falls on this truth. As Paul put it, "If Christ has not been raised, then our preaching is in vain and your faith is in vain" (1 Cor. 15:14). The early Christians were utterly convinced that Jesus had been raised and that his Holy Spirit dwelled within them.

What was the evidence that convinced them? First, there were many eyewitnesses. Luke told us that Jesus carried out a crucial postresurrection ministry among the apostles. "To them he presented himself alive after his passion by many proofs, appearing to them during forty days, and speaking of the kingdom of God" (Acts 1:3). There were other eyewitnesses as well. Paul listed them in 1 Corinthians 15. Besides the apostles, he revealed that Jesus "appeared to more than five hundred brethren at one time," most of whom were living at the time of Paul's writing. He also "appeared to James, then to all the apostles" and finally, to Paul himself (15:6-8).

There are three major reasons why these are witnesses to be believed. For one thing, they professed this belief and propagated it in peril of their lives. If the resurrection was untrue, they had nothing to gain and everything to lose. Second, when some of them—Peter, John, and Paul—began to record this great truth in Gospels and letters, there were other eyewitnesses who could have corrected any untrue parts of their testimony. They, too, were risking their lives to believe and share this truth.

In addition, there was the empty tomb. This was a great embarrassment to Jesus' enemies who had sealed the tomb and set a guard (Matt. 27:65-66). It became necessary for them to resort to subterfuge in an attempt to explain what had happened (Matt. 28:12-13).

Most important of all was the transformed lives of people, then and now. Peter is an example. Prior to the resurrection he denied his Lord three times. He trembled in cowardice before the accusing finger of a little maid. In utter defeat, he wept bitterly and finally returned to his fishing. Following his discovery of the risen Lord and after the forty-day resurrection ministry, we find Peter boldly preaching despite threats of Jewish leaders and rejoicing when called upon to suffer for his faith.

The transforming power of the risen Lord is seen even more powerfully in the case of Paul. If you can imagine the head of the Ku Klux Klan becoming overnight a champion of black civil rights, you can sense something of the radical nature of the change in Paul. One day he is seen studying at the feet of Gamaliel, leading the Jewish movement to oppose "the Way." Then we find him in the dust on the Damascus road, surrendering to the Lord he opposed and soon preaching fervently the very faith he disdained. The catalyst of such change was his discovery of the risen Lord. What is even more relevant to the present situation is the fact that every gospel-preaching church has transformed members who credit the same discovery to be the basis of their change.

This is powerful evidence. Christians believe that, when it is considered with an open mind, it is too compelling to cast aside.

Other Religions

The Question and the Anticipated Answer

Quite frequently, persons who receive our witness want to know our attitude toward other religions. Is Christianity as exclusivistic as they suspect, or can it somehow make room for other faiths within its latitude of acceptance? Overseas work and travel, expanding knowledge and awareness of foreign neighbors via the media, planeloads of foreign students on our campuses, and increasing religious pluralism at home have all contributed to the new urgency of these questions.

Many who ask would like to hear that all religions are good, that all lead to the same God, and that any sincere, practicing religious person is safe and secure. Our answer, however, must be in accord with the Scriptures, and it must please God and not men. At the same time, it must reflect a Christlike spirit of humility and sensitivity regarding the feelings and the religious and cultural heritage of other peoples. Only within that framework can the uniqueness of the good news secure an appropriate hearing.

Christianity Confronting Other Religions

The first question has to do with what guidance the Scriptures give us. Here there is no disappointment. The New Testament commissions mandate taking the message to the whole world. The gospel is clearly for all men, prior religious ties affording no exception.

Jesus himself was engaged in a struggle for truth, and he did not hesitate to point out the error of the Sadducees in regard to the resurrection. He warned of the false teaching (leaven) of both the Sadducees and Pharisees (Mark 12:18-27; Matt. 16:6).

Paul's encounter with the people of Zeus and Hermes and their priest at Lystra (Acts 14:11-18), the idol worshipers at Athens (17:18-34), and the worshipers of the goddess Artemis at Ephesus (Acts 19:8-27) show that early Christianity was in a life and death struggle with the religions of the day. The fact that these people already had religious beliefs or that certain philosophies already claimed their allegiance in no way discouraged Christians from sharing their faith or proclaiming Christ as the way of salvation.

For these early Christians such witness was a matter of carrying out their mission under the leadership of the Holy Spirit, as well as a response of loving obedience to the commission given them. Jesus was Lord. They must do as he had directed when he said, "You shall be my witnesses in Jerusalem and in all Judea and Samaria and to the end of the earth" (Acts 1:8). Witnesses today are no less under constraint. Contrary to many contemporary voices, the sincere witness must work to find Christlike ways of sharing the gospel with persons of other faiths.

What is to be shared is the absolute uniqueness of Jesus, God incarnate, the Savior, who went to the cross and was raised by the Father to reign as living Lord. According to Hugo Culpepper, "Without detracting from the atonement, there is need for a great emphasis on the incarnation in the Christian message amid the religions. . . . God really was in Jesus Christ. God really came once for all into the existence of mankind. This is unique amid the religions" (Culpepper 1977, 206).

J. N. D. Anderson has written, "The ultimate difference is that other religions teach people that what they must do is somehow climb up to heaven to discover God. . . . When you turn to the message of Christ, you get the pedagogical answer that this can't be done. . . . It's precisely at that point that we find the uniqueness of Jesus Christ, which put in childlike terms is this: God didn't stay right out there beyond us somewhere. He came down to be one of us, to meet us in our need" (Anderson 1983, 7).

In his death Jesus made atonement for sin, and in his resurrection he demonstrated his victory and that of the believer over the grave.

The answer to the question about other religions is summed up in the uniqueness of Jesus Christ. Our mission is to see that every person in the world has the opportunity to know him.

Christians have over the years seen other religions in various ways. For example, they have been seen as wholly without merit, as a preparation for the gospel, as a demonic substitute for the gospel, or as having certain "values" but in improper "balance and relationship" (Anderson 1983, 7; Newbigin 1978, 191-96). It is probably best to recognize that all religions have positive as well as negative elements, and similarities as well as differences. For whatever is good in them we can give credit to God, for he has lightened every man (John 1:9), and he causes light to continue to shine in the darkness (John 1:5) while not leaving himself without witness in the world (Acts 14:16-17). Whatever is good has its origin in God. But it is truth in the person of Jesus that saves. It is this that Christians are commissioned to share with the world.

The Spirit of Sharing and Dialogue

The spirit in which this is done is of primary importance. It calls for the deepest humility and the keenest sensitivity. The witness must remember that it is by grace alone he or she has received the truth that is to be shared (1 Cor. 4:7). There is no place for even a hint of arrogance or superiority.

It is important also to be aware that there are things to be learned as well as shared. Such sharing must be dialogic. One-way communication simply will not produce the desired results.

Such are some suggested answers for those seriously concerned about puzzling questions. Skill in answering problems comes with experience and study. Every witness should keep a journal after the manner of some of the great saints of other years. Great experiences should be recorded in learning encounters and preserved. Such a practice will enhance learning and increase facility in dealing with these common obstacles to belief. There will be other days when the review of those recorded events will bring an encouragement and inspiration to the heart.

---

[1] Foust credits James Kennedy as the source of this illustration.

12
Training Laypersons for Witness

"I have sung in the choir here for years," he said. "It used to be that when the invitation was extended, I wondered if anyone would come accepting Christ. Now, I only wonder how many will come accepting Christ." That was the comment of a happy layman in a burgeoning church where scores of trained laypersons had become life-style witnesses. The church had been transformed and was growing dramatically.

It is not enough to understand that laypersons are commissioned to witness and that they did so with telling effect in the early church. Step-by-step training plans must be offered and implemented if local churches are to enjoy a laity capable of witness today. Moreover, there is needed a tenacity of spirit that will not accept defeat and that persists in effort until an effective program of life-style lay witness is functioning powerfully in the church.

Training witnesses is no empty vision. It can be done. It has been done and is being done.

In 1739, John Wesley embarked on a program to disciple his converts. They were of limited education, and training materials were few. Most societies began with no building or meeting place to call their own. Nevertheless, Wesley molded a force of lay preachers and trained Christians that became directly or indirectly the greatest moral force in the nation. Thousands were converted, inhuman labor practices changed, prisons reformed, and churches revived. The forces that did away with slavery were set in motion, and the founders of many significant social institutions were raised up.

Trained life-style witnesses are evident in some churches today. Consequently, those churches see new converts every week and enjoy an expectant atmosphere only possible for truly evangelistic congregations.

Such training is no easy task. It requires toil and persistence, so much, in fact, that many churches never seriously try. Those that do will suffer disappointments and failures along the way, but in time they will celebrate successes and victories as well.

Rarely can a training plan or program be used without adaptation. Every situation is different. Churches do not come from copy machines. What has worked well in one church may prove a complete failure in another. Thus, local church leaders must be prepared to think through any potential training program and tailor it to fit their situation.

Since previous chapters of this book have dealt with subject matter to be taught, this segment will outline a step-by-step procedure for inaugurating a training program and some suggestions and principles for making it work.

Step One: Forgetting Past Failures

Previous Fruitless Attempts

Many churches have sponsored witness training programs before only to see them fail. While a few persons may have become witnesses, the vast majority has continued with sealed lips as before.

Failure results from many causes. Poor teaching, inadequate models, overabbreviated training, lack of priority for evangelism in the church program, and failure to provide for experiential learning under skilled supervision are a few. Negative feelings about such programs and a decided reluctance to begin another are natural results of such experiences. These attitudes are understandable, but they must be left behind if witnesses are to be prepared.

A New Beginning

There is a key on my small calculator marked *C*. When I punch it, the machine clears. All previous figures are canceled, and it is ready to start afresh as if it had not been used before. All previous records of either proper calculation or of human error are done away.

As nearly as possible, leaders must "punch their *C* button." Both past successes and discouragements must be laid aside and a new effort launched if witnesses are to be trained.

It may not be easy. The laws of inertia tell us that it requires much more energy to get something started than it does to keep it going. Fortunately, we do not depend simply on human power.

Determine to begin with as few as one, if that is all that God raises up. Resolve to stay at it until that person becomes a witness. Then trust God to give others.

Baptize the effort in prayer and show a spirit of optimism and expectancy. Be encouraged by churches that are enjoying success in similar efforts and trust God to do a significant work for his glory. These things are altogether necessary because the next step is to provide a good example!

Step Two: Offering a Good Model

The Pastor's Responsibility

Charles Kraft has pointed out that "the major thing a professor [or a preacher] communicates is . . . what he does, not what he says. Indeed, the main thing we learn from professors and preachers is how to be professors and preachers, not as we think, the messages they articulate verbally!" (1979, 31). This being the case, the witnessing pastor does much to teach others to be witnesses just by being one himself.

Modeling must begin with the pastor. Responsibility extends to staff members and other leaders as well, but the pastor's model is crucial. Since he is chief trainer, results can only be meager if he does not demonstrate fruitful evangelism on a consistent basis. The trainees must know that he practices what he preaches and engages in what he teaches. He will take them no farther than he has gone. His teaching must have credibility based on performance.

A Method of Jesus

Jesus modeled this principle supremely. He gave the disciples ample opportunity to observe his witness. He never asked them to do what he did not do himself. He thoroughly demonstrated his method before he sent them to try. He poured his life into theirs, spending the major part of his time with these who would carry the most responsibility. Modern pastors frequently find themselves doing just the opposite in the press of ministry activity.

A Method of Paul

We saw in chapter 2 of this book that Paul sometimes invited people to imitate him. To the Philippians he wrote, "Brethren, join in imitating me, and mark those who so live as you have an example in us" (3:17. See also 4:9; 1 Cor. 4:16; 11:1). A student once asked me if I didn't think this indicated that Paul was an egomaniac. I didn't, but his question caused me to give some thought as to why Paul dared to so challenge his churches. I concluded that he simply understood how important it was for them to observe and follow a good model. Two factors made it imperative. One was that they were first-generation Christians. Their knowledge was limited, and good models were few. At the same time, models of raw paganism were everywhere. The heathen temples out of which they had been won were ever ready to welcome back defeated Christians. Second, many of the basic elements of Christianity were expressed in abstract terms. Faith, hope, and love could best be understood when seen actually operating in the life of a person. Paul was faith on foot, hope in the flesh, and love personified. He knew that he was a vital part of his message.

To see good models today is hardly less important. Pagan sanctuaries of other kinds invite people just as urgently, and faith, hope, and love are still best understood when manifested in living flesh.

When the eighteenth century Moravian Brethren leader, Count Nikolaus von Zinzendorf, was asked the secret of his unflagging commitment and tireless missionary zeal, he replied that he had taken his meals at August Francke's table while studying at Halle. The faith, prayer, and Christian demeanor of that godly man had challenged him to serve Christ unreservedly (Taylor 1964, 238-39).

In our time, James Kennedy, founder of Evangelism Explosion, reveals that it was the example of a witnessing pastor who had invited him for an evangelistic meeting that revolutionized his ministry and caused him to see the possibilities of winning large numbers of people to Christ (Kennedy 1977, 6).

A Principle of Modern Management

The ability to motivate is now a large concern of business management. A high standard of performance on the part of leadership or, in other words, a good example is a recognized principle of motivation. On the other hand, poor performance on the part of management is a demotivating factor.

In the Christian realm, primary motivation comes from within. It has to do with the indwelling Christ and the ministry of the Holy Spirit. This is so significant for the Christian life that many Christians are reluctant to recognize or discuss human factors. Yet they are important also.

Modern management has done considerable research into the problem of human motivation and has concluded that a skilled leader can do much to help persons be at their best in the workplace. While there are Christian writers who are reluctant to apply management experience to Christian problems, others, like Kenneth Gangel, have already done so. He believes many churches are missing the benefits of solid research that would be of considerable value in helping both leaders and those who follow them (Gangel 1974, 84).

To lead Christians to become effective witnesses is the most difficult task of the church. Every possible human skill must be offered to the Holy Spirit to help bring it about.

Besides the one mentioned above, there are many other motivational principles that can make the difference between a successful training class and a failure. For example, good communication is a definite positive factor in motivation. Persons have a basic need to be informed. They do not like to be passed over when information is sent out.

Even more important is the magic of two-way communication. Good leadership now listens as well as talks. This means deeper involvement with people and real concern for their feelings and opinions. Such things as giving recognition when it is due, showing genuine interest and personal concern for people, helping them to be involved, and to have responsibility that is challenging are all elements known to help persons be at their best.

While ever on guard against anything that smacks of manipulation, the thoughtful Christian leader will be open to learning and applying new leadership skills. Some, like those mentioned above, can be put to use immediately.

Step Three: Praying for Appropriate Workers

A Command of Jesus

As "Jesus went about all the cities and villages, teaching . . . preaching . . . and healing," what he saw moved him to the very depths (Matt. 9:35). "Harassed and helpless" persons were everywhere (9:36). They were people suffering spiritual neglect and despair and unable to help themselves. Two pictures came to his mind. One was of shepherdless sheep, suggesting vulnerability to marauders and other dangers. The other was of a ripe harvest field, but with few laborers to bring in the grain, a picture of eminent spoilage and tragic neglect.

This was the world as Jesus saw it. What makes this particularly noteworthy was that there was no lack of religious workers. Counting the priests and sect members such as the Pharisees, Sadducees, and many others, they numbered in the thousands. They were very concerned with the law, especially things such as circumcision, sabbath keeping, and maintaining the ceremonial matters at the Temple. Their whole lives revolved around religious activities, but they were not harvesters (Stagg 1955, 90).

What could be done? The one remedy that Jesus offered came in the form of a command. "Pray therefore the Lord of the harvest to send out laborers for his harvest" (Matt. 9:38). Jesus gave few such commands to pray for specific things. Aside from the Lord's Prayer, they can be counted on the fingers of one hand. Here was Jesus' own word about how to deal with the harvester shortage.

Many have thought this command applied to the raising up of preachers and missionaries. Its application, however, is far broader. It is the God-given means of raising up the harvesters that every church must have.

This does not mean that the church is to pray and nothing else. As in most matters of Christian service, there is both a human and divine area of activity. The pastor and other leaders can suggest to likely persons the possibility of God's call to personal evangelism training and invite them to pray. God can direct his leaders to contact proper persons even as he prepares the hearts of the potential harvesters. God often uses a human word to make his call to specific service known.

The phrase "send out laborers" is surprisingly strong. The Greek verb is almost "thrust out" or even, "force out." Why would Jesus have used such a forceful term for the divine activity of sending? Is it not expressive of the reluctance of most people to serve in the harvest? Does not God often have to "thrust out" his reticent, excuse-making servants? This is one reason why prayer is so crucial in personal evangelism. Meeting the need of enough harvesters will have to come as a result of obedience to the command to pray.

A Method of the Early Church

It was while the Antioch church was "worshiping the Lord and fasting" that the Holy Spirit directed the sending out of Barnabas and Saul for a larger church planting, harvesting task (Acts 13:2). We are not told the content of their praying (implied with worshiping and fasting), but the same spiritual dynamics seem to be in operation. What is clear is that the church was praying, and the Holy Spirit was sending (Acts 13:2-4). It was just after Peter prayed on the housetop that the message came that sent him to Cornelius's house on an evangelistic mission.

While there is no lack of perfunctory praying today, the paucity of fervent, specific prayer for harvesters may be one of the major failings of the church. In the light of Jesus' firm command, it is not amiss to suggest that if the church prayed as it ought to pray, it would have the harvesters it ought to have.

Continuing Prayer

When a proper group has responded, prayer has only begun. Continuing petitions must be offered for the spiritual health and progress of the trainees. Looking back again to chapter 2, we note that, while there was much teaching in the early church and a remarkable spirit of evangelism, courses in methods and techniques of witness were, doubtless, nonexistent. Theirs was an overflowing witness like that of the apostles who had declared, "We cannot but speak of what we have seen and heard" (Acts 4:20). They had tasted the "living water," and it had become a spring within them (John 4:14). That sort of witnessing is the goal of our praying. We need to be witnesses who retain a deep sense of wonder at what God has done for us and a spirit of excitement about being children of God. Only concerted praying can produce that.

Step Four: Securing Commitments

A Formal Agreement

When those approached about the training have prayed and indicated a favorable response, they should make a commitment to the task. One good method is to gather them into a group for devotion and prayer. Explain the urgency of the task and the seriousness with which a person should follow God's leading. A word about the certain opposition of the adversary and the temptations to quit and take the easy way is also wise. Following a prayer commending them to God, have them sign a commitment card. The commitment should be something similar to the following:

> Having sensed God's call to train myself as a personal witness and, understanding that following his leading is my highest duty, I prayerfully commit myself to complete the basic course in theory and practice.

Date_____   Signature_____

Make clear that it is not a pledge to the pastor or to the church but a commitment to the Lord. The signed card adds to the formality and the sincerity of the intent. Such a pledge helps persons sustain their resolve through times of weakness. It also enhances faithful attendance at the training sessions. Some may want to add a maximum number of allowed absences to the commitment or otherwise specify faithful attendance.

A Definite Time Frame

The card should state the length of the basic training time. Six months is best in that it will include a minimum of two classroom courses and several months of weekly supervised visitation. Some will doubtless combine the two courses into one, but it is always dangerous to take shortcuts. It takes time to develop a witness, and to cut corners will be to repeat the mistakes of most attempts in the past.

Advanced courses should be ready and waiting for those who want to go on. They should not be offered, however, until the basic period of commitment is over, lest they detract from the emphasis on supervised visitation.

Step Five: Offering a Specific Curriculum

Theological and Practical

Basic training should include both theological and practical emphases. Theological themes for witnessing, designed to help the trainee understand the message, would be a logical first course. A "how-to" course of practical guidance for visiting and sharing one's faith should follow within two or three weeks. Weekly visitation should begin immediately thereafter, and each gathering should include ten to fifteen minutes of review and further instruction in response to needs that arise.

Be creative in planning the two courses. A weekend retreat may be a good means of handling one. An all-day Saturday course could take care of another. Two concentrated evenings a week apart could also be used. Good meals and varied learning activities help long sessions to be palatable.

Appealing and Engrossing

At all costs, make the course sessions interesting. If the pastor is not the instructor, spare no effort to secure a skilled, enthusiastic teacher with a keen sense of humor. He or she should be an experienced witness with personal experience to share. Most trainees will have worked all day or all week and would like to be at home with their families. Dullness is often a terminal disease for efforts of this kind.

What is even more important, get a teacher who can relate to people personally. It is not enough to be a good model although that is always a pressing concern. The best teaching grows out of relationships. Jesus lived with his disciples and was vitally involved in their total life experience. His teaching was a part of all that happened to them hour by hour. From this standpoint, the teacher is more important than the particular material selected to be taught. In a very real sense, the teacher is the material taught.

Work to build an academic atmosphere. A pleasant room of a size that fits the class, comfortable chairs, tables for note taking, a chalkboard, an overhead projector, and other visual aids are essential tools. Plan to use all of them in varied activities of learning. Let the class enjoy role play and dialogic participation. Never let a session drag. Have coffee available for before and after and a snack for breaktime. These training activities will build a group relationship, and the fellowship times will be especially rich.

If possible, videotape or at least audiotape each class session. If a person is compelled to miss, makeup will be no problem. If that is not possible, offer makeup sessions at convenient times so that no one has to miss a single session. Such efforts add to the atmosphere of serious purpose that must pervade these courses and encourages people to be faithful.

Affirming and Motivating

The pastor should go out of his way to show personal interest in each trainee. Even if he is not the teacher (and it is far better if he is), he must be there if the program is to succeed. This may not be possible in extremely large churches, but even then the pastor should put in some appearances. What, after all, is more important than witness training? This is an opportunity for motivational activity that comes from the heart. Words of encouragement should be spoken, and the trainees should know that the pastor is praying for them daily. Magnify the task and opportunity constantly. Express appreciation for their faithfulness and anything else that merits comment.

The more personal time the pastor can spend with individuals, the greater the likelihood of producing fruitful witnesses. If the pastor is a good model, this could well be the most productive work that he can do.

Advanced Study

Sincere witnesses soon recognize the need for further training. They encounter questions they cannot answer, situations they cannot handle, and needs they cannot meet. A continuing curriculum should be designed for that purpose. The following is a suggested list of practical subjects that should be of help to those zealous to win others:

1. Advanced Personal Evangelism. This course may include case studies of witnessing situations, handling difficult questions, dealing with hostility, further investigation of Jesus' methods, communication principles, and other matters based on needs of the specific group.
2. Doctrine of Conversion. This could be a thorough study of this doctrine and other New Testament metaphorical concepts that relate to it. Cases of conversion in the New Testament and psychology of conversion would be included.
3. Evangelistic Ministries and Cultivative Witnessing. A particularly needful area of emphasis today is that which shows Jesus constantly meeting needs of those he encountered. Serving people in the light of personal needs is one good method of relating to indifferent, satisfied persons. Discovering gifts and how to develop and use them would be a major emphasis.
4. Pastoral Care. Instruction concerning ministry to the sick, the suffering, the grief stricken, the anxious, the hurting, the depressed victims of broken marriages, and numerous other situations is extremely helpful. How to serve such persons in the name of Christ, and how to sense appropriate evangelistic opportunities would be valuable emphases.
5. Christian Ethics. This course would help lay witnesses in understanding a Christian approach to such issues as abortion, homosexuality, illegitimacy, child abuse, battered spouses, racial issues, and pornography.
6. Personal Christian Life. This course would help the witness understand the necessity of a consistent and growing Christian life. The devotional emphasis and spiritual discipline would be important emphases.

Each particular situation will dictate the order in which they are offered, and whether other subjects may be more pressing.

Other Possibilities

Some denominations have a vast array of prepared courses for which only a good teacher is needed. For example, the Southern Baptist Seminary Extension Department has complete curricula at different levels to meet almost every need. They may be taken either by correspondence or in a class setting. If courses of that type are used, they should be slanted by the teacher to meet the particular needs of persons who are trying to become efficient witnesses.

Some churches will want to develop their own program. I visited a large London church during sabbatical leave that offered an impressive schedule of quality courses which included beginning and intermediate New Testament Greek. All courses were taught by Christian tutors or professors from the universities in London. The program was popular and well attended. I visited the church on Sunday night, and, had I not arrived early, I would not have found a seat. It is a great evangelistic church with a constant influx of new believers. There is that exciting atmosphere that only an evangelizing laity can create.

Most churches are small and could not offer such a program alone, but several together might. A quality program costs money; but if a trained, witnessing laity is the hope of the world, it is worth large expenditure.

Step Six: Magnifying Experiential Learning

Definition

Experiential learning is that "in which the learner is in direct touch with the realities being studied" (Keeton 1982, 618). It is learning by doing. On-the-job training is the popular term today. It has already been mentioned that actual visitation evangelism in the company of experienced persons is part of the training, but it is so indispensable that it merits some additional comments.

Importance and Intent

There are many things that can only be learned by doing them. No one learns to swim by reading an instruction manual by the side of the pool or learns to play the piano by attending lectures on music. No one wants to fly with a pilot who has only read about airplanes or have a root canal by a dentist who only attended discussion groups on the subject. This does not mean that the reading, lectures, and discussions are not valuable. In each case, however, skill in the particular activity comes from both academic and practical endeavor. Winning persons to Christ is that kind of skill. Following a study of the subject, persons only become proficient by actual practice of the art.

Supervised visitation permits the trainee to assume gradually increasing responsibility for the interviews. He or she increases in confidence and skill until the supervisor is no longer needed. Then, the trainee becomes a trainer.

A Missing Element

In the past, experiential learning of any consequence has been the missing element in most course offerings. That deficiency manifested itself in the fact that few who took the courses ever became consistent witnesses. On the other hand, the relative success of programs such as Evangelism Explosion has been due, in large part, to the continuing emphases on experiential learning. Continuing in this activity until the trainees have adequate confidence and skill is the most difficult part, but it is also the most productive. No scheme that omits this will enjoy any large measure of success.

Additional Values

It is important that the trainees and their supervisors all visit on the same night so that a report session can be held immediately thereafter. After sessions, sometimes called report sessions, are necessary and valuable for several reasons. Some will have had disappointing experiences. They will need to both talk about them and learn from them as well as hear affirmation and encouragement from the group. Others will have encountered problems, needs, unusual situations, and, perhaps, strange people. These provide great learning opportunities. Unusual problems or questions can become research assignments for the next week. The whole group can think together about how they might handle these situations or persons, and how they can meet uncovered needs.

Though these sessions must be brief, they afford opportunities for the application of theological and ethical concerns to life situations. In a continuing program, some poverty-stricken people will certainly be found. What should be the response of the church? Some will encounter situations of injustice. What can be done? Homes torn by adultery, narcotics, and alcohol are legion, and always there are hurting people because of them. New immigrants will be encountered along with changing communities. Each of these situations afford opportunities to apply the Spirit of Jesus to contemporary situations. Trainees learn not only how to share their faith in words but also to manifest it in loving deeds.

There is no one best way of training laypersons. Most programs in print represent some pastor's experience and relative success. A course planned and structured by the local pastor, if carefully and wisely done, can have advantages over using someone else's prepared material. That is what I would recommend if it is feasible at all. This chapter has suggested steps to be taken and usable materials are happily abundant.

Many churches today have no witness-training program. This is an almost unforgivable omission. If careful plans for training were executed and repeated appropriately, many churches would be revolutionized. It is being done effectively by some. Nothing less can suffice for the many.

Reference List

Abelson, Robert P., et.al. eds. 1968. *Theories of Cognitive Consistency: A Sourcebook*. Chicago: Rand McNally Co.

Aldrich, Joseph C. 1981. *Life-Style Evangelism*. Portland: Multinomah Press.

Arn, Win. 1979. "People Are Asking. . . ." *Church Growth: America*. (March-April): 11.

Anderson, J. N. 1970. *Christianity and Comparative Religion*. Downer's Grove: Inter-Varsity Press.

_____. 1983. "Do All Religions Lead to God?" *Radix*, May/June, 3-7.

Argyle, Michael. 1975. *Bodily Communication*. London: Methuen and Co.

Armstrong, Ben. 1979. *The Electric Church*. Nashville: Thomas Nelson.

Bangham, William. 1974. *The Journey into Small Groups*. Memphis: Brotherhood Commission, S.B.C.

Barclay, William. 1964. *New Testament Words*. London: SCM Press.

_____. 1972. *Turning to God*. Grand Rapids: Baker Book House.

_____. 1979. *Introducing the Bible*. Nashville: Abingdon Press.

Barrett, C. K. 1957. *A Commentary on the Epistle to the Romans*. New York: Harper & Brothers.

Barry, F. W. 1965. *A Questioning Faith*. London: Bloomsbury Press.

Bavinck, J. H. 1960. *An Introduction to the Science of Missions*. David Hugh Freeman, trans. Grand Rapids: Baker Book House.

Beck, Kenneth H., and Clive M. Davis. 1978. "Effects of Fear-Arousing Communications and Topic Importance on Attitude Change." *The Journal of Social Psychology*. 104:81-95.

Bibby, Reginald W. 1978. "Why Conservative Churches Really Are Growing." *Journal for the Scientific Study of Religion*. 17(2):129-137.

Blauw, Johannes. 1962. *The Missionary Nature of the Church*. London: Lutterworth Press.

Borg, Dennis R. 1981. "Christian Witness Is Dialogue, Not Monologue." *Christianity Today*. 27 Mar., 31.

Bounds, E. M. 1907. *Preacher and Prayer*. Chicago: The Christian Witness Co.

Brehm, Jack W. 1966. *A Theory of Psychological Reactance*. New York: Academic Press.

Brown, Charles T., and Paul W. Keller. 1979. *Monologue to Dialogue: An Exploration of Interpersonal Communication*. Englewood Cliffs: Prentice-Hall.

Brown, Dale. 1978. *Understanding Pietism*. Grand Rapids: William B. Eerdmans Publishing Co. Citing Richard, Marie E. 1897. *Philip Jacob Spener and His Work*. Philadelphia: Lutheran Publication Society. 53-54.

Buursma, Bruce. 1983. Fresh Crop of TV Evangelists. *Chicago Tribune*, 10 July.

Camargo, Robert. 1982. Testimonials—The Most Powerful Form of Advertising. *The California Southern Baptist*. 22 April, 13.

Carlsmith, J. Merrill, and Alan E. Gross. 1969. "Some effects of Guilt on Compliance." *Journal of Personality and Social Psychology*. 11 (3):232-39.

Coleman, Robert E. 1963. *The Master Plan of Evangelism*. Westwood, NJ: Fleming H. Revell Co.

Culpepper, Hugo. 1977. "The Christian Message Amid the Religions." *Review and Expositor,* 74(2):199-208.

Dayton, Edward R., and David A. Fraser. 1980. *Planning Strategies for World Evangelization.* Grand Rapids: William B. Eerdmans.

Discipler. 1978. Fort Worth: International Evangelism Association. 4(1):1.

Dodd, C. H. 1936. *The Apostolic Preaching and Its Developments.* New York: Harper & Brothers.

Drakeford, John. 1976. *The Awesome Power of the Listening Ear.* Fort Worth: Latimer House. Sound Cassette. 4:9.

Drummond, Lewis A. 1972. *Leading Your Church in Evangelism.* Nashville: Broadman Press.

E & E Newsletter. 1983. Washington, D. C.: Baptist World Alliance Division of Evangelism and Education. Special Edition, May, 1-4.

Edgemon, Roy. 1980. "Evangelism and Discipleship." *Review and Expositor.* (Fall): 539-547.

Edwards, Gene. 1962. *How to Have a Soul Winning Church.* Montrose, CA: Rusthoi Publications.

Emmert, Philip, and William C. Donaghy. 1981. *Human Communication: Elements and Contexts.* Reading: Addison-Welsey Publishing Co.

Engel, James F. 1979. *Contemporary Christian Communications: Its Theory and Practice.* Nashville: Thomas Nelson Publishers.

Engel, James F., and H. Wilbert Norton. 1975. *What's Gone Wrong with the Harvest?* Grand Rapids: Zondervan Publishing House.

Ferm, Robert. 1959. *The Psychology of Conversion.* New York: Fleming H. Revell Co.

Fisher, Fred L. 1964. *Prayer in the New Testament.* Philadelphia: The Westminster Press.

Ford, Leighton. 1966. *The Christian Persuader.* Philadelphia: The Westminster Press.

_____. 1977. *Good News Is for Sharing.* Elgin, IL: David C. Cook Publishing Co.

Fore, William F. 1979. "Electronic Church." *Ministry.* Jan.

_____. 1981. "A Critical Eye on Televangelism." *The Christian Century.* 23 Sept.

Foust, Paul J. 1973. *Reborn to Multiply.* St. Louis: Concordia Publishing House.

Freedman, Jonathan L., Sue Ann Wellington, and Evelyn Bless. 1967. Compliance Without Pressure: The Effect of Guilt. *Journal of Personality and Social Psychology.* 7(2):117-124.

Friedrich, Gerhard. 1964. εὐαγγελίζομαι *Theological Dictionary of the New Testament.* Vol. 2, Gerhard Kittel, ed. Geoffrey W. Bromiley, Trans. and ed. Grand Rapids: William B. Eerdmans.

_____. 1965. κηρύσσω *Theological Dictionary of the New Testament.* Vol. 3, Gerhard Kittel, ed. Geoffrey W. Bromiley, Trans. and ed. Grand Rapids: William B. Eerdmans.

Gangel, Kenneth O. 1974. *Competent to Lead.* Chicago: Moody Press.

Green, Michael. 1970. *Evangelism in the Early Church.* Grand Rapids: William B. Eerdmans.

Griffin, Emory A. 1976. *The Mind Changers.* Wheaton: Tyndale House Publishers.

Gutzke, Manford George. 1975. *Plain Talk on Mark.* Grand Rapids: Zondervan Publishing House.

Hadden, Jeffrey. 1980. Some Sociological Reflections on the Electronic Church. Paper presented at Electronic Church Consultation of the Communication Commission, National Council of Churches. New York, 6-7 Feb.

Hadden, Jeffrey and Charles E. Swann. 1981. *Prime Time Preachers: The Rising Power of Televangelism.* Reading: Addison-Wesley Publishing Co.

Haenchen, Ernst. 1971. *The Acts of the Apostles: A Commentary.* Oxford: Basil Blackwell.

Hastings, James, ed. 1955. *Encyclopedia of Religion and Ethics.* Vol. 3. New York: Charles Scribner's Sons.

Havlik, John. 1976. "Theology for Growing an Evangelistic Church." *Growing an Evangelistic Church Guidebook.* Atlanta: Home Mission Board of the SBC.

_____. 1980. *Where in the World Is Jesus Christ?* Nashville: Broadman Press.

Hendricks, William L. 1977. *The Doctrine of Man.* Nashville: Convention Press.

_____. 1980. *A Theology for Children.* Nashville: Broadman Press.

Higbee, Kenneth L. 1969. "Fifteen Years of Fear Arousal: Research on Threat Appeals: 1953-1968." *Psychological Bulletin.* 72(6):426-444.

Horsfield, Peter G. 1982. "Religious Broadcasting at the Crossroads." *The Christian Century.* 27 Jan.

Hughes, Robert Don. 1984. "Models of Christian Missionary Broadcasting." *Review and Expositor.* Roy L. Honeycutt, ed. 81(1):31-42.

Humphreys, Fisher. 1974. *Thinking About God.* New Orleans: Insight Press.

Hunter, George G., III. 1979. *The Contagious Congregation.* Nashville: Abingdon Press.

Jauncey, James H. 1972. *Psychology for Successful Evangelism.* Chicago: Moody Press.

_____. 1978. *One-on-One Evangelism.* Chicago: Moody Press.

Jemison, Hedwig. 1980. *Clothing Men of the Cloth.* Ministry. July, 4-6.

Johnson, Cedric B. and H. Newton Malony. 1982. *Christian Conversion: Biblical and Psychological Perspectives.* Grand Rapids: Zondervan Publishing Co.

Jones, E. Stanley. 1968. *A Song of Ascents: A Spiritual Autobiography.* Nashville: Abingdon Press.

Katz, Elihu. 1968. "On Reopening the Question of Selectivity in Exposure to Mass Communication." *Theories of Cognitive Consistency: A Sourcebook.* Robert P. Abelson et. al. eds. Chicago: Rand McNally Co.

Keeton, Morris T. 1982. "Experimental Education." *Encyclopedia of Educational Research.* Harold E. Mitzel, ed. Vol. 2. New York: The Free Press.

Kennedy, D. James. 1977. *Evangelism Explosion.* Rev. by D. James Kennedy and Archie B. Parrish. Wheaton: Tyndale House.

Khang, James. 1972. "The Rich Rewards of Creative Listening." *Christian Life Magazine.* 23 Feb., Citing Barbara, Dominick A. 1974. *The Art of Listening.* Springfield: C. C. Thomas.

Klapper, Joseph T. 1973. "The Social Effects of Mass Communication." *Basic Readings in Communication Theory.* C. David Mortensen, ed. New York: Harper and Row.

Kraft, Charles H. 1979. *Communicating the Gospel God's Way.* Pasadena: William Carey Library.

_____. 1983. *Communication Theory for Witnesses.* Nashville: Abingdon Press.

Ladd, George Eldon. 1974. *A Theology of the New Testament.* Grand Rapids: William B. Eerdmans Publishing Co.

Landry, Sabin. 1980. "The Training of Lay Persons for Personal Witnessing." *Review and Expositor.* Roy L. Honeycutt, ed. 77(4):549-60.

Lane, Margaret. 1980. "Are You Really Listening?" *Reader's Digest,* Nov., 183-88.

Leavell, Roland Q. 1979. *Evangelism: Christ's Imperative Commission.* Rev. by Landrum P. Leavell II and Harold T. Bryson. Nashville: Broadman Press.

Lenski, R. C. H. 1943. *The Interpretation of St. Matthew's Gospel.* Columbus: The Wartburg Press.

_____. 1944. *The Interpretation of the Acts of the Apostles.* Columbus: The Wartburg Press.

Levinson, Daniel J. 1979. *The Seasons of a Man's Life.* New York: Alfred A. Knopf.

Lewis, Gordon R. 1974. *Judge for Yourself.* Downer's Grove, IL: Inter-Varsity Press.

Little, Paul. 1966. *How to Give Away Your Faith.* Downer's Grove, IL: Inter-Varsity Press.

Manson, T. W. 1951. *The Teaching of Jesus.* 2nd ed. Cambridge: The University Press.

McDill, Wayne. 1979. *Making Friends for Christ.* Nashville: Broadman Press.

McGavran, Donald. 1970. *Understanding Church Growth.* Grand Rapids: William B. Eerdmans.

McGuire, William J. 1968. "Selective Exposure: A Summing Up." *Theories of Cognitive Consistency: A Sourcebook.* Robert P. Abelson et. al. eds. Chicago: Rand McNally Co.

McPhee, Arthur G. 1978. *Friendship Evangelism.* Grand Rapids: Zondervan Publishing Co.

Mewborn, C. Ronald, and Ronald W. Rogers. 1979. "Effects of Threatening and Reassuring Components of Fear Appeals on Physiological and Verbal Measures of Emotion and Attitudes." *Journal of Experimental Social Psychology.* 15:242-53.

Miles, Delos. 1975. "Towards a Descriptive Definition of Evangelism." Paper delivered as an evangelism lecture at Golden Gate Baptist Theological Seminary.

_____. 1981. *Church Growth A Mighty River.* Nashville: Broadman Press.

_____. 1982A. *Master Principles of Evangelism.* Nashville: Broadman Press.

_____. 1982B. *How Jesus Won Persons.* Nashville: Broadman Press.

Miller, Keith. 1977. *The Becomers.* Waco: Word Books.

Molloy, John T. 1975. *Dress for Success.* New York: Warner Books.

Montgomery, Jim. 1978. "Religious Broadcasting Becomes Big Business Spreading Across the U.S." *The Wall Street Journal,* 19 May.

Moody, Dale. 1981. *The Word of Truth: A Summary of the Christian Doctrine Based on Biblical Revelation.* Grand Rapids: William B. Eerdmans Publishing Co.

Mortensen, C. David. 1972. *Communication.* New York: McGraw Hill, citing Ekman, P. and Freisen, W. V. 1968. Nonverbal Behavior in Psycotherapy Research. *Psychotherapy.* 3:181.

Moule, C. F. D. 1953. *An Idiom Book of New Testament Greek.* Cambridge: The University Press.

Murphy, Edward F. 1975. *Spiritual Gifts and the Great Commission.* South Pasadena: Mandate Press.

Neighbour, Ralph. 1982. *TOUCH Ministries: Basic Training Manual; Touch Ministries Seminar; TOUCH Basic Training.* Project 180 Field Test Edition. Houston: TOUCH Publications.

Neil, William. 1973. *The Acts of the Apostles.* New Century Bible. Greenwood: Attic Press.

Nelson, Martin L. 1982. "What's Behind the Discipling of Korea?" *Global Church Growth Bulletin.* 19(2):173-75.

Newbigin, Leslie. 1978. *The Open Secret.* Grand Rapids: William B. Eerdmans Publishing Co.

Nicholas, Daniel J. 1983. "Baptists Ready to Take Acts on the Road." *Religious Broadcasting.* June.

Niles, D. T. 1962. *Upon the Earth.* London: Lutterworth Press.

Packer, J. I. "Conversion." *The New Bible Dictionary.* J. D. Douglas, ed. Grand Rapids: Eerdmans Publishing Co. 250-52.

Peters, George W. 1972. *A Biblical Theology of Mission.* Chicago: Moody Press.

Petty, Richard E. and John T. Cacioppo. 1981. *Attitudes and Persuasion: Classic and Contemporary Approaches.* Dubuque: Wm. C. Brown Co.

Pollock, J. C. 1963. *Moody: A Biographical Portrait of the Pacesetter in Modern Mass Evangelism.* New York: Macmillan Co.

Pope, M. H. 1962. "Proselyte." *The Interpreter's Dictionary of the Bible.* Vol. 3. George Butterick, ed. Nashville: Abingdon Press. 921-31.

Princeton Religion Research Center and Gallup Organization. 1981. *Religion in America.* Princeton: P.R.R.C. and Gallup.

_____. 1982. *Religion in America.* Princeton: P.R.R.C. and Gallup.

Ramsey, Howard. 1981. "Changing Statistics Through C.W.T." *Home Missions Notebook.* Atlanta: Home Mission Board of the S.B.C. 2:3 July.

Robertson, A. T. 1922. *A Harmony of the Gospels for Students of the Life of Christ.* New York: Harper and Brothers Publishers.

Rogers, Everett M. and F. Floyd Shoemaker. 1971. *Communication of Innovations: A Cross-Cultural Approach.* 2nd ed. New York: The Free Press.

Roozen, David A. 1978. *The Church and the Unchurched in America.* Washington, DC: Glenmary Research Center.

Rutenber, Culbert. 1960. *The Reconciling Gospel.* Nashville: Broadman Press.

Sanders, J. Oswald. 1966. *What of the Unevangelized.* London: Overseas Missionary Fellowship.

Schaller, Lyle. 1972. *The Change Agent.* Nashville: Abingdon Press.

Seamands, John T. 1981. *Tell It Well: Communicating the Gospels Across Cultures.* Kansas City: Beacon Hill Press.

Sears, David O. "The Paradox of De Facto Selective Exposure Without Preference for Supportive Information." *Theories of Cognitive Consistency: A Sourcebook.* Robert P. Abelson et. al. eds. Chicago: Rand McNally Co.

Severin, Werner J. and James W. Tankard, Jr. 1979. *Communication Theories: Origins, Methods, and Uses.* New York: Hastings House Publishers.

Shostrom, Everett L. 1967. *Man, the Manipulator.* New York: Bantam Books.

Simons, Herbert W. 1976. *Persuasion: Understanding, Practice and Analysis.* Reading: Addison-Wesley Publishing Co.

Sogaard, Viggo. 1980. "Communicate the Gospel." *World Evangelization.* Wheaton: Lausanne Committee for World Evangelization. 6-8 June.

Southard, Samuel. 1962. *Pastoral Evangelism.* Nashville: Broadman Press.

_____. 1981. *Pastoral Evangelism.* Rev. ed. Atlanta: John Knox Press.

Spring, Beth. 1982. "Pat Robertson's Network Breaks Out of the Christian Ghetto." *Christianity Today,* 1 Jan.

Stagg, Frank. 1955. *The Books of Acts: The Early Struggle for an Unhindered Gospel.* Nashville: Broadman Press.

_____. 1962. *New Testament Theology.* Nashville: Broadman Press.

Stoeffler, Ernest F. 1973. *German Pietism During the Eighteenth Century.* London: E. J. Brill.

Stott, John R. W. 1959. *Fundamentalism and Evangelism.* Grand Rapids: William B. Eerdmans Publishing Co.

_____. 1971. *One People.* Downer's Grove, IL: Inter-Varsity Press.

_____. 1975. *Christian Mission in the Modern World.* Downer's Grove, IL: Inter-Varsity Press.

Strathman, H. 1967. μάρτυς, *Theological Dictionary of the New Testament.* Vol 3. Gerhard Kittel, ed. Geoffrey W. Bromiley, Trans. and ed. Grand Rapids: William B. Eerdmans.

Swann, Charles. 1980. "Varieties and Appeals of the Electronic Church." Paper presented at Electronic Church Consultation of the Communication Commission. National Council of Churches. New York: 6-7 Feb., 1980.

Sweazey, George. 1978. *The Church as Evangelist.* San Francisco: Harper & Row, Publishers.

Taylor, James A. 1979. "No Miracles from the Media." *The Christian Century,* 30 May.

Taylor, John V. 1966. *For All the World: The Christian Mission in the Modern Age.* Philip E. Hughes and Frank Colquhoun, eds. Christian Foundational Series. Philadelphia: Westminster Press.

Taylor, Mendell. 1964. *Exploring Evangelism.* Kansas City: Beacon Hill Press.

Tippett, Alan R. 1977. Conversion as a Dynamic Process in Christian Mission. *Missiology* 5:203-21.

Truett, George W. 1917. *A Quest for Souls.* J. B. Cranfell, ed. Philadelphia: American Baptist Publication Society.

Turlington, Henry E. 1969. "Mark." *The Broadman Bible Commentary.* Nashville: Broadman Press.

U. S. News and World Report. 1980. "Secrets of Being a Better Listener: An Interview with Lyman K. Steil, an Authority on Communication," 26 May, 66-67.

United States Department of Commerce. 1982-83. *Statistical Abstract of the United States.* 103rd ed. Washington, D.C.: Bureau of the Census.

Wagner, Peter. 1979. *Your Spiritual Gifts Can Help You Grow.* Glendale: Regal Books.

_____. 1981. "Where Growth Flows from Prayer Mountains." *Global Church Growth Bulletin.* 18(5):136-37.

Watson, David. 1976. *I Believe in Evangelism.* Grand Rapids: William B. Eerdmans Publishing Co.

Watson, Goodwin. 1966. "Resistance to Change." Goodwin Watson, ed. *Concepts for Social Change.* Cooperative Project for Educational Development series. Vol. I. Washington, D.C.: National Training Laboratories. Reproduced by Bennis, Warren G., Kenneth D. Benne, and Robert Chin. 1967. *The Planning of Change.* 2nd ed. New York: Holt, Rinehart and Winston.

Wellborn, Stanley N. 1982. "Ahead: A Nation of Illiterates?" *U. S. News and World Report,* 17 Sept., 53-56.

Winn, Marie. 1977. *The Plug-In Drug.* New York: Viking Press.

Wolf, Tom. 1979. "The Biblical Pattern of Effective Evangelism." *The Pastor's Church Growth Handbook.* Win Arn, ed. Pasadena: Church Growth Press. 110-16.

Wood, Barry. 1977. *Questions Non-Christians Ask.* Old Tappan: Fleming H. Revell Co.

Wood, Skevington. 1966. *Evangelism: Its Theology and Practice.* Grand Rapids: Zondervan Publishing House.

Working Together. 1983. Richmond: Foreign Mission Board of the SBC.

World Evangelization. 1982. Evangelization/Church Growth Advances in French Canada. Publication of the Lausanne Committee for World Evangelization. Bulletin 28: Sept.

Yao, Margaret. 1979. "Big Pitch for God: More Churches Try Advertising in the Media." *The Wall Street Journal.*

Zimbardo, Philip G., Ebbe B. Ebbeson, and Christina Maslach. 1977. *Influencing Attitudes and Changing Behavior.* 2nd. ed. Reading: Addison-Wesley Publishing Co.

G. WILLIAM SCHWEER, native of
Missouri, is E. Hermond Westmoreland
Professor of Evangelism, Golden Gate
Baptist Theological Seminary, Mill
Valley, California. Earlier he was pastor
in Missouri and Illinois. For fifteen years
Schweer was missionary to Indonesia
where he served as president,
Indonesian Baptist Seminary,
1970-1972. He is a graduate of the
University of Missouri (B.S.) and
Central Baptist Seminary, Kansas City,
Kansas (B.D., Th.M., Th.D.). Dr. and
Mrs. Schweer have three children:
Merilee Ann, Mark, and Clark. This is
his first book with Broadman.